LOVE OF TWO LANDS

THE PURSUIT OF FREEDOM IN IRAN

A Memoir/Documentary

HABIB ESLAMI

ISBN-10: 1451576854
EAN-13: 9781451576856

I dedicate this book to Neda Agha-Sultan, Sohrab Arabi, Farzad Kamangar, and all the 2009 post-election victims in Iran who became the silent voices of freedom. I also dedicate this book to the brave mothers of Neda, Sohrab, and Farzad: Hajar Rostami, Parvin Fahimi, and Saltaneh Rezaee, respectively. In addition, the book is dedicated to all the youth and struggling people in Iran.

The love of one's country is a splendid thing.
But why should love stop at the border? ~Pablo Casals

Freedom may be the soul of humanity,
but often you have to struggle to prove it. ~ Lech Walesa

AUTHOR'S NOTES

As a tribute to my late father, my teachers, and all who have had a positive impact on my life, I have written this blend of stories and anecdotes about my life experiences in both Iran and America. The voices of the young and tireless freedom fighters of Iran give me the inspiration to share my own tales as well as the stories of those whose lives have touched mine. Political unrest, struggles for freedom, diverse culture, devout people, and ancient Iranian history give *Love of Two Lands* a unique flavor while conveying the message of appreciation and respect to those of us fortunate enough to live in a democratic society.

For some characters of the book, fictitious names have been used in order to shield identities of the individuals and their secrets.

ACKNOWLEDGMENTS

First and foremost, I want to thank my late father and my lovely mother for their unconditional love and support of every step of my life.

I have acknowledged many people who have had a positive impact on my life throughout this book. Several people have helped me with the book. I want to thank Linda Eastlake for reading my manuscript and helping me with the editing of the first draft of the book. She has been so kind and very encouraging. I also thank Professor Eastlake, my esteemed colleague, who made the suggestion to have his wife Linda read the manuscript. I would like to thank him for some of his useful editing tips as well. I am so thankful to my friend Mr. Mike Potash for his insightful and constructive comments on portions of this book. I am also thankful to my long-time friends Dr. Bijan Vasigh and his wife Behnoush for their kind words and encouragement.

I am grateful to all of my colleagues who read portions of this narrative and encouraged me to publish it, especially my good friend Dr. Tej Gupta. I thank Mr. William Cummins, author, publisher, engineer, and motivational speaker for his unselfish advice. I appreciate the editorial team at the CreateSpace publishing company for their kind and favorable feedbacks. My thanks go out to my friend Alain H, who introduced me to Mr. Erik Calonius, the author of *The Wanderer*, a former reporter, editor, and London-based foreign correspondent for *The Wall Street Journal*. I am thankful to Mr. Calonius for his advice on publishing and for introducing me to an excellent editor, Ms. Laura Fogarty. I sincerely appreciate Ms. Laura Fogarty for editing the final draft of my book and for her positive feedbacks and kind words about my book. I also want to thank my good friend Dr. Massoud Noghrekar for his encouraging words. I like to extend my gratitude to Mr. Marc Bernier, the WNDB-AM 1150 Daytona Beach talk show host and special assistant to Dr. John Johnson, the president of Embry-Riddle Aeronautical University for his willingness to read the manuscript and for his encouragement.

I want to thank my children Saum, Sara, and Sina for being inspirational factors in my life. My daughter Sara helped me with the cover image and I love her for that.

Most importantly, I want to thank my wife, Mitra, for her support, patience, kindness, and for her love throughout the writing of this book.

PROLOGUE

The first time Ahmadinejad ran for president on June 17, 2005, he was not a well-known political figure in Iran. Six other candidates[1] had been approved by *Shora-ye Negahban*, the Guardian Council[2] to run for president as well. During the presidential campaigns, Ahmadinejad was behind in the polls, and his name did not surface as frequently and favorably as Rafsanjani, Moeen, Karoubi, and Ghalibaf. He was the mayor of Tehran but not known to all Iranians. It was astonishing to many Iranian people, including me, that he finished second to Rafsanjani. However, neither Rafsanjani nor Ahmadinejad secured 50 percent of the votes to be elected as the ninth president. So, according to the constitution, the two candidates with the highest votes were mandated to run against each other one week later.

I am not sure if Ahmadinejad was really elected by the Iranian people the first time around. In fact, many people believe that the election was rigged.However, during his runoff campaign versus Rafsanjani, he did not speak of the Holocaust, nor did he speak of wiping Israel off the map of the world. He never mentioned that he was going to arrange a conference on the Holocaust the first few months after taking office. In other words, he did not show any signs of bigotry and hatred—his distinctive characteristics. He did not bring up nuclear issues at all. He spoke of more freedom for Iranian youth. He campaigned for a better economy

---

1   Akbar Hashemi Rafsanjani, the fifth and sixth president, the chair of the Expediency Discernment Council, also the chair of the Assembly of Experts. Mehdi Karoubi, the former speaker of the parliament. Mohsen Mehralizadeh, the former president of the National Sports Organization. Mostafa Moeen, the former minister of science, research, and technology. Mohammad Bagher Ghalibaf, the former commander of the police force and now the mayor of Tehran. Ali Larijani, the supreme leader's representative in the National Security Council. He was the mayor of Tehran before he became the president.

2   *Shora-ye Negahban*, Guardian Council, is comprised of 12 members. Six of the council members are appointed by the supreme leader, and the other six by the Iranian parliament. The first six are the "Islamic Jurists," specializing on Islamic laws. The latter six are the jurists specializing in other types of laws.

and more. The Iranian people embraced him as a person who might be able to fight the elite corruption of the cleric regime.

After almost four years, he had yet to fulfill his promises. Not only did he not fight the corruption, he became a source of corruption himself. Not only did he not solve the immediate and imminent problems that the country was facing, including inflation, unemployment, price gouging, drugs, prostitution, and poverty, he caused the deepening of such problems. In addition, under Ahmadinejad, street arrests of the youths for "bad hairdos," or "bad *hejabi*," ("unacceptable dress for women") increased. Even worse, barbaric public executions, stoning, and hanging of people, including teenagers under the age of eighteen, increased. Further international isolation of the country increased. The number of political prisoners increased. The unrest in the universities escalated and the list goes on.

I was baffled to hear that the "supreme leader," Ali Khamenei, in his speeches a few months before the tenth presidential campaign, praised Ahmadinejad, referring to him as a "brave person" and encouraged him to run for the presidency of the country again. I personally don't think Ahmadinejad is brave, and I am certain that a vast majority of Iranian people are in agreement with me. He is, in fact, a puppet and a coward. If he were brave, he would not kiss the hands of the tyrant, the supreme leader, and would not be subservient to him. If he were brave, he would stand up to the supreme leader and his corrupt cleric regime to tell them firmly that enough is enough. Enough of hatred, enough of lies and deception, enough of blaming America, the West, and the late shah for the Islamic Republic's inability to solve the country's economic, judicial, and social crises. The supreme leader in Iran is supposed to be the country's spiritual leader and moral authority. However, the current supreme leader's hunger for power, his lack of respect for his own people, and his contempt for human rights and human lives are the characteristics of a despotic ruler, not a spiritual leader. These characteristics are far from any religious values. A spiritual leader must be a messenger of peace, not of war; must be a source of love, not of hate; must be the owner of hearts and not of earthly possessions—and must be a moral authority, not a commander of armed forces. A spiritual leader must inspire the government to build houses and shelters for needy people, not to build more weapons. A spiritual leader is the one who brings honor and dignity to his nation, not shame, and disgrace.

In every speech that the supreme leader makes, he repeatedly uses the word *doshmanan*, "enemies." The people whom he often refers to as "enemies" are Iranian citizens asking for the basic necessities of life: food, shelter, jobs, security, humanity, social justice, and social freedom. These people are ordinary citizens not enemies. For over three decades, they have been deprived of their basic rights; they have been under the threat of war, under reign of terror, under fear of prosecution and persecution, and under the hateful statements and propagandas. The people of Iran cannot even have a simple gathering of friends and relatives in the privacy of their homes without being invaded by government thugs. The only person who could have put a stop to all this nonsense was the supreme leader. He could have halted the criminal and inhumane acts of the government against people. Instead, he chose to turn his back on them and sided with criminals. Thus, he is the enemy of the people—not other way around. Why should a religious leader use the word enemy when referring to his fellow citizens?

Almost two weeks before the tenth Iranian presidential elections, on May 30, 2009, I left the United States for Iran to be a part of historical events and one of the most crucial presidential elections in my motherland. That was my very first opportunity to participate in a presidential election after the revolution. I observed extreme enthusiasm and positive energy in the people of Iran and especially the youth, who were hoping for a big change. The messages of change by American President Obama resonated with Iranian youths. They too wanted change and were inspired by President Obama's "Yes We Can" speeches. They thought they had the power to bring about change. They thought they could bring freedom, justice, equality, prosperity, brightness, and hope for a better future.

The vast majority of Iranian people were tired of Ahmadinejad's incompetence and his hateful messages. They were tired of Ahmadinejad's mishandling of the economy. They were tired of Ahmadinejad's deceptive "halo"[3] speeches, his phony smiles, his arrogance, and his thuggish demeanor. They wanted change. They wanted peace. They wanted fairness. They wanted someone who could sing their songs. They wanted an honest person as their president. What choices did they have? Only those who had been approved by the Guardian Council: Mehdi Karoubi; Mohsen Rezaee;[4] Mahmud Ahmadinejad, the incumbent president, and Mir Hossein Mousavi, the former prime minister (1981-1989).

---

3   In September 2005 Ahmadinejad, just after the 9th presidential elections, attended the United Nation General Assembly in New York. According to a video clip, he told a top cleric, Ayatollah Abdollah Javadi Amoli, that a "halo of light" had enveloped him and that the crowd stared at him unblinkingly during his entire speech at the UN. Ahmadinejad claimed that a member of the (Iranian) delegation told him that a light surrounded him (Ahmadinejd) during his speech. "I sensed it myself too ... I felt the atmosphere changed. The audience did not blink for 27, 28 minutes. I'm not exaggerating when I'm saying they didn't blink. Everybody had been astonished ... they had opened their eyes and ears to see the message from the Islamic Republic." The clip first surfaced in November 2005, prompting analysts to wonder whether Ahmadinejad was really claiming that he was a divine leader. During 2010 presidential campaign, when the reporters asked him about his "halo speech," Ahmadinejad denied the story!

4   Rezaee was the founder and commander of the Army of the Guardians of the Islamic Republic (AGIR). Also, he was a top member of the Expediency Discernment Council, and the founder of the Revolutionary Guard

After twenty years of keeping a low profile and staying away from mainstream politics, Mir Hossein Mousavi announced his candidacy on March 9, 2009. He stated his main goals: institutionalization of freedom of speech, freedom of press, social justice, equality, fairness, rooting out corruption, and more. He spoke about privatization of government-owned radio and television networks. He criticized Ahmadinejad's misuse of the economy and mismanagement of the oil profits. During the heyday and peak of high oil prices, in the mid to late 2000s, Middle Eastern countries profited with a great deal of revenues. Ahmadinejad's government, in his four years as president, earned more than $272 billion in oil and gas revenues, owing in part to oil prices reaching as high as about $147 a barrel.[5] By comparison, Iran's oil and gas earnings during eight years of Ahmadinejad's predecessor, reformist president Mohammad Khatami was $172 billion.[6] For a third world country not much bigger than the State of Alaska, $272 billion is a substantial amount of money.

Even Tehran's conservative mayor, Mohammad Baqer Qalibaf, has been quoted as saying, "What kind of management is this? Not only did people's livelihoods not improve when oil prices were $140 a barrel in comparison to when they were $16, they worsened."[7] When the reporters asked Ahmadinejad whether he envisaged the fall of oil prices, he responded, "When the prices go up, they do not fall down!" Mousavi criticized him for not coming up with a plan when the oil prices fell. He also criticized Ahmadinejad for wasting the Iranian assets by giving away gifts to individuals, officials, and many rural sectors without any explicit contract for their return. Ahmadinejad's creation of "a gift-based economy" or the so-called "alms-based economy" was his main ulterior motive to gain popularity. He succeeded among some uneducated people of rural areas and those who benefited from the gifts. However, his generous and uncontrolled spending of the country's assets resulted in corruption, high inflation, banking irregularities, and bureaucracy. Mousavi, on many occasions during his campaign, warned the people of Iran of the dangerous path that Ahmadinejad was steering.

Mr. Mousavi and his wife, Dr. Zahra Rahnavard, started a tireless campaign vowing to dissolve discriminatory laws against women in Iran and to put an end to the aggression of the so-called morality police against the youth. Mousavi voiced strong opposition to the brutality of police forces in Iran. He indicated in his speeches that he would demand that the control of law enforcement be transferred

---

5   http:www.rferl.org/content/Irans_Economy_Takes_Center_Stage_IN_Increasingly_Bitter_Campaign/17 52031.html
6   Ibid.
7   Ibid.

from the supreme leader (elected by the eighty-six-member Assembly of Experts) to the president (elected by the people, if there is no cheating). He also wanted control of the national radio and TV networks to be transferred from the hands of the supreme leader to private ownership. Mousavi spoke about creating foreign policies that would reduce tension between Iran and the international community—foreign policies that would take Iran out of isolation and would protect the country's national interests. He spoke about a fair and balanced relationship with the Western world. He not only opposed Ahmadinejad's opinion that the Holocaust was a "myth," he condemned Hitler's massacre of Jews.

Regarding the Iranian nuclear issues, Mousavi believed in Iran's right to acquire peaceful nuclear energy under the nuclear nonproliferation treaty. He had mentioned on many occasions that if elected, his policy would be to provide "guarantees" that Tehran's nuclear activities would never be diverted to non-peaceful aims.[8] Mr. Mousavi's intelligent, honest, and gentle responses to all questions attracted waves of the young, the educated, and intellectuals in Iran. For these groups, the choice was obvious. They considered Mousavi as their voice and the most viable option. They demonstrated their enthusiasm for a brighter and more blissful future on the streets of Tehran weeks before the Election Day. They had no doubts that their candidate would win.

During those couple of weeks of intense campaigning by all parties, Mousavi's camp was by far the most energetic, most organized, and most vital. An overwhelming majority of Iranian people in Tehran supported Mousavi. I witnessed that myself. I was told by a reliable source that he observed the same trend in most other major cities in Iran.

In spite of problems and doubts that I had regarding Mousavi, he became my favorite candidate after considering the alternatives. The biggest problem I had with Mousavi was that he was an element of the Islamic Republic—he was a believer of the whole establishment of Khomeini's *Velayat-e-Faghih* ("Guardianship of Jurist") doctrine. He had served as prime minister for eight years (1981-1989). He handled the economy during the war very well and made the right decisions on food rationing at crucial times. As prime minister, he stood up to the authoritarian ruling of the then president, Ali Khamenei, now the supreme leader. Nevertheless, why did he remain indifferent during the senseless and inhumane executions without trials and the massacre of dissidents in prisons that took place in 1988-1989? Why did he not join Ayatollah Montazeri and other opposition voices against the ferocious criminal acts of the regime? Why did he choose to stay

---

8   Press TV. IR (English language global news network owned by Islamic Republic), 2009-04-14. Retrieved 2009-07-01.

silent and never condemned the brutality of the regime for all those years? To this date these questions remain unanswered.

Ahmadinejad made a fool of himself during the televised presidential debate with Mr. Mousavi. Instead of debating Mousavi, he bashed former presidents, Mohammad Khatami, and Akbar Hashemi Rafsanjani, and Rafsanjani family. Mousavi criticized Ahmadinejad for attacking the former presidents who were not even there to defend themselves. He tackled Ahmadinejad's policies by implying that his style of management was based on "adventurism and instability, theatrical behavior, machismo and sloganeering, extremism and radicalism, hallucination and superstition, deception and secrecy." Ahmadinejad tried to change the theme of the debate again by attacking people such as the former speaker of the parliament, Mr. Nategh Noori, and his son, accusing them of making themselves rich through money laundering. He then accused Mr. Mousavi's wife, Dr. Zahra Rahnavard, of completing two master's degrees while serving in the government and earning a doctorate degree without taking "the entrance exam."[9] Iranian people who watched the debate thought that Ahmadinejad's attack on his opponent's wife was vicious, uncalled for, and cheap. Mr. Mousavi defended his wife like a gentleman and proudly mentioned his wife's accomplishments.

During the Karoubi-Ahmadinejad debate, Ahmadinejad again made a fool of himself by showing charts indicating that unemployment rate was increasing in the whole world but decreasing in Iran under his administration. Also, he mentioned that the inflation had dropped down to below 15 percent in Iran while it was increasing in the whole world including all the oilexisting Persian Gulf countries. Mr. Karoubi responded, "The Central Bank has declared that the inflation was a little over 25 percent. You have dropped it to 14 percent in a couple days!" Ahmadinejad stated that those charts were provided to him by the Central Bank of Iran. The day after the debate, the Central Bank of Iran announced that the inflation rate was indeed 25 percent.

Almost forty-eight hours before the election, on June 10, I had a conversation with one of my friends who used to work for the government. He basically told me that he smelled a rat; he talked about cheating, and voter fraud. I asked him why and he responded, "There are no more than 45 million eligible voters, but they (the Interior Ministry) printed 72 million ballot sheets."

Two days later, on Friday, June 12, I took my birth certificate, went to one of the districts (in Iran, the voters can go to any district they wish), and stood in line. Most of the people in front of me were young. An older fellow and his wife stood behind me, grumbling loudly, "I want to see how they could rig the election

---

9   In Iran, it is required of everyone to pass "entrance exams" to enter the master's and doctorate degrees.

this time." He continued saying, "Throughout the contemporary Iranian history, I don't think we have had a more incompetent, irrational, and impudent politician than Ahmadinejad." I voted for Mousavi, and so did everybody else, to the best of my knowledge.

It was almost midnight and I was glued to the TV and dozing off. The telephone rang; it was my friend on the phone. He said, "I have a strong feeling that they will announce Ahmadinejad as the winner."

"How could that be?" I asked.

"I cannot tell you the details. I can only tell you that they don't care about the popular vote in this country," my friend said.

I woke up early morning on Saturday, June 13. I turned the TV on. To my dismay, Kamran Daneshjoo[10] projected that Ahmadinejad was the winner of the election by a big margin. It was astonishing to me how quickly they reached this decision. I could not believe my eyes and ears. I thought I misunderstood him. A few minutes later, he appeared on TV again and repeated the same results. I could not accept that. I could not have imagined that they would so obviously rig an election. I could not believe that they would put aside such a gentle and intelligent person (who is, after all, one of their own) in favor of a not-so-intelligent, not-so-knowledgeable person, an impolite street thug like Ahmadinejad with a record of four years of failure as president!

After breakfast, I decided to go for a walk and check of the news headlines at the closest newsstand. An older person passed by and said, "Can you believe this? Can you believe how they are playing with the minds of the people?"

"No, sir, I can't. I am as shocked about the news as you are," I said.

At the newsstand, people had no fear of expressing their contempt for the government. I heard someone shouting that Khamenei, his son, and Mahsouli, the interior minister, rigged the election and stole people's votes. That was the first time I heard of Khamenei's son having a role in the election fraud. I wanted to join the crowd and express my displeasure of the action of the government, but I had promised my mother not to enter into any political debates. That evening, I was invited to my brother's house along with a group of other people. In the middle of our dinner, we heard the clamor, "*Allah-o-akbar*" ("God is great"), "*Marg bar diktator*" ("Death to the dictator") from the surrounding neighborhood. I had the urge to join with the voices, but my brother would not let me. The next day

---

10   Kamran Daneshjoo was an Interior Ministry senior official and the head of the State Election Headquarters during the election. He is now the minister of science, research, and technology. Kamran Daneshjoo is one of the most controversial characters of Iranian politics today. There are many controversies surrounding this man. One can search through Google to find out more.

millions of Iranians poured into the streets and demonstrated peacefully against the government. I was saddened to hear that the peaceful demonstrations by the people were crushed and that a few young people were killed. From that moment on, the Green Movement became a national symbol. "Where is my vote?" became a motto used by anti-government demonstrators to tell the whole world that the Iranian government had stolen their votes. Ahmadinejad had the audacity to call the protestors *"khas va khashak"* ("dirt and dust"). It was sickening to hear the person who has been the source of all the nuisance, instability, and economic disaster in Iran ever since he became the president calling the peaceful demonstrators "dirt and dust."

Demonstrations, uprisings, nighttime shouting of *"Allah-o-akbar"* and *"Marg bar diktator"* by the people from the rooftops all over Tehran continued until June 18, the day of my departure. My sister asked me why I was so sad, why I looked so pale. I felt I was leaving behind not just a few loved ones but millions of young brothers and sisters. I left Tehran in tears.

It was early in the evening when I returned to Orlando International Airport. My then twenty-year-old son, Saum, whom I love and adore so much, picked me up from the airport. I was so glad to see him, but I could not hide the sadness in my face. We stopped by a restaurant to have dinner. He is an intelligent kid; he could tell that I was depressed. He asked me if everything was okay. I could not tell him how I felt. He would not understand. He has lived all his life in a free country. He would not understand why the young people his age or younger are fighting and dying for freedom in his father's homeland. He would not understand what it is like to live under a tyrannical regime. He would not understand why the young people would be arrested for playing loud music in their own cars. He would not understand why the people do not have the freedom to dress any which way they want. He would not understand why the people in his father's homeland do not have the freedom to talk about freedom, to read about freedom, to write about freedom, or to struggle for freedom.

It was late in the evening when I got home to Daytona Beach. My son went his own way. My wife was still in Iran. I was dead tired and lonely at home. I turned the TV on and changed the channel to CNN. All the news on CNN revolved around Iran and the uprising by the people. I decided to go to bed and wake up early to watch the Friday sermon to be given by Ali Khamenei, the supreme leader, followed by his speech. I thought he was going to do what the shah did when the uprising started in 1978—to tell the people of Iran that he saw their uprising, to apologize for mistakes of the past, and to promise to fix wrongdoings by the government. I thought Khamenei was going to announce the annulment of the election and ask the people of Iran to vote again. How naive I was! That did not happen. Instead, he said that the election results were final and that the people would be held "directly responsible" for violence and bloodshed. Instead of calling for calm and restraint, he gave signals to his bloodthirsty *basiji*[11] people to use violence on any further demonstrations. He had declared war on his own people.

In response, immediately after Khamenei's Friday sermon, the human rights monitor Amnesty International issued a statement saying, "Khamenei's sermon indicates the authorities' readiness to launch violent crackdowns if people continue to protest which may cause a widespread loss of life."[12]

Hassiba Hadj Sahraoui, deputy director of Amnesty International's Middle East and North Africa program,[13] went on to say, "We are extremely disturbed at statements made by Ayatollah Khamenei which seem to give the green light to security forces to violently handle protesters exercising their right to demonstrate and express their views."

On the next day, June 20, 2009, millions of the unhappy people of Iran poured into the streets to have a peaceful protest against Khamenei's declaration of war and his hateful speech against the people. Predictions by Ms. Hassiba Sahraoui turned to reality; the peaceful rally of the Iranian people turned bloody. Neda Agha Soltan was murdered for participating in the peaceful rally around six-thirty that evening.

The whole world watched Neda's innocent face smothered in blood. One of the basijis was identified as her murderer. Many people who were present at the scene attested to this. Instead of calling for the arrest of the real murderer, the government-controlled media blamed Neda's death on a young doctor who tried to save her from dying. In addition, Neda's tragic death received such world-wide media attention that prompted the Islamic Republic to come up with different scenarios depicting her death as a premeditated murder by foreign countries. But Neda was not the only victim in the peaceful demonstration. What about the deaths of Sohrab Arabi, Ashkon Sohrabi, Taraneh Mousavi, Moustafa Ghanyan, Kianoosh Asa, Mohsen Rohulamini, Masood Hashemzadeh, Mehdi Karami, Mobina Ehterami, Fatima Barati, Meisam Ebadi, Tina Soodi, and many other

---

11   Basij literally means mobilization. Basij force serves as an auxiliary force engaged in activities such as internal security as well as law enforcement auxiliary, the providing of social service, organizing of public religious ceremonies, and more famously moral policing and the suppression of dissident gatherings. Basiji people receive orders from the Pasdaran (the revolutionary guards) or the supreme leader. Basij force was founded by Ayatollah Komeini in 1979. In this book basiji is referred to a volunteer militia person belonging to the basij force. The word basijis is used as the plural of basiji.

12   www.cnn.com/2009/WORLD/meast/06/19/iran.../index.html, updated 9:34 p.m. EDT, Friday, June 19, 2009.

13   Ibid.

peaceful demonstrators, who were randomly arrested, raped, tortured, and killed?[14] They were all very young, beautiful, and innocent.

I felt sad, useless, and helpless that I couldn't be with my compatriots. I felt like writing an open message to the supreme leader stating: "Khamenei shame on you. What do you think you have gained by destroying the lives of all these innocent people? You have brought about more instability, further isolation, and endangerment of the country. Have you no shame? Have you no heart? Have you no remorse? But these young lives that you have destroyed, have not died in vain; their bodies are gone, but not their souls."

---

14   For a list of those killed in the protests after June 12, 2009, presidential election in Iran, one can refer to the following sites:
http://enduringamerica.com/2009/09/08/irans-victims-the-72-people-killed-in-post-election-conflict/
http://iran.whyweprotest.net/missing-persons/2346-list-killed-arrested-english.html

GROWING UP IN IRAN

PART I

O N E

Political unrest and turmoil marked the year1952 in Iran. It was the year after Dr. Muhammad Mossadeq[15] became the prime minister, and a year before the Shah was brought back to power through a CIA-engineered coup. Dr. Mossadeq had the support of many Iranians, including my father. In my youth, I once asked my father who Dr. Mossadeq was. He replied, "Dr. Mossadeq was an honest politician, a freedom fighter, a patriot, and a true believer of democracy for Iran. He was not anti-Shah, nor was he anti-monarchy. He was against dictatorship. The Shah was young and inexperienced. He should have listened to the sixty-two-year-old prime minister instead of opposing him. We would have been in much better shape; we would have been another Japan." My father also believed that the Shah was a good person and had a big dream for the country.

In recalling his life as a young man, my father told us, "In those days, the future was uncertain. Life was extremely difficult for people who did not have a steady job. I was not even certain about my marriage. Having a baby was the last thing on my mind."

Two years after my parents had married, my mother was lonely and pregnant in a rental room, and my father was in the hospital suffering from tuberculosis. According to my mother, the room was the smallest of six in the house. The largest bedroom and the only kitchen were occupied by the landlord and his wife.

---

15   Dr. Mossadeq was a Western-educated politician and a secularist. He was a lawyer and a prominent parliamentarian before he became the prime minister. He was perhaps the first democratically elected prime minister. As Prime Minister, he carried out several important social and political reforms to benefit workers, farmers, and ordinary people. He started his "nationalistic movement" against the absolute monarchy and for nationalizing the Iranian oil. He was against the British oil domination of Iran. In those days, the British owned the Anglo-Iranian oil company and were controlling the Iranian oil. It was due to Dr. Mossadeq's due diligence and his struggle for better trade deals for the Iranian people that *Majles,* the Iranian parliament, passed a bill nationalizing the oil industry in Iran. Dr. Mossadeq was named as the "Man of the Year" by *Time* magazine in early 1952.

The rest of the bedrooms were rented to other families. Renters utilized each room as both bedroom and the kitchen. Small kerosene heaters provided heat during the bitter cold winters in Tehran, and they were often utilized to cook food as well. Small fans cooled down the rooms during intolerable, hot summers in Tehran.

Agha Joon, My father had been hospitalized for more than one week with TB when my mother felt the signs of labor—dizziness, sharp pains in her stomach, and numbness in her arms. She was in tremendous pain, screaming for help. The landlord was intolerant of having kids in his house. My mother had no one to turn to. Her family resided in a town in Northern Iran, which was known then as Shahsavar,[16] and since the revolution as Tonekabon. It is situated almost 260 kilometers from Tehran, in the province of Mazandaran on the shore of the Caspian Sea.

To make matters worse, the property owner and his wife didn't want the baby to be delivered in their house and demanded that she leave. There were no telephones back then, and not many people could afford a car. They typically rode their bikes to work, used the public transit system, or resorted to chariots. The only person she could turn to was my uncle, Sarrullah, my father's only brother. With the help of neighbors, she somehow managed to get herself to my uncle's house. Immediately after arriving at my uncle's house, my uncle's wife, whom I would come to love and respect, sought the help of a midwife in their neighborhood to deliver the baby. I was born on the night of June 10 in my uncle's house.

I was my mother's fourth child and my father's first. My mother was first married to a young merchant at the age of fourteen in Shahsavar. He was twenty-two. My mother was a blonde, blue-eyed girl in a small countryside community not far away. She was the talk of the town. She was my grandmother's youngest and her most favorite child. She does not remember much about her father other than the fact that he was an equestrian and a hunter. My mother's first husband was good to her. They were very happily married and had three daughters together, Molook, Maasoomeh, and Molood. They lived in a huge house belonging to my mother's in-laws. The house was partitioned into several smaller homes, each of which had

---

16 *Shahsavar* means "the king on a ride." It was named Shahsavar in honor of Reza Shah, who often visited that town on his royal horse while the city was being renovated and roads were being built. The name of the city was changed to its original name of Tonekabon after the revolution. Reza Shah was the founder of the Pahlavi dynasty and the first king of the Pahlavi era. Many Iranians believe that he was one of the greatest leaders of all time in Iran.

at least one bedroom and a kitchen. My mother and her first family lived in one of them.

My mother's first husband was a successful young businessman who worked for his father, a rich and influential person in Shahsavar. He came home one evening complaining about a headache and fatigue. He told my mother that he needed to rest. After about an hour, he got up extremely pale and continued complaining about the headache. My mother, no more than seventeen or eighteen at the time, sensed the seriousness of the situation and sought her brother-in-law for help. He came to the house, lifted her husband off the ground by his arms, and took him to the hospital. By the time they arrived, however, it was too late. My mother's husband passed away. To this day, they are not sure what caused his death. He was too young for his life to end so abruptly. Their youngest child was not even a year of age when he died. My mother, being so young, blamed herself for his death. Her life had been shattered before her eyes. Her father-in-law forbade my mother to remain in his house. When she begged him to allow her to take her children with her, he refused. He gave her not more than forty-eight hours to leave. My uncle, Daei Mousa (Moses), my mother's oldest brother, picked her up from her in-laws and took her back to their mother. She stayed at her mother's house, living with the misery of her husband's death and the separation from her children. She was given the right to visit her daughters at the leisure of her ex-father-in-law once or twice a year.

My mother stayed at her mother's house for about two or three years until one of my father's cousins, Yazdan, introduced her to my father. We used to call him Yazdan *Amoo* , Uncle Yazdan. My father was in his late twenties and my mother barely twenty. She was in Shahsavar and my father in Tehran, but they met in the rural district of Taleghan, a beautiful rural area about 140 kilometers from downtown Tehran. My mother's and my father's relatives used to go there every summer for its pleasant climate and its bucolic surroundings.

T W O

My father learned of my birth while he was still in the hospital. He was over-whelmed with joy and couldn't wait to be released. The moment, unfor-tunately, was tempered by the state of my parents' marriage, which was tenuous at best. They didn't have much in common and often didn't get along. It was a rebound for my mother—still mourning her late husband and missing her kids. She was not quite happy at home, nor did she want to stay with her mother and brothers. My father had his own family issues. His mother and some of his rela-tives made it known that they did not approve of his marrying a widow with three children of her own.

Before my mother found out that she was pregnant and after my father was diagnosed with TB, they sat down and had a serious talk about ending their mar-riage. There was no cure for TB at that time, and many people died of the dreaded disease. He told her, "You are young, attractive, and might have a better chance with someone else. You may not want to be stuck with an unhealthy man."

My mother seriously contemplated calling it "quits." However, divorce was her last resort. She decided to go back to her family to consult with her mother and her brothers. She left Tehran for Shahsavar. She stayed with them until she found out that she was pregnant. She then told her mother, "I want this child to be raised with both parents under the same roof." She left Shahsavar the next day with her brother, my uncle Isa (Jesus). My uncles Mousa and Isa were both very much protective of their youngest sister, Saltanat, my mother. They had two more sisters—my aunts Farangis, the oldest of the sisters, and Safieh, the most gullible of all—but they were more fond of my mother than the other two. Their eldest brother was killed in a hunting accident when my mother was only five years old.

Shortly after I was born, my father was released from the hospital feeling much better but not completely free of TB. My mother and I were still staying at

7

the house of my uncle Sarrullah when my father came by to pick us up. He was so glad to see his newborn. "What should we name him?" my father asked his older brother. My father always consulted Uncle Sarrullah on family matters. Their relationship seemed unlike most brothers today. My father was extremely respectful of his older brother. He never called him by his first name. He called him *dadash,* which, like *baradar,* is the Persian word for "brother," only more formal. My uncle Sarrullah was a charismatic, wise, experienced, and handsome man. He had gained the respect and love of the whole Eslami family. Many of our relatives sought his advice and consultation in their daily business affairs. My cousins Guity and Morteza, both very successful in their lives, owe their success to their father, my uncle Sarrullah. I also benefited a great deal from my uncle's wisdom and advice. He suggested naming the newborn Habib, after my grandfather who had died a few years before I was born. Everybody liked the idea, and so the name stuck.

Agha Joon worked as an equestrian in his youth and traveled on horse from one location to another, carrying goods—rice, grains, tea, and so on. During summers, he would travel from a small town near Shahsavar called *Ghale-Gardan* to Taleghan, which would take at least a week. The horse road was bumpy, mountainous, and very dangerous. You had to be skillful to survive. He carried enough food, mainly bread and cheese and sometimes *ghorme,* a smoked meat, to last them for about a week. My uncles Mousa and Isa often traveled along the same horse road, and that's how my father got to know my mother's family. My father and my uncle Isa had good singing voices and they entertained each other along the way.

"Life was so simple and so pure, no automobiles, no machines, no cheating, and no competitions," my father used to say. However, the road was treacherous. They would often encounter dangerous animals on their way. Tigers, wolves, and jackals were often gunned down by the travelers. My father was not fearful of animals, and he never carried a gun. His philosophy was, never harm any of God's creatures. "Wild animals only attack humans if they are provoked and threatened," he would often say. I remember my mother chasing after a scorpion that appeared in our house. My father asked my mother not to harm the creature. He gently picked up the scorpion and carried it out of the room. We once had a cat in the house that adored my father, and every evening just before he came home from work, the cat would wait at the door to greet him. My father would always bring the cat a treat or something to eat.

On another occasion, when I was about nine or ten years old, my father was put in charge of a huge warehouse in a secluded area northwest of Tehran. The warehouse was probably twice the size of a football stadium, housing products such as tractors, cars, big boats, and lift trucks. A family of four—husband, wife, two children, and their dog were living in a corner of the warehouse. My father kept track of all the products inside the warehouse and did the inventories, while the family was in charge of protecting and watching over all the products. The warehouse was burglarized several times. Spare parts, hub cabs, and other smaller items were stolen. Therefore, the family was given a watchdog to help guard the items inside the warehouse. The dog was like the classic "junkyard dog." My father used to take me with him, and sometimes my brother Iraj and I would accompany him to work. One early morning, as my father and I entered the warehouse, the dog ran toward us; my father immediately took me under his arms, sat down, and stared into the dog's eyes. I was scared to death; the dog was angry and barked at us menacingly. There was absolutely no sign of fear in my father's eyes. He started talking to the dog and the dog gradually backed down. My father got up and walked toward him, talking all the while as the dog began to bark again. He kept talking and walking toward the dog. I pleaded to my father not to get too close. With another step, he reached the dog and patted him on the back. Just then, the father of the family entered the warehouse and rushed over to protect us from being torn to pieces. How astonished he was to see that the dog and my father had become fast friends.

Before relocating to Tehran, my father continued working as an equestrian between Tonekabon and Taleghan for a number of years while his brother Sarrullah studied in Tehran. Tired of working as an equestrian in the countryside, he moved to Tehran to find a better employment. He worked many different jobs, from doing sidewalk sales to working in small food stores, until he settled in at an ice cream parlor near downtown Tehran. Business was poor for the old man who owned the shop before he hired my father, but my father's hard work and devotion to his job turned the man's fortune around. During the night at the shop, my father would study on his own to improve his reading and writing. The owner, impressed with his honesty and hard work, came to regard him as one of his sons. The old man did not trust his own children and wanted to turn over a small part of the ownership of the shop to my father so he could continue working there. His children had other ideas. As the business grew and the old man got sick, they took over the business and fired my father after he had worked there for almost three years. He really liked the ice cream shop and the old man, but he had to move on. After my father's departure, business in the ice cream shop gradually suffered, and a couple of years later, they closed down the shop for good.

My father realized that in order to find a better job, he had to study much harder. Though he never had the benefit of a formal education, he learned how to read and write. He also taught himself arithmetic and bookkeeping. He learned much from his brother Sarrullah, other relatives, and friends. When he wanted to know something, it became an obsession for him. He would even ask questions from whoever happened to be near him at that moment. He developed excellent handwriting and spelling. He was quick and accurate with addition, subtraction, multiplication, and division. My friends who had seen my father demonstrate his skills were amazed to hear that he had never gone to school.

After looking for a job for about six months or so, he found a job as a host at a small motel near that ice cream shop. He worked there for nearly one year learning the ins and outs of the business. The owner of the motel decided to rent the place, so my father was about to lose yet another job. He consulted with Uncle Sarrullah. Together they came up with the idea of renting the place themselves, but they didn't have enough money, so they decided to find a partner. They did find a partner—a selfish, middle-aged mullah who owned other businesses. It turned out that the mullah was of little help. He collected the paychecks at the beginning of each month while my father ran the business. My father devoted a lot of time and effort to make sure that the customers were happy. His hard work and dedication paid off as the business grew and made a decent amount of money. The mullah had many connections—lawyers, bankers, judges, and some government officials. Using his influence and deception, he snatched the business from my father's hands by tricking him into signing papers that would turn over his share of the business. My father was an honest man who trusted people too much, and this time it cost him dearly. He could not believe that a clergyman would do this to him.

"Some of the mullahs, but not all, are not practicing Muslims, they are not in touch with reality, and they are not concerned about people as Prophet Muhammad was. These people would have fought Prophet Muhammad if he was alive today," my father often would tell me.

My father was a true believer of Islam. He never missed the prayer, *Namaz*. He always read the Quran in the morning before going to work. He used to go to the mosque often. On Thursday nights after evening prayer, he would recite the Quran and then would go outside with a big plate full of dates or Persian cookies to distribute among people on the crowded sidewalks. Sometimes he would ask us to do that.

THREE

My mother and I stayed in my uncle's home for about one week. My father was finally dismissed from the hospital and he came to pick us up. My grandmother, Shah Sultan, who at the time was staying at my uncle's, decided to come with us in order to take care of her son as he recovered from TB and to help my mother around the house. The relationship between my mother and grandmother was stormy at times. They had different styles of management around the house; they were both stubborn and strong willed. They constantly argued.

My father was torn between the two women. On one hand, he loved and adored his mother so much, and the word "mother" was holy and godly to him. On the other hand, he didn't want to hurt his wife's feelings.

Going back to the rental room was not very pleasant for my parents because they did not want to deal with the grouchy property owner and his wife. My father managed to find another room to rent in another house. We left that house about a week later to move to another hellhole owned by another very grumpy family. My parents and my grandmother did not have nice things to say about that family.

I was probably not even a toddler when I got sick. It was pneumonia at first that turned into whooping cough. It turned more severe by the day. I lost so much weight. From a chubby little boy I turned into a tiny, pale, and boney one. My parents, my grandmother, and the rest of our relatives were worried. The doctors didn't have any answer as to what was wrong with me, and they almost gave up on me. My parents and my grandmother prayed for me and did *nazr*, vowing to give away some money to the needy people, or to go on a pilgrimage, if I recovered. My mother and grandmother started treating me with herbal medicines and feeding me properly. We had some little stores in the bazaar, which were selling those kinds of medicines. Now, there are many of them in Iran. Most Persians are strong

11

believers of the herbal medicines. They are deeply proud of their foremost physician, Abu Ali Sina[17] who treated his patients with herbal medicines.

I gradually got better, and in a matter of six months, I was healed completely. My parents took me to the holy city of Mashhad, 850 kilometers east of Tehran, to the Shrine of Emam (Imam) Reza for a pilgrimage and to fulfill their *nazr*.

When we came back from our trip, life was as usual; Mother would be working around the house and Father was struggling to make ends meet. My grandmother was doing her usual things until my brother Iraj was born. He was born, a healthy boy, and life was not getting any easier for Agha Joon. My brother looked very much like me. Most often, we were mistaken for twins. However, personality wise, we were two different people. He was hyperactive, outgoing, and always in a fighting mood; I was much more reserved and a peacemaker.

When Iraj was about six months old, my father was given one month to find another place to live. Not very many people in Iran were willing to rent to couples with kids, especially as young as we were, and there was no such thing as apartment complexes back then. My parents had a hard time finding places to rent. They finally found a place to rent, just a room, not very convenient at all. However, the good news for Agha Joon was that he landed a job with a reputable company, Press Express in downtown Tehran. An Iranian-Armenian, Mr. Malekian, owned this company. It was a big company doing shipping, airborne, and trading goods with a lot of other countries, including the old Soviet Union, but mostly European countries. In addition, they did ticketing for travel by air and by the sea. Yazdan Amoo was already working there and, upon recommendation of Uncle Sarrullah, he helped my father find that job.

My father was hired as a blue collar worker in charge of opening and closing the company and scheduling people to stay overnight as night watchman. During the daytime, he was in charge of the kitchen, making tea and coffee for the employees. It was a hard job but stable, secure, permanent, and best of all, the pay was better than the previous jobs he held.

Most of the employees of this company were Persian-Armenian. Mr. Malekian was an intelligent executive and yet a very kind and caring person. He used to speak in many different languages: Farsi, Armenian, English, French, Dutch, and a little Russian. I remember one day I was sitting on a chair near the entrance door looking at the replicas of the big boats, ships, and airplanes placed on the

---

17   *Abū 'Alī al-Ḥusayn ibn 'Abd Allāh ibn Sīnā'*, known as Abū Alı Sınā by Persians, or Ibn Sina in the Arab world or Avicenna in Greek (980-1037BC) was a Persian physician, mathematician, philosopher, astronomer, and Islamic scholar. He wrote numerous treatises on a variety of subjects, many of them burnt during the Mongolian invasion of Iran, nevertheless 240 of them survived. His well-known books, *The Book of Healing*, and the *Canon of Medicine* were used as standard medical text at many different medieval universities.

flat surface pedestal by the window when Mr. Malekian showed up to work. All the employees in the lobby rose to their feet, bowing to him and paying him respect. As he was taking the stairs to go to his office, he turned back and slowly walked toward me; again, all the employees got up. As he came to me, everybody was looking and probably thinking, "Oh boy, Karim (my father) is in trouble." He walked closer and closer to me. I got up and said, *"Salam, agha"* ("Hello, sir").

"Salam, pesar" ("Hello boy"). He sat right next to me.

"How are you?" he asked.

"Khoobam mercy, I am well, thank you," I said.

"What is your name?" he asked.

"My name is Habib Eslami," I said.

"Are you Karim's son or Yazdan's?"

"Karim's son."

"What would you like to be when you grow up?"

"I am not sure, but I like airplanes. Maybe I will be a *ranandeh havapeyma,* airplane driver."

He laughed, "You mean, *khalaban,* pilot."

"Baleh, agha" ("yes, sir") I said.

At this time, he lifted one of those replica airplanes and asked me, "Do you like this?"

"Yes, I do," I said. He gave it to me.

He also gave me a piece of a chocolate bar, which was rare those days in Iran, probably imported. *"Mercy, agha,* thank you, sir." He tousled my hair and left to go to his office on the second floor. My father's kitchen was also upstairs. Mr. Malekian asked my father to his office. Agha Joon was wary and concerned that he might be reprimanded for bringing me to work.

"Karim, I like that little boy of yours."

"I will not bring him back any more."

"No, Karim, he is smart and a well-behaved kid. You can bring him any time."

My father often told us such stories about our childhood. Sometimes he would take my brother Iraj, but seldom both of us together. It was a joy for me to go there with my father, especially when it was his turn to be the night watchman.

The nights that he stayed at the company, he would clean the place after everybody was gone and then he would cook, make tea, and read me nighttime stories until I fell asleep. One of those nights, as my father was sweeping the floor, he found a big stack of money wrapped with a rubber band. He picked

13

up the money and hid it somewhere safe. The amount of money was large, large enough to solve much of my father's financial problems. The next day he went from one office to another. He would ask people whether they lost anything. The company was huge with many offices. He literally went to every employee until he finally found the owner of the money. He had gained the love and respect of everyone at his workplace. He used to help needy people; he would give them money, buy them food, and buy things for their children. One winter evening, as my father and I were going home after a long day at work, the weather was bitterly cold and we both were wearing our overcoats. We got off the bus and started walking toward the house when we noticed a homeless man sleeping on the sidewalk with his money jar next to him. My father put some change into his jar and we kept on walking. After walking for a few feet, he paused and turned to me and said, "Son, I want you to stay put and I will be right back." I was probably seven or eight years old. I was just wondering what he was trying to do. He went back towards the homeless man, took his overcoat off, and put it on him.

"Why did you do that?" I asked my father.

"He needed that. I can afford to buy another one. He can't," my father said. He went on saying that it is one's moral and religious duty to help others. "Son, life is not just you and the people around you; life is about giving, sacrificing for the good cause, and sympathizing with people's sorrow. When you help people, you can be rest assured that you will receive help when you need it. There is more joy in giving than receiving."

After hearing those words, I turned to my father and said, "I want to give my overcoat to the homeless man as well. Maybe he has a son my age." My father smiled and said, "Let's go home, son."

When we got home, my mother looked at my father and said, "What happened to your overcoat? Did you give it away again?"

My parents were tired of renting and dealing with the property owners. Agha Joon worked in the company for a while. He saved some money, borrowed some, and with the help of my grandmother and after consulting with Uncle Sarrullah, he managed to buy a small two-bedroom house with a decent-sized kitchen in the west of Tehran. The houses were reasonably inexpensive in that part of the city. Not too long after buying that house, my mother gave birth to my brother Nasser, a green-eyed, good looking smiley little boy. He was an easy going kid and hardly ever cried.

A few years later, my parents added one more story to the house with two more bedrooms. We moved upstairs and rented out the two bedrooms downstairs.

My parents never treated any of their tenants the way they had been treated. They would always consider the tenants as part of the family. The tenants usually left for reasons such as job relocations or buying houses of their own and so on, but never for harsh treatment. They usually left with tears. When the tenants were under financial pressure, my father would not charge them rent. On some occasions, he even helped them financially.

FOUR

During the summer of 1958, when I was barely six years old, my grandmother recommended registering me for a Quran class. My mother found a Quran class in the neighborhood and registered me there for very little money. The teacher was a tiny but tough little old lady. Not only would she have us memorize some verses in the Quran, she expected perfect Arabic pronunciations. If we made any mistake or if we were a minute late to class, she would punish us. The punishment was to hit us with a stick on the palm of our hand. I did not like her and was not motivated to attend her class at all, although I always enjoyed listening to my father singing and reciting Quran. I cried every morning when my mother tried to get me ready for that class.

One day after I was beaten by the lady, I snuck out of the class and left. While trying to run away, I could hear the old lady shouting, "Come back, or else you will be punished more severely next time."

When I got home earlier than expected, my mother asked me, "What happened?"

I told her that the teacher beat me with a stick.

My mother got mad and took me back to that school and yelled at the lady, "How dare you raise your hand to these little kids? Instead of teaching them, you are terrifying them." That was the end of my going to that class. Late September 1958 my mother registered me at Farmanieh Elementary School. We had to be vaccinated before entering the first grade, so my poor mother took me from one clinic to another. Boys' and girls' schools were separated back then.[18]

---

18   It was during mid 1970s that government officials decided to overhaul the whole educational system in Iran and make it more westernized. As a result, they categorized the school system into elementary school, middle school, and high school. One of their plans was to integrate boys' and girls' schools. First, they started the plan at the middle school. Mullahs adamantly resisted this idea. However, that happened after I graduated

Farmanieh Elementary School was far from our house, and I didn't have a very good feeling about going to school because of my bad memories of the old lady. Our first-grade teacher was a very nice lady. She was not anything like the old lady, but I did not like school. Homework assignments were long and not fun at all. I had no desire to do school work at home. My grandmother was always the source of encouragement and inspiration for me to do my homework.

In the first grade, I was always very quiet and hardly ever conversed with anybody. One day, my teacher asked me a question in class. I knew the answer, but I kept quiet and said nothing. She repeated the question. Again, I kept quiet. "I am talking to you. Why don't you answer me? Are you deaf?" she yelled. Everybody started laughing.

The bell rang and we all went into the yard. I had to do something, I was afraid that the kids would make fun of me by calling me deaf or other names. I went toward the main door. The door attendant was busy talking to people, and I snuck out of the door and ran as fast as I could. While running, I would pause after a few steps to look back and to make sure that the door attendant was not running after me. I was so relieved when I finally got home. My mother was surprised to see me home so early. I told her the whole story.

The next day, I left the house unwillingly. I was afraid that I was going to be punished by Mr. Meshkatian, the dean of our school. My mother noticed the fear in my eyes, and, without my knowledge, she followed me to school. We were lined up from grades one to six, said the prayer, repeated the pledge of allegiance, which was the tradition in those days, and as we were going to our classroom, I was called to go to the office and report the reasons for my skipping classes on the previous day. I went to the office and, to my surprise, I saw my mother there yelling at the teacher and asking why she humiliated me in front of the whole class. That was an embarrassing moment for me, but I was proud of her for sticking up for me.

I was very much afraid of Mr. Meshkatian. He was very rough with students, and he would punish those who came late to school. One day I got up late and was late for school. I told my mother that I was going to have to skip school because there was no way that I could get there on time and Mr. Meshkatian would punish me. My cousin Zahra, Uncle Mousa's daughter, was staying with us during that time. My parents treated her as their own daughter, and we loved her as one of our sisters. She took me to school that day and used her charm to talk Mr. Meshkatian out of punishing me.

---

from high school. During my time, we had only elementary and high school. The government separated boys' and girls' schools again after the revolution.

Another time, my then three-year-old brother Nasser had disappeared for hours. My mother was crying hysterically and we were all looking for him. My father came back from work and left the house in a haste to look for his little boy. We were all worried that something drastic might have happened to him. The whole neighborhood got involved. Nasser was a good looking and smiley kid; everyone in our neighborhood loved him. After searching for him for more than half-a-day, it was around midnight that cousin Zahra showed up carrying Nasser on her back. She had done it by going from one police station to another. According to cousin Zahra, when she finally found him in a police station, he was sitting with a bunch of police officers, smiling at everyone and eating food with them. Some police officers jokingly asked cousin Zahra if they could keep him there. The whole neighborhood celebrated the safe return of Nasser. Zahra was one of my heroes. She was loved by everyone in our family. Every time I had a problem, I would go to her for solution.

One early morning in my second grade, I went to school and noticed a number of buses lined up. We were told that classes were cancelled. Students were all happy about the good news, but we were all curious as to what was happening. Then we learned that they were going to take us to greet the president of the United States of America. We were taken by the bus, and each of us was given small flags of Iran and America. We were lined up along a street that ended up with the airport and asked to wave the flags. After waiting for a while, we observed a number of police officers on their motorcycles followed by a number of black limousines. Then a convertible slowly passed by with the Shah and President Eisenhower standing and waving their hands for people. Everybody waved the flags and enthusiastically applauded and greeted the two leaders. That was my first time looking at the Shah's face live. One of the streets in Tehran was named Eisenhower shortly thereafter. After the revolution, they changed it to a different name.

After the welcoming ceremony ended, I tried to sneak out of the crowd and go home. I slowly started walking away from the rest of the students when I noticed a tall and handsome but scary-looking guy standing in my way. He said, "Where do you think you are going, boy?" Then he grabbed my hand and took me to the bus! That person was none other than the infamous dean of our school, Mr. Meshkatian.

Another good reminiscence of that year was the wedding ceremony of the Shah and Ms. Farrah Diba, his third wife. The celebration took one week and to the best of my recollection, schools were closed for the whole week.

FIVE

September 21, 1959, I started the second grade in the new school. The new school was much closer to my house and the school environment was more relaxed, and we did not have Mr. Meshkatian there. However, going back to school and thinking about doing homework again was not exciting for me at all. In addition, being bullied and harassed by a kid in the neighborhood named Kian made me dislike school even more.

In those days, the teachers assigned a great deal of reading, writing, memorizing, and doing arithmetic problems on a daily basis. It was really too much for an eight-year-old to digest. I didn't have anybody around the house to help me with my homework. My father worked long hours, and my mother, although a very smart lady but she didn't know how to read or write. My cousin Zahra was attending evening school and didn't know much more than I did. My grandmother Shah Sultan was always encouraging me, bringing me fruits, cookies, candies, and giving me incentives to do my homework. Every time I finished my homework, she would give me a pat on the back and show me love. Her way of showing love and attention was not kissing, blabbering, and hugging as most Persians do. She expressed her love and affection in a magical way that is hard to explain, but it always worked.

Weekends were always relaxing for everybody, and Thursday evenings were my favorite because we did not have to go to school the next day. On Fridays, we stayed at home, listened to the radio, and had gatherings of relatives and friends. Telephones were luxury items, and only rich people could afford having phones. Therefore, guests would show up without any prior notifications. My poor mother had to cook for so many people on Fridays. Sometimes my father would invite his co-workers and their families for lunch or dinner. I especially enjoyed the visit by one of my father's friends, Mr. Ashok, who had a pretty daughter named Anna. At

21

my young age, I had a big crush on Anna. Every time they visited us, Anna and I played for hours; we read books together and laughed aloud.

Mr. Ashok was an Iranian-Armenian. He was a devout Christian and my father a devout Muslim. Yet religion was never a barrier between the two and never a topic of their conversation. Mr. Ashok had a high position at the company, but he was a humble person and down to earth. He considered my father as one of his best friends. Mr. Ashok lost his young wife to an unknown disease. He was extremely depressed and decided to send his children, Anna, and her younger brother, to their grandmother in Armenia. About a year later, Mr. Ashok decided to join his kids in Armenia. He often expressed his anger that Armenia was a part of the Soviet Union; he never wanted to live under the Communist rules. He was proud to be an Iranian and to be free to practice his religion. His last day at work, I happened to be there, and he was sad and in tears. He shook hands with everyone and said, "Good-bye." I don't forget the emotional moment that Mr. Ashok had with my father. They both had a hard time saying good-bye to each other. They were both in tears. He then came to me, gave me a big hug, and said, "You have the greatest father in the world."

In those days, other than family gatherings, the main source of entertainment at home was radio. I was very much interested in listening to the radio because the programs were very entertaining and fun to listen to. After school, often I would hang out with my friends in the neighborhood or my brother Iraj, playing soccer, or volleyball, and go home just before my father's arrival. We had to wash our hands, feet, and faces every time we came home or else my mother would not let us eat. After dinner, I would do some homework and listen to the classical Persian music and the nighttime stories on the radio before going to bed. Unlike Thursday nights, Friday evenings were not very exciting for me because I had to go back to school the next day. Thinking of being bullied by Kian was scary.

The birth of my brother Ahmad was a joyful moment in my life that year. Ahmad was the best-looking kid in our alley. Nasser and Ahmad both had the prettiest green eyes in their childhood, but they turned darker later on. I was always proud of my little brother, Ahmad. I used to take him everywhere with me. Kian used to make fun of me by telling other kids in the neighborhood that my little brother was my bodyguard. He would never try to harm me when I had my little brother with me. The people in our alley would come to our house just to pick him and play with him.

One day on my way home after school, I saw Kian bothering a kid. As soon as he saw me, he came towards me, and I started running. He tripped me; I fell down and got hurt. He ran away. With the help of a classmate, I managed to get up with scratches and blood on my hands and pain in my chin and all over my body. The pain got worse by the minute. I asked my classmate not to tell my mother what happened. I went home and expectedly, my mother asked me, "What happened?"

"I was running too fast and fell down," I said. She put some *dava ghermez*, red medicines, on my hands, bandaged them, and asked me to take a rest. That evening my father and my grandmother came home. I was glad to see my grandmother, who had just come back from my uncle's house.

The next day I woke up feeling even worse. The pain became unbearable and I started developing fever, coughs, sore throats, and severe body aches on top of my pain from bruises and injuries. My parents took me to the doctor, and he diagnosed me with meningitis. It was a dangerous disease back then, and some young kids had died from it. The doctor prescribed some medicines and ordered complete rest until I healed completely. Because of good care by my mother and grandmother, I felt better a few days later. I enjoyed staying at home and not going to school for a while. I hated going back to school because I was afraid to encounter Kian again, but I vowed not to run away from him this time. I saw him a few times from afar and tried to avoid him as much as I could. The school year ended successfully without any more incidents with Kian.

A few days after the school year ended, we departed to the countryside, Taleghan. That is what we did during most summer holidays. Other than my father, who had to work, the whole family—my mother, my brothers, Iraj, Nasser, Ahmad, and my cousin Zahra—used to pack our clothes and leave Tehran for Taleghan by bus and would stay there for almost the entire summer. The center of *Taleghan* is a small town called *Shahrak*, which means small city. Shahrak is the main connecting point for all the villages. In those days, the buses would travel to Shahrak only.

From Shahrak onward, people had to either walk or rent a donkey, mule, or a horse to get to their desired destination. Now, the roads are all paved and the transportation is much easier than before. Luckily, my uncle Mousa and sometimes my uncle Isa and often one of his friends used to come to Shahrak to get us. Cousin Zahra, my brother Iraj, and I would normally walk while mother and my brothers Nasser and Ahmad rode on a horse. A donkey would often carry our bags and suitcases. It would take us almost one hour to get to my mother's birth village, *Harandj*. It was tiresome to travel such a long distance, but fun and joyful. Often we would stop by a nearby spring to take a break, to drink, and to have some snacks, I mean real snacks; local breads, cheese, and fruits. There are many springs in Taleghan, and the landscape is absolutely pure and breathtaking.

My grandmother Jaan Jaan Naneh, uncle Mousa and his family, and some summer times, Uncle Isa and his family would come to *Harandj* from their town in Tonekabon. They always arrived there before we did. It was always a joyous reunion. My aunt Farangis used to live there for the whole year. We would all stay at my grandmother's house. Every family would bring food like rice, flour, tea, and sugar to last for three months. Together, they would cook food, bake home-made breads, make tomato paste, jelly, and more. Ladies used to get together at least once a week to bake local breads. The kids had a lot of fun sitting around the rounded in-ground clay oven to watch women bake breads. There was no electricity in most villages let alone refrigerator, so for meat supplies, they used to bring "Ghorme Meat," (smoked meat) in big clay jars which would last for months. On rare occasions, they would buy lamb from local shepherds which were not cheap. Most families had their own chicken farms, and they would most often slaughter their homegrown chickens. For dairy products, most families had their own cow(s) at home. They milked cows usually early mornings and would make their own cheese and yogurt. Everything was homemade. Other than lamb, they seldom bought anything from stores.

For breakfast, most often, we would eat bread, butter, and cheese with tea, and occasionally we would make Persian omelets (a mixture of sautéed onions, eggs, and tomatoes in a pan). Lunchtimes and dinnertimes were always fun. We would all sit together, a crowd of probably twenty, around a big rectangular dining cloth, eat together, laugh, and enjoy each other's company. After lunch, the adults would normally take a nap. The kids would pretend to take a nap; we would whisper to one another and giggle. That would sometimes get on my uncles Mousa's and Isa's nerves. My brother Iraj was the most hyperactive kid, and he hardly ever followed the rules and orders. After our nap, we would go mountain climbing, hiking, or go to the garden to pick Persian berries, apples, plums, cherries, apricots, and peaches.

There are several villages in Taleghan surrounded by mountains, valleys, small and narrow canyons, rivers, and natural springs. Some of the villages are located on the hills and some in the valleys. To the north of Taleghan there are the well-known Alborz Mountains. The highest peak in the Alborz Mountains, which is about 5,671 meters, is situated in Taleghan. Harandj is located on the hilltop. To the east of *Harandj* there is a narrow canyon called Band-e-Bonak, to the west a village called *Hassanjun*, to the north Alborz Mountain and to the south a village called *Koolaj*, known as the little Swiss. The word *Harandj* comes from the combination of *Har* and *Gandj* and means "every treasure." Rumor has it that gold and silver treasures have been buried in different parts of *Harandj* and some fortune hunters go there every year to dig such treasures. The well-known Persian writer Jalal-e-Al-e Ahmad and the well-known spiritual-leader Ayatollah Mahmud Taleghani[19] were both from Taleghan and they are considered as two of Iranian most distinguished revolutionary leaders.

Although there were no TVs and no amusement parks, no restaurants and no electricity in Taleghan, we would never get bored there, and there was always something to do. My favorite thing to do was to go hiking, mountain climbing, and camping with my uncle Mousa or sometimes with the whole family. Often I would hang out with my friend Mohammad. One day as I was headed to Mohammad's house, I got attacked by a number of killer bees and was stung on my hands and face. My grandmother came to my rescue and put some herbal medicines on the stings to calm the burning sensation. The next day my face was swollen. It took weeks to heal.

On another occasion, Mohammad and I contemplated going to the Band-e-Bonak Valley during an evening. To go to this valley, we had to go down a very steep and somewhat dangerous hill. Down in the valley there was a river and several small springs. The valley was long and narrow; to the north of the valley, there was a beautiful narrow waterfall, flowing into a small pond with clean water, and usually women, and especially young ladies, would go there to wash clothes and to socialize. To the south of the valley, there was nothing exciting but just the river and some walnut trees. Mohammad and I used to go there often to pick fresh walnuts. Sometimes, we would take bread and cheese with us there, and eat them with fresh walnuts. The blackness as a result of peeling the walnuts would stay on our hands for days. We had a lot of fun doing that. However, you had to be a daredevil to go there during late evenings or nighttimes.

One evening, around sunset, Mohammad and I decided to go there. We were probably ten or eleven years old. Mohammad had warned me about the danger that we might be facing—being attacked by wolves or jackals or being abducted by genies! In those days, there were myths and stories about genies. I was really

---

19   Ayatollah Mahmoud Taleghani was born on September 9, 1911 in the village of Gilyard Taleghan. He learned much of Islamic lessons from his father. He continued his education in Razavieh and Faizieh Qom. He started his political activities against Reza Shah in 1938. He was imprisoned for his lectures on Islamic values and against ruling of Reza Shah in 1939. After Reza Shah, Taleghani became even more politically active against the new king, Mohammad Reza Shah. Between the ruling of Reza Shah and his son, Taleghani was imprisoned a dozen times. He was a founding member of the Freedom. He was a big supporter of Dr. Mossadeq's nationalization of oil but against secularism. During 1979 revolution he was Khomeini's biggest ally. However, immediately after the revolution, Khomeini and Taleghani started having differences over different issues; Khomeini was leading the government towards totalitarianism whereas Taleghani was pro-democratic establishment. The differences between the two leaders became more obvious in April of 1979 when Taleghani warned against the return of dictatorship. Taleghani died in September of 1979.

determined to go down there. By the time we got there, we were out of breath and thirsty. As soon as we got to the river, we noticed several hundred snakes in the water. We got scared and decided to climb up the incline as fast as we could. We climbed almost halfway up when I fell and rolled down the hill and injured several parts of my body. The hill was mainly comprised of small rocks and sand. Poor Mohammad ran towards me to my rescue. Luckily, my injuries did not seem very serious, and I immediately got up and asked Mohammad to run. It was very dark and we could hardly see the ground in front of us. We were afraid that we would get stung by snakes. The snakes in Taleghan are very poisonous. When we finally reached to the top of the hill, I noticed pain all over my body. I couldn't walk straight. I was limping. Mohammad accompanied me to the door and left. My mother and the rest of my relatives had been looking for me. They asked me for explanation, and I told them the story. "Are you out of your mind? Going to the valley at this time," my mother exclaimed. "You could have gotten yourself killed."

One of my most favorite things to do in Taleghan was to go to my uncle Mousa's field to plow using the cattle. When the crops of grain or wheat were harvested, they used cattle again to trample the crops in order to take the seeds out of their shells. Everything was done by hand; no advanced technology was used. The workers were compensated with meals, grains, and maybe a little money. My uncle and his workers were not farming for business but for self-usage only. I would take over for one of the workers occasionally for fun. For lunch, we would take local homemade bread and cheese with grapes, or watermelon, or Persian melon, or cantaloupe. Often we would take tomatoes and cucumbers and sometimes hard-boiled eggs or boiled potatoes. We always carried a couple of blankets to use as lunch pads and to take a nap after lunch.

Some Thursday evenings my father used to come to visit. He would bring lots of food, fruit, rice, tea, cookies, and so on for everybody to share. It was always a joy for my brothers Iraj, Nasser, Ahmad, and I to see Agha Joon. He would leave on Friday afternoons to get ready to go to work the next day. It was sad to see my father leave. We would sometimes beg him to stay longer. Some summers, however, he could take a longer vacation. He sometimes would take my brother Iraj and me to his birth village, *Segran*, on foot of course. It was quite a long walk from Harandj to Segran. It would take hours to get there. We would stay at our relatives' houses for a few days. We would enjoy the warmth of the people of Segran.

We normally would stay in Taleghan for almost the entire summer, if not more, and would come back to Tehran a few days before school started on the first day of fall, *Mehr the first,* September 22. The last day of our stay in Taleghan was usually sad; it was hard for my mother and me to say good-bye to everyone and especially to my grandmother, Jaan Jaan Naneh. She would always cry and make every one of us cry. Sometimes, she would come with us to Tehran and stay with us for a while, but most of the time, she would stay with my uncles, Mousa and Isa up north. Very seldom she would stay in Taleghan with my Aunt Farangis for the entire year.

The new school year started. It was the fall of 1960 and I started the third grade. The first few days of school were peaceful, and there was no sign of Kian. I was hoping not to see him ever again. It would have been a nightmare to confront him after having such a great time in Taleghan.

However, my nightmare came true; one day as I was walking to my house with one of my classmates, Kian came up to me and started bullying me again. "Listen, Kian, I don't have anything against you, and I want you to stop bothering me." He pushed me around and challenged me to a fight. He pushed me to my limit. He was bigger than I was. I could not defend myself standing up, so I quickly bent over, grabbed both of his legs, and pinned him down hard and beat him on his face left and right until I felt that he was almost unconscious and defenseless.

"Stop, stop, he's had enough," a friend of Kian yelled.

"I will stop if he promises not to harass me or anybody else," I said. I got a bit concerned because I thought that he might not get up. I stayed there to make sure that he was not seriously hurt. I felt so bad. After a few minutes, he got up. I went to him and asked him whether he was okay. He looked down and didn't say anything. I could tell that he was embarrassed. He left. A number of students who were watching the fight cheered and clapped for me. Kian never bothered me again.

SIX

My father was getting tired of working for other people. He took a leave of absence from work for a period of almost two years, from part of 1960 to 1962, to start his own business. He used to travel to the northern province of Mazandaran frequently. Often we wouldn't see him for months. My brothers and I were so attached to Agha Joon; his absence was hard. Unfortunately, that business which seemed to be profitable at first turned out to be a disaster. My father lost a lot of money and incurred a lot of debts to particularly a person who had fraudulently caused him all the troubles. When he finally came back to Tehran, he found out that he had lost his job and shortly after, he lost his mother. To make long story short, we went through one and a half years of protracted hardship. My father had far too much pride to discuss his problems with people. My witty mother sought help from her brother, Mousa and my father's brother, Sarrullah. Together they brought up the matter to the attention of a very influential relative who was a well-respected member of Ministry of Justice at the time, and with his help; they managed to wipe out all of my father's debts. Then again, my astute mother persuaded my father that he should make an attempt to see Mr. Malekian to get his old job back which he finally did. Mr. Malekian did not hesitate to allow my father to go back to work in the company again. That's when my father was put in charge of the big warehouse, as mentioned before.

The loss of my grandmother, Shah Sultan, in early March 1962, was devastating to me. I loved her so dearly, and to this day, I have not forgotten her constant care and attention for me. I can never forget my father's devotion to and his love for his mother. He used to feed her, dress her, give her medicines, and carry her on his back down the stairs to take her to the bathroom. My mother also used to take care of her in my father's absence.

Another sad memory of that year was the Boein Zahra[20] earthquake, which touched me deeply. Just before the start of the fourth grade, I was at my uncle's house. My cousin Shaheen, the daughter of Uncle Yazdan, had come to visit. We decided to go see the well-publicized American movie about Genghis Khan. There were six of us. The movie theater, Universal, was packed with people on the first floor and the balcony. We could only find tickets for the rooftop. The movie got to an exciting scene when Morteza whispered to me, "Habib, stop shaking the chair." Guity asked Shaheen to settle down and not be nervous. All of a sudden, Uncle Sarrullah told us that it was an earthquake and gently asked us to get up and leave. Immediately, after my uncle used the word "earthquake," the people behind us started shouting, "Earthquake!" People rushed to the exit door on the rooftop. It was just about to get chaotic when my uncle asked people for calm and restraint. The next day we were informed of a strong earthquake, centered in the town of Boein Zahra, which caused several thousand deaths and the destruction of more than one hundred surrounding villages. It was a terrifying earthquake with strong aftershocks that pulled the people of Tehran out of their houses for a few nights.

I remember that my all-time favorite champion, Gholam-Reza Takhti, the wrestling champion of the world and the most popular sportsman in Iran, used his influence to gather donations and financial support for the earthquake victims. He went street-to-street and door-to-door asking people for help. He inspired other champions and celebrities to use their fame in order to collect donations for the victims. People's love and respect for him grew further, and he became the people's champion from that moment on.

One of my fondest memories in the fourth grade was the discovery of my singing talent by my cousin Zahra and some of her friends. I came home one day; Zahra and a couple of her friends were at home. They were listening to the radio, dancing, talking, and having a great time together. She wouldn't dare do that when my mother was around. My mother and my three younger brothers were visiting *Khale Safieh*, Aunt Safieh. One of Zahra's friends was a very pretty girl by the name of Nadia. She used to live in the same alley and was a very popular girl in the neighborhood. Not only was she pretty, she was outgoing and witty. The boys in the neighborhood would go nuts for her. I had a crush on her too, even though she was much older than I was. The radio started playing the music of one of my favorite singers, Akbar Golpayegani, also known as Golpa. I was singing along and enjoying myself when I noticed that the girls became quiet, turned off the radio, and gathered around me. "What?" I said. They asked me to continue.

---

20   Boein Zahra is a town in the province of Qazvin. Qazvin province is located approximately 165 kilometers northwest of Tehran.

I was too shy and had no idea that they liked my voice. They asked me to continue. I sang one of Golpa's songs and they liked it. They all kissed me on the cheek. "I had no idea he could sing like this. I guess he inherited that from both of his parents," cousin Zahra said.

A few days later as I was passing Nadia's house, she grabbed my hand, pulled me to her house, took me to a room, and asked me to sing. I refused and she insisted, "Please, do it for me."

"How can you say no to a beauty like that?" I thought to myself. I did sing a song, she asked me for another, and after finishing my second song, I heard clapping and shouting "bravo" from the other room. Nadia's parents, Mr. and Mrs. Bahmani, and her brothers and sisters were all present and listening in that room. Mr. and Mrs. Bahmani were a great couple and well respected in our alley. I never forgot Mr. Bahmani's big smile, his friendly and fatherly attitude. Occasionally he would come to the gathering of the boys and would tell us stories or give us candies. Everyone in our alley loved him.

A few days before *Chahar Shanbeh Suri*,[21] the last Wednesday before Persian New Year, on my way to school with a bunch of kids, I hurled a small firecracker (popper), which accidentally popped in front of a Volkswagen Beetle. The car stopped. The driver got out of the car and grabbed me by my neck and pushed me into the back seat of the car next to a lady. There was another guy sitting in the front seat. These guys started yelling at me, cussing me out, and threatening me. I was scared and had no idea where they were taking me. The lady was much more poised and asked for restraint. She gently asked me, "Why did you do that, young man?"

"I am so sorry, it was just an accident." I said. She insisted that they should release me and take me back. They took me to a police station and lodged an official complaint against me. The chief of police apparently told them that I was a minor, there were no casualties, and they couldn't do much. However, they threatened that if I ever engaged in such acts again, they would punish me. The police told them that they were responsible to take me back where they picked me. Incidentally, they had picked me up from a nearby steel factory where one of my cousins by the name of Mirza, the eldest son of Aunt Safieh, worked as a blacksmith.

---

21   The last Wednesday of the year before Persian New Year is called *Chahar Shanbeh Suri* (Chahār shanbe-Sūri). Chahar Shanbeh means Wednesday and Suri means red. It symbolizes the importance of the Sun as the source of energy. This is an ancient Persian festival that goes back to 18th century BC. The celebration usually starts in the evening, with people making bonfires in the streets and jumping over them singing *zardi-ye man az to, sorkhi-ye to az man*. This statement literally means my paleness (sickness) is yours and your redness (health and beauty) is mine. Bonfires symbolize the sun; they are lit to "keep sun alive." After the revolution, the government of the Islamic Republic tried hard to abolish the festivity but never succeeded.

They took me back there, and as soon as I got out of the car, I noticed two of the workers, one being my cousin, standing right in front of the car. A bunch of other workers surrounded the car.

My cousin Mirza shouted at the driver, "He is just ten years old, how dare you take him away?" Another fellow challenged the driver to get out of the car. I was frightened of the whole situation and blamed myself for causing all the trouble. At this point, my cousin Zahra and her friend Nadia arrived at the scene. They each gave me a big hug and tried to comfort me. Nadia went to the driver, and yelled, "You coward, why don't you get out of the car? Why don't you pick on someone your own size?"

Nadia was a one of a kind, a girl who knew how to take care of herself in a male chauvinistic society, especially in the west of Tehran, which was known as the place for street thugs. Rumor had it that one day Nadia was riding on a bus; a bunch of guys on the same bus started harassing her. She slapped one of them across his face. When they got off the bus, the guy followed her and started using foul language and sexual slurs against her and her family. As he got closer to her and tried to touch her, she pulled a big knife out of her stocking and told the guy, "If you touch me, the biggest parts of your body will be your ears." As she scared the man away, her spectators applauded.

Today women in Iran do not dare defend themselves against street thugs the way Nadia did, for lack of self-esteem. The cleric regime in Iran has absolutely no respect for the rights of women. The so-called "morality police" in Iran are themselves harassing women and getting away with it. As a result of the brutality of the current regime and the lack of respect for women, we have the biggest percentage of prostitutes ever in the history of Iran. Our women are selling their bodies to make a living or to support their families.

Nadia's younger brother Majid was a playmate and a classmate of my brother Iraj. He was a nice-looking kid, polite, smart, and well liked by the kids in the neighborhood. Unfortunately, during one of my visits to Iran, I learned that he was executed by Khomeini's regime for being "activist against the government." Majid was in his early twenties. I was also told that his older brother became extremely depressed and got into drugs and was found dead on the sidewalk of one of the streets in Tehran. Drugs, addictions, and lack of confidence and self-esteem are also the products of the cleric regime today. A big number of our youths are either committing suicide or overdosing on drugs.

I have no idea what happened to Nadia and the rest of her family. I cried when I was made aware of what happened to her brothers.

SEVEN

The next academic year, as usual, started on September 22, 1962. Our fifth-grade teacher's name was Khanoom Taheri. She was a nice lady and a good teacher. She was petite but tough. We had a bunch of tall and older-looking kids in our class who used to sit in the back row—some of those guys had failed the fifth grade a few times.

At the beginning of the school year, those kids tried to control the class, but later on when they found out how tough she was, they backed down and acted more civilly. For example, one day Hamid, one of those fellows, had brought pictures of Marilyn Monroe, Jane Mansfield, and Brigitte Bardot to class and was circulating them among the students. We were giggling and passing the pictures around. Khanoom Taheri noticed that students were not paying attention to the board and to her teaching; she paused, walked slowly toward one of the kids who was trying to pass the pictures to the next, and snatched the pictures from his hands. She found out who the source of the trouble was and asked Hamid to step forward.

"Why were you disrupting the class?" she asked.

"I didn't mean to disrupt the class; I just asked them for their opinion about something."

"What opinion?"

"I just wanted to know which one of these ladies I should marry. Maybe you could give me an opinion."

Everybody laughed. She paused until we finished laughing. Then she embarrassed the crap out of Hamid, and showed him and the rest of the class that she could not be messed with.

I was not a studious student and did not well in my first and second tri-annual exams. I was weak in several subjects and after the death of my grandmother; I did

33

not have much motivations to study. I was very much concerned that I could fail the whole year and have to repeat the fifth grade. That would have been a disaster. Not only would it be embarrassing for me, for my parents as well. Therefore, I decided to study hard for the final exams to catch up with all of the subjects that I performed poorly in my previous exams. However, Math was my hardest subject in Khanoom Taheri's class. I was just not getting it.

A few weeks before the final exams in early May 1963, as I was leaving school with my classmate, Amir, we noticed a demonstration by a number of young and old people shouting, *"Marg bar shah"* and *"Dorood bar Khomeini,"* "Death to the Shah" and "Long live Khomeini," and other slogans in support of Khomeini.

"Who is Khomeini?" I asked Amir.

"I don't know exactly who Khomeini is, but I think he is a religious figure," he said. "My father has been talking about him for the past few days."

We then noticed a number of police cars came to the scene and tried to disperse people. "Run, run, they might shoot at us," Amir said. Amir's house was much closer to school than mine was. He offered to take me to his house, and I declined because I didn't want my mother to get worried. I was so scared and ran as fast as I could. That was the very first time that I had heard of Khomeini.

I told the story to my father and asked him about Khomeini. "I don't know much about Khomeini, but I know that he has a lot of followers and some people consider him as a *marjaa taghlid* (literally translating, it means source of imitation in matters of Islamic rules and principles)," my father said. "He is an anti-government activist and doesn't agree with the Shah's policies."

"But why?" I asked.

"Politics is dirty and I want you to focus on your studies and never think about politics. If you see any of your friends talk about politics, move away from them."

I would often ask my father questions like, "Do you have a *marjaa taghlid?*"

"No, I am wise enough to go by my own instincts and not to follow any particular person except God, Prophet Mohammad and the twelve imams."

"What about a person who was born in a Jewish family, a Christian, or a Zoroastrian family? Why is it that I hear from my theology teacher or some friends that no religion other than Islam will be accepted on the Judgment Day?"

"Son, all of us are God's creatures. Those so-called Muslims who consider their own religion as the supreme religion and discriminate against other religions are not true Muslims."

"What about Baha'is (Baha'i people)? Is Baha'i faith real? Is it blasphemy to associate with Baha'is? Is it against Islam to shake hands with them? Is it true that they are allowed to marry their own children or brothers and sisters?"

"Son, Baha'is are God's children too. They have the same rights as anybody else. You have seen me shaking hands with Mr. Rabbani and going to his house many times, haven't you? These allegations against Baha'is are spread by the hate mongers and they are far from truth. Son, claiming supremacy of any type is bad, whether it is religious supremacy, racial, language, or nationalistic supremacy," My father used to tell me these words often.

Mr. Rabbani was a Baha'i religious leader in the neighborhood who used to be a devout Muslim. He was a well-educated person, and I occasionally went to him with any questions regarding Persian literature, history, and poetry.

There was another Baha'i family in the neighborhood, the Nouzari family. They lived two houses down from ours. Mr. Nouzari's younger brother used to live with them. He was attending a university in Tehran. It was very prestigious to be a college or university student back in those days. When I was in the sixth grade, I would sometimes go to him with any math and science questions that I had, and he was always courteous with me and patiently answered my questions. I used to be very shy and had too much pride to ask questions from people, but he made me feel at ease asking him questions.

Sadly, the people in our neighborhood, and especially those from a different alley (our rival alley) did not treat these two families with respect. The people in that particular alley were mostly uneducated, religiously fanatic, and very backward. One day, as I was walking home, I noticed a big crowd of people in our alley talking and whispering. As I got closer to our house, I noticed bloodstains everywhere. One of the kids by the name of Touraj from that alley was present at the scene. He was known as a bigmouth, short, and chubby Touraj. I asked him, "What happened?"

"Mrs. Nouzari got what she deserved," he said.

"What do you mean by that?" I asked.

"She was beaten by a number of people, including me," he said.

"But...why?" I asked

"Because she is a Baha'i," he said. "Baha'is are bastards."

"People who beat up a defenseless lady are bastards," I said.

"You are a Baha'i lover and we will take care of you, too," he threatened me.

"Get out of here and go back to your own alley and never come back here again," I told him.

Apparently, she got into an argument with one of the ladies in the neighborhood; it quickly turned into a fistfight with hair pulling. A number of people, including people from the next alley, showed up on the scene and beat Mrs. Nouzari unmercifully. She was rushed to a nearby clinic. I saw Mr. and Mrs. Nouzari that evening and noticed bruises on Mrs. Nouzari's face, forehead, and bandages on her head and hands. I was relieved to learn that she was going to be fine.

I told the story to my father. He became very angry and said, "This is inhumane, and those who committed this act must be prosecuted and punished!"

A few days later, chubby Touraj and some of his friends, tried to approach my brother Iraj and me while we were walking towards home. They were following us and we started walking fast. They caught up with us in our alley. They started provoking and challenging us for a fight. We were surrounded by these guys and there was no way to escape. My brother Iraj threw punches at one of them and knocked him down. They surrounded him. As I tried to defend my brother, their gang leader, Farzad scratched my face and left bloody scratch marks. Shortly after, a number of kids in our alley came to our rescue. Farzad kicked me in my shin; that really hurt. He threw another kick at me; I grabbed him by his foot. He fell down. I punched him once and told him, "You are lucky I am not a dog like you who scratches people's faces. I want you to leave our alley immediately." We gradually overpowered them and made them run.

All of a sudden, one of the girls in our neighborhood by the name of Soraya screamed, "Habib, watch out!" Chubby Touraj had a big rock in his hand, and he had targeted my head. I turned around and he threw the rock at me. I reacted quickly and ducked my head. The rock hit the concrete electric pole. Soraya and I ran after him and caught him. Soraya insisted that she would take care of him.

I grabbed him by his shirt collar. He pleaded to me not to hit him. I said, "I am not going to hit you; I'll let someone else do the job for me." I turned to Soraya and said, "He is all yours."

She slapped him across his face and told him, "You dirty little pig, go back to your dirty alley and dirty friends, and do not ever come back here again." I was so proud of Soraya and thankful to her; she saved me from a big injury or perhaps a fatal injury that day.

I did very poorly on it on the final exam. Usually, back in those days, they would give us the transcripts for the whole year a few weeks after the end of the final exams. The day I went to get my transcripts, I was extremely nervous. I was unsure of a few subjects, especially math. To the best of my recollection, according to the school regulations back in those days, failing more than four subjects would result in repeating the whole year. Failing four subjects or less meant that we had to retake exams on those subjects by the end of the summer. We had only one chance to retake the exams; failing any of the subjects again would result in lagging behind for one year. On my way to school, I kept thinking, "What will happen if I have to start the fifth grade all over again? What will happen if I fail math? In either case, how am I going to look at my parents' faces?" I was having an anxiety attack. I had decided if I flunked the whole year, I would run away forever.

I got my transcripts for that year and, sadly but expectedly, I had flunked math. I took it very hard. I didn't know what to do. "Too bad Zahra is not living with us any longer. I am really missing her. She is the only one who could comfort me on occasions like this," I was muttering to myself. I was too shy to go to Uncle Sarrullah's house. Then it just dawned on me that there is one more person who I could turn to and that was my *khale,* Aunt Safieh. Her house was a good walking distance from the school.

On my way to her house, I saw one of my classmates, who asked me, "How did you do, Habib?"

"Oh, shut up!" I muttered. I kept on walking. It was around noon when I got to *Khaleh* Safieh's house. She was surprised to see me. I had never gone there alone. She asked me if there was something wrong. I told her the story; she comforted me by her kind and encouraging words.

That evening my father and my cousin Morteza showed up at my aunt's house. They were furious. They had been looking for me all over the place. I was ashamed and speechless. "What is going on? Why didn't you tell your mother where you were going?" my father asked. I told them the story.

My cousin said, "At least you did not fail the whole year. That happens to many students. You shouldn't have run away from home for just failing one subject." They took me home. My mother was relieved to see me. My father did not say a word to me for a few days.

I didn't understand his silence, so one day, I went to him and asked, "I know you are upset with me, but why don't you talk to me? Why don't you tell me what's on your mind?"

"Son, I am not upset with you because you failed one of your subjects. I am upset with you for not telling anybody where you were going. You got everybody worried. That's what bothered me the most." He continued, saying, "Son, failing a subject was not your choice, but running away from home was your choice, and that was the wrong choice. I have no doubt in my mind that you will pass the subject if you focus on it and organize your thoughts."

"What if I don't pass the subject?" I asked my father.

"That is not the right attitude. You will pass," he said.

I repeated my question, "What if I don't?"

"You do your best, you will achieve the best," he said.

"Are you going to be very upset with me if I fail the retake exam and have to repeat the whole year?" I asked.

"Not if you do your best," he said.

"One last thing, son, behind every failure, there could be a victory or more failure. People who are determined and have a positive attitude in life will achieve victory. Conversely, people who have no direction in life and have a negative attitude will bring more failure to their lives." After hearing those words, I decided to make this failure a milestone of my academic life.

Along the same line many years later, I read a Persian article about a successful man who was asked by a reporter, "What made you so successful?"

"Two words: Good decisions."

"What made you reach good decisions?" the reporter asked again.

"Two words: Bad decisions."

EIGHT

The uprising and anti-Shah campaign orchestrated by Khomeini and his Bazaari followers spread all over Tehran and were especially prevalent in the holy city of Qom where Khomeini resided. Tensions boiled over in early October 1962 when the Shah's government established new laws that turned over election responsibilities to city and provincial councils. These laws removed the requirement that people elected to the *Majlis,* parliament, or to any other public office, be sworn to the Quran. Khomeini and a number of 'Ulama' (religious scholars) interpreted this as allowing religious minorities such as Baha'is and Jews to serve in those capacities. Additionally, the new laws gave women the right to vote—a provision thoroughly denounced by the mullahs. Khomeini also opposed a provision calling for the draft of young clergymen for military duty—an obligation from which they had previously been excluded. The clergy, led by Khomeini, railed against these laws for being un-Islamic and in violation of the 1906 constitution. They called a meeting at which they made the following decisions: 1. to demand that the Shah nullify the new laws, and 2. to admonish all clergy in Tehran and other cities as to the danger of such laws and the need to resist them. Unsurprisingly, many grand ayatollahs gave Khomeini their support. On November 29, 1962, the government of Prime Minister Alam, under pressure from the ayatollahs, rescinded the new laws—a victory for Khomeini and the mullahs. Women protested the government's decision by staging a demonstration in front of Prime Minister Alam's Headquarter on January 7, 1963. Alam, succumbing to the pressure, made a speech promising a positive resolution in accordance with the women's demands.[22]

---

22   Translated from the *Rouz Shomar-e-tarikh-e-Iran az mashrouteh ta enghelab-e-eslami, Jeld-e Dovom,* Chronology of Iran (1896-1979), Vol. 2 by Bagher Agheli, *Nashr-e Goftar,* 1995, pages 145, 147.

Shah was making advancements on what he called "The White Revolution"[23]—a series of social reforms ostensibly designed to usher Iran into the modern age. But he had ulterior motives as well—to wrest the support of the peasants and working class people." In early January 1963, the Shah called for a referendum on the first six principles of his White Revolution. In spite of Khomeini's attempts to persuade people to abandon the referendum, they voted to adopt the first six principles on the day of *Sheshom Bahman mah-e 1341*, (January 26, 1963)—a vote in which women were allowed to participate for the first time. Two days later, the Shah made a speech expressing its successful passage and described it as: "A historic event and, a legitimate and sacred revolution."[24] During the same speech, the Shah stated that in the near future, with everyone's cooperation and hard work, Iran would become a free country with equal rights for men and women that would parallel the most developed countries in the world. A few days later, President John F. Kennedy congratulated the Shah for his success in the referendum.[25] On February 28, women representatives marched in front of the Shah's *Marmar* Palace and thanked him for the new freedoms granted to them.[26]

Khomeini accused the Shah of being anti-Islam and claimed that his White Revolution was in violation of the Islamic faith. Many of the Shah's opposition leaders labeled him as a puppet of the United States and claimed that the White Revolution was dictated to the Shah by President Kennedy. On June 3, 1963, the day of Ashura (see footnote 28), Khomeini made a fiery speech in *Madreseh Faizieh-e-Qom* (Theology school in Qom) denouncing the Shah's reforms and

---

23   White Revolution was a series of reforms that the Shah launched in 1963. One of the main objectives of the White Revolution was to abolish feudalism and begin land reform programs in order to help the peasants in the rural and village areas. Through land reform, the Shah hoped to ally himself with 1.5 million families of peasants living in the countryside. In addition to land reforms, Shah presented five other principles: nationalization of forests and pasturelands, sale of government factories to finance the land reforms (privatization of the government owned enterprises), profit sharing of the industrial workers in the private sector enterprises, extending the right to vote to women (this principle was particularly criticized by the mullahs), establishment of the literacy corps (through this principle, the Shah wanted to abolish illiteracy in Iran). The Shah called for a national referendum in 1963 to vote for or against the reforms. According to the government officials at the time, a vast majority of people voted yes in favor of the reforms. The Shah gradually added 13 other principles through a period of 15 years (1963-1978), including the health care reform.
24   Translated from the *Rouz Shomar-e-tarikh-e-Iran az mashrouteh ta enghelab-e-eslami, Jeld-e Dovom,* Chronology of Iran (1896-1979), Vol. 2 by Bagher Agheli, *Nashr-e Goftar,* 1995, page 150.
25   Ibid.
26   Ibid, page 151.

asking people not to celebrate *Eid Nowruz*[27]. He called the Shah "a despicable person" and equated him with the Yazid.[28]

After Khomeini's speech, uprisings and violent demonstrations erupted in Qom and other parts of Tehran in which several people were killed or injured. Many young clergy were being arrested in the streets of Qom and drafted into military service. Khomeini began circulating leaflets asking people to mourn the martyrs of Qom. A rumor quickly spread among my relatives that Yazdan Amoo had been shot by the soldiers. When I heard, I cried. How tragic that such a good, kind, and joyful soul might now be dead. In fact, it turned out that he had been caught in the middle of gunfire as he was trying to run from the scene. At some point, he fell down hard on a sidewalk and passed out. When he regained consciousness, he found himself in a hospital surrounded by a doctor and nurses, and assuming that he had been shot, perhaps mortally. To his surprise, the doctor and nurses told him that he had not been shot at all and he would be just fine. I can recall being overjoyed to hear the good news. This became a funny story among some of my relatives. Even Yazdan Amoo was able to see humor and he would often humorously tell the story during the occasional gatherings of relatives.

Televisions and telephones were luxury items that few people could afford, and the newspapers and radio stations were being censored. The only source of information was word of mouth. While our parents tried to keep unpleasant news away from us, my friends and I were curious about what was happening. We wondered whether the Shah was going to be toppled. We were concerned that Iran could become a battleground for foreign invaders.

---

27   Nowruz literally means "New Day." Eid Nowruz means New Year festivity. Nowruz marks the first day of spring (usually on March 21) and the beginning of the year in Iranian solar calendar. The moment the sun crosses the celestial equator and equalizes night and day is calculated exactly every year. Thus, Nowruz could occur on March 20 or most often on March 21. It is believed that Nowruz was established by Prophet Zoroaster. It is originally a Zoroastrian festivity and has been celebrated by Iranians and many other countries in the world. On the day of Nowruz, Iranian families visit each other starting with the elderly and celebrate the event. The UN's General Assembly in 2010 recognized the International Day of Nowruz, describing it a spring festival of Persian origin, which has been celebrated for over 3,000 years. During the meeting of *The Inter-governmental Committee for the Safeguarding of the Intangible Heritage* of the United Nations, held between 28 September – 2 October 2009 in Abu Dhabi, Nowrūz was officially registered on the UNNESCO List of the Intangible Cultural Heritage of Humanity.
28   Yazīd Ibn Mu'āwiyata Ibn Abī Sufyān (645CE-683CE) was the second caliph of the Umayyad Caliphate (and the first one by heredity), ruling for three years from 680 CE until his death in 683 CE. The period of Yazid's ruling is thought of as a disastrous period for Muslims, especially Shia Muslims. During his reign, Hussein Ibn Ali, the third Shia imam, was murdered and beheaded by one of Yazid's men, Shimr Ibn Thil-Jawshan in the battle of Karbala in 680 CE. This atrocious crime took place in the month of Muharram. Revenge for Husayn's death was turned into a rallying cry that helped undermine the Umayyad caliphate, and gave impetus to the rise of a powerful Shia movement in Iran. The anniversary of Hussein's *Shahadat* ("martyrdom") is called 'Āshārū (*"tenth"* day of Muharram) and is a day of mourning for Shia Muslims.

The situation continued to get worse. Curfews were instated in Tehran and Qom. The Shah and Ayatollah Khomeini began a battle of words. Shah told Khomeini: "Do not make me put on my father's boots."

"Your father's boots are too big for you," Khomeini replied.

Our final exams coincided with the peak of the uprising, and my mother and I were concerned about the safety of Agaha Joon, as his workplace was located in the center of Tehran, the heart of the demonstrations. All this made it hard for me to concentrate on my studies. While the uprising spread to several big cities such as Mashhad, Isfahan, Tabriz, and Shiraz, it was not an organized effort and was eventually suppressed by martial law. The rioting died down after the arrest of Khomeini in June of 1963. He was jailed for a year and then exiled to Iraq.

Shah accused the mullahs who led the uprising of being elements of the British government and warned them not to get involved with politics. He called them the "Black Reactionaries." I think the Shah's biggest mistake was using violence against the demonstrators—and especially the clergy, who were extremely influential at that time. He might have achieved his objectives through negotiations rather than sending troops and thugs to kill his opponents. Violence begets more violence, more vengeance, and more retaliation. This is a fact of life. I believe the Shah would have been more successful had he given the people more of a chance to get to know the mullahs instead of combating them. In the end, it seems that he paid too much attention to the will and desire of the clergy. Today, the term "violence" applied to the suppression of the Iranian people by the cleric regime is a weak euphemism; Ferocious killings, crimes against humanity, and mass murder better describe the ongoing campaign of terror by the leaders of Islamic Republic. In time, history will judge the current regime for what it is; despotic, authoritarian, and immoral.

N I N E

A few weeks after my fifth-grade final exams, my father contracted a rental agreement for the rooms downstairs to a family of four, Mr. and Mrs. Bozorgy and their two daughters, Zarrin and Parvin. Zarrin was a gorgeous girl with beautiful big green eyes. When I first noticed her, I just couldn't believe my eyes. I thought she was a knockout. Not only was she beautiful, she was sociable, naughty but polite. She was about a year younger than I was but well developed for an eleven-year-old girl. The first day I met her, she shook my hand and said, "You must be Habib because I have already met Iraj, Nasser, and Ahmad."

"You are correct," I said. "What is your name?"

"My name is Elizabeth Taylor," she said. "I am just kidding; my name is Zarrin but I want to be an actress like her one day."

Two or three days later, while I was studying, Zarrin came upstairs to visit and asked me what I was doing, "I am studying," I said.

"It is summer. Why are you studying?" she asked.

"Do you really want to know?" I asked.

"Don't tell me that you are studying for a retake exam," she said.

I felt embarrassed. I turned red and shamefully said, "Yes, I am."

"What subject?" she asked.

"Math," I said.

Then she enthusiastically said, "Don't you worry, Gholam is good at math. I will ask him to teach us both."

"Who is Gholam and why do you want to study with me," I said.

"Gholam is a family friend. I'd like to be your companion and to get prepared for next year," she said. I accepted. Gholam came to the house almost every day; he unselfishly tutored both of us free of charge. He enjoyed doing that. Not only did he teach me math, he helped me boost my confidence. I felt that I was ready to take the retake exam. However, a few days before the retake exam, I was having nightmares and anxiety attacks about failing. I had lost my appetite and a lot of weight.

The day came. I was getting ready to go to school. My mother insisted that she wanted to come with me. Before the exam started, she had a chat with Khanoom Taheri. There were a number of us in a big classroom. Khanoom Taheri and couple of other teachers from other sections were administering the exam. They handed out the exam, I looked at all the questions, and I was confident that I could do them all. Halfway into the exam, I lost track of the time and thought that I was running out of time. I became extremely nervous. I lost my train of thought and started panicking. Khanoom Taheri came toward me, comforted me, and told me to calm down. I was complaining that time was running out. She assured me that there was plenty of time left and that she would give me more time if I needed it. She then glanced through my exam and told me that I was on the right track in all of the problems. I was on a roll after that. Khanoom Taheri was so nice to me that day. I could have kissed her. I felt good coming out of that exam.

I was still worried and negative thoughts would cross my mind, "What if I fail?" A few days later, my mother went to school to see Khanoom Taheri without my knowledge.

She came back with the good news: "You passed the exam."

"How do you know?" I asked my mother.

"I just talked to your teacher and she gave me the good news off the record," my mother said. I thought my mother was making it up to make me feel better until I got my official records a week or two later. Sure enough, I had passed the exam. The day that I got my official records, Zarrin and Gholam came to me and congratulated me for my success. I thanked Gholam for his time and his help. Zarrin told me that she had a surprise for me.

I remember that the Bozorgi family went to the movies quite often and occasionally they took me with them. Zarrin was always fascinated with the female stars in the movies, and her passion was to become an actress one day. A few days before my exam, I had mentioned to her that I would have liked to see a Persian movie about two twin brothers who were separated at birth and after living through years of trauma and harsh circumstances, they found each other. Zarrin and her family took me to see that movie—that was the surprise.

Zarrin and I got along great. We had to see each other every day; we had at least one meal a day together. We studied, shopped for groceries, played games, sang songs, and had a lot of fun together. We were becoming addicted to each other. Zarrin came to me one day and said, "We are going to go for a short, three-day vacation; I want you to come with us."

"I am afraid I can't, because I don't think my parents would allow me to leave the house for three days," I said.

"Don't you worry; I will talk to Mr. and Mrs. Eslami. They both like me, and I am sure they are not going to say no to me," she said. She sure was charming and well liked by my parents. Her father was a bus driver. He borrowed a minibus from his company every time they travelled.

We packed the next day and left for a small community in the countryside near Tehran called *Eivan Darakeh*. We were hosted by a family, friends of the Bozorgi family, who owned a big house located in a corner of a huge garden of fruits and flowers. The weather was very pleasant in that town. After dinner, the women got busy cleaning, and the men started playing backgammon. Zarrin and I started playing card games. Nighttime was cold in that town even in summer. Around bedtime, Zarrin came to my bedside to make sure that I had enough coverage. We chatted some more and went to sleep. We got up early in the morning. After breakfast, we went for a long walk around the town. That evening Zarrin asked me to go for a walk in the garden. We picked some fruits and chatted for a long while. It was becoming cold and she was shivering; I wrapped my jacket around her shoulders. She asked me to sing a song for her. I did and she liked it.

"With this voice you could become a famous singer like Golpa. You really should pursue this," Zarrin said.

"I am not sure if that's what I want to do," I said.

"What do you want to be?" she asked.

"Maybe an engineer or a teacher."

"How about becoming a doctor?"

"Never! I can't imagine dealing with blood or dead bodies," I said.

"That's what I want to do when I grow up. I want to become a doctor," she said.

"You are too pretty to become a doctor. How about an actress? Have you given up that dream?" I said.

"You know that's just a dream. Not very many Persian girls will have the opportunity to become an actress unless they are unattached to their family. My father would never let me pursue that dream," she said. Then Zarrin very quietly whispered to my ears, "Do you like me?"

"Of course I do," I said.

"You see nobody is around, you can kiss me if you want," she said. I gently gave her a kiss on the cheek. "You could do better than that," she said.

"What do you mean?"

"Let's do it the way we see in the movies." At this time, we were whispering to each other and trying to make sure that nobody was around. We did kiss each other on the lips once. We immediately got up and decided to leave. "Do you think that we committed a sin?" she asked me.

"According to Islam, yes, we did. We shouldn't have even held hands together," I said.

She then raised her voice and asked, "Is it a sin for a boy and a girl to love each other?"

"No, it is not, but we are way too young to talk about love," I said.

"Do you love me?" she asked.

I vividly remember that I said, "Yes, more than I love myself."

"Would you marry me if we were at the right age?"

"Yes, I would."

Although the relationship between us was just a puppy love, but I will never forget that evening and Zarrin's beautiful face.

The Bozorgi family left our house a few weeks later. We kept in touch off and on for about a year or so then, we lost touch. Years later, I heard from a mutual friend that Gholam and Zarrin got married. That was shocking news to me, as Zarrin had always considered Gholam as an older brother or maybe even an uncle.

T E N

Fall of 1963, the first day of school, Mr. Zamani, a well-known and well-respected teacher in our elementary school and a good friend of Mrs. Taheri, showed up in class and introduced himself as our sixth-grade teacher. It was my last year in the elementary school; the final exam was a common exam for all the sixth-graders in the country. We were lucky to have Mr. Zamani as a teacher. He taught all of the subjects except the physical education class. He had the reputation as a serious teacher, tough but fair. He was known as a teacher who prepared his students well to pass the difficult nation-wide common final exams—standard exams for all six graders across the whole country. His first two tri-annual exams before the final were hard and challenging. I was under the impression that Mrs. Taheri had talked to him about me, probably as a student who barely passed the fifth grade.

I was determined to study hard and do very well in all of my subjects. That was my promise to my parents as well. This class was very different from my fifth-grade class; students were much more disciplined and academically sound. They were mostly attentive and quick to answer Mr. Zamani's questions. At the beginning, I was nervous and thought that I was going to have a hard time competing and catching up with the class. In particular, three of my classmates were sharp: Mehran, Behrouz, and Shamon. Mehran was the captain of the class. Shamon was excused from attending Quran and theology sessions because he was Jewish.

I remember one day in our Quran class, Mr. Zamani asked if anyone could recite the Quran verses with a good voice. Some of the students who knew that I could sing shouted, "Eslami, sir." Mr. Zamani turned to me and said, "Habib, go ahead and try."

I turned red and bashfully said, "If you don't mind, I will practice some verses and try next time." That was okay with him.

47

Mr. Zamani was a well-dressed teacher; he always appeared in class with a tie and nice suit. He did not strike us as being a practicing Muslim. However, he took his theology and Quran classes very seriously. He read the Quran verses with an excellent Arabic pronunciation and translated them in simple and meaningful Persian words.

With the help of my father, I practiced the verses that we were taught, and in the next Quran class, Mr. Zamani pointed at me and asked me to start. I did, and he really liked it. He complimented my voice that day. My recitation of the Quran verses at the beginning of each Quran period became a routine. Surprisingly, in one of the Quran sessions, Shamon attended the class and asked for permission to sit in.

"Of course, but what made you decide to come to class?" Mr. Zamani asked.

"I came to hear Habib reciting the Quran," Shamon said.

Mr. Zamani turned to me and jokingly said, "See, Habib, you even inspired a non-Muslim student."

Two month into that school year, President John F. Kennedy was assassinated on November 22, 1963. The next day school authorities raised the school's flags half way up. Everybody was talking about Kennedy's death during the break in our schoolyard. The majority of the students expressed sorrow, while a few called Kennedy the enemy of Islam. In our school, some teachers announced moments of silence for the death of the American president, and for that matter the government and many people in Iran expressed sympathy with American people. As previously mentioned many of the Shah's adversaries claimed that the White Revolution was dictated to the Shah by President Kennedy. On the contrary, the article by April R. Summitt[29] proves this claim to be false. President Kennedy tried to persuade some Middle Eastern leaders including the Shah of Iran to make some reforms, in their countries, but not dictated any details. The Shah has been doing reforms regardless—he was determined to push his "White Revolution" forward. In part of the article it is stated:

> "The story of American relations with Iran during the Kennedy Administration (1961- 1963) is one of misunderstandings and missed opportunities. President John F. Kennedy's policy toward the Middle East illustrates the agency and unexpected power wielded by nation's peripheral to the main thrust of the Cold War. In spite of careful planning in Washington, Middle East leaders sometimes manipulated and thwarted Kennedy's policy toward the region. The US-Iranian relationship during the Kennedy Administration is one example. Shah

---

29 *"For a White Revolution: John F Kennedy and the Shah of Iran,"* by April R. Summitt, Middle East Journal, vol. 58, No. 4, Autumn 2004.

Muhammad Reza Pahlavi of Iran used American fears of Communism to gain increased financial aid, military support, and influence in the United Nations. The Shah, however, mostly sought to bolster his faltering regime by exaggerating the external threats to his power. Kennedy and his State Department fell victim to the same fears of instability and Communism and ignored those who argued for a fresh approach in American relations with Iran. The Kennedy Administration is an excellent case study for the nature of power relationships during the Cold War because it came during a period in which policy shifted because of the actions of local players.' In most cases, successful policy toward the "Third World" occurred only when the interests of a superpower and the non-superpower state converged. In spite of Kennedy's resolve to change the American approach to the Middle East, the Shah managed to pose as a reformer, thus assuring a steady flow of dollars."

Anyhow, our physical education period in the sixth grade was intense but fun. During the first half of the period, we had to do warm-ups. During the second half, we sometimes played volleyball, often soccer, occasionally ping-pong, and seldom basketball. Other than ping-pong tables that were set in a large room, the rest of the games took place in the schoolyard. We did not have a separate gymnasium, not in our school. During one of our PE periods, we were left to do whatever we wanted to because our PE teacher did not show up. It was cold outside. We had to do something in order to keep warm. Behrouz came up to me and said, "Habib, let's fight; I am Sonny Liston and you are Cassius Clay."

We were playing around, throwing fake punches, and pretended that we were fighting. I paused and curiously asked Behrouz, "By the way, who are these people that you just mentioned?"

"Haven't you heard of these people?" Behrouz asked.

"No, I have not," I said.

"They are all over the media."

"But we don't have television," I said. "Now, could you tell me who these people are?".

"Sonny Liston is the boxing champion of the world, and Cassius Clay is the challenger, and they are scheduled to fight in a few days," Behrouz said.

"Which countries are they representing?" I asked.

"They are both Americans, dummy."

"How do I know? I told you we don't have television. We don't get the newspaper, and I don't have time to listen to the radio anymore." I said. "How could two people from the same country fight against each other and bring so much publicity?"

Behrouz started explaining what professional boxing was and briefly educated me about the past American boxing champions.

"How do you know all these?" I asked him.

"I read about them in magazines and newspaper articles," he said.

"Can I borrow those magazines?" I asked.

"Yes, of course. Come to my house. I will give you some."

Behrouz was an amazing kid—not only was he smart academically, he was knowledgeable about everything else. He read newspapers, magazines, story-books, cartoon books, and more. Behrouz was a bundle of energy. I went to his house quite often; we studied together, and played different kinds of dice games. Often he would challenge me for a boxing or a wrestling match.

The Cassius Clay-Sonny Liston boxing match was the hot topic of the students during the break the day before the fight. The kids were talking about them enthusiastically and they were betting on them. The majority of the kids were betting on Sonny Liston. Behrouz was saying that Clay would not stand a chance against Liston; other fellow classmates, including me, were rooting for the under-dog. I read about Cassius Clay's victory in the newspaper. Behrouz was in disbelief and was disappointed that he lost his bet.

From that moment on, I became interested in American boxing and a big fan of Cassius Clay. Reading sports magazines and sports columns in newspapers became one of my hobbies in my teens and in college years. I read sports maga-zines and newspaper articles that dealt with professional boxing. I learned about Sugar Ray Robinson, Joe Louis, Rocky Marciano, Jack Dempsey, Floyd Patterson, Sonny Liston, and Cassius Clay. They all had one thing in common with me—they all came from poor and hardworking families. I especially enjoyed reading about the pluckiness and sportsmanship of Floyd Patterson and Rocky Marciano. It was interesting for me to learn that Floyd Patterson, after knocking his Swedish oppo-nent unconscious, picked him up in his arms and waited for the doctor to come to the ring, or that Rocky Marciano went to the dressing room after knocking out his idol Joe Louis, cried, and hugged him. In addition, I was particularly inter-ested in reading about Iranian wrestlers, soccer players, and weightlifters. I also was very much interested in British soccer tournaments—World Cup and Asian soccer games.

I remember in the previous year, when I was in the fifth grade, my father often talked enthusiastically about the newly appointed prime minister, Has-san Ali Mansour. He was charismatic, young, and dynamic. He was an excellent speaker and never used cue cards when he was giving speeches. My father was always talking very highly of him and was very optimistic that the country would be advancing in the right direction under his leadership.

Unfortunately, his time was short. He was gunned down as he was leaving the parliament on February 21, 1964. He was rushed to the hospital and was pronounced dead a few days later. His assassin was twenty years old and a member of Fadaeian-e-Islam. It is believed that Mr. Rafsanjani (the fourth president of the Islamic Republic) was, at the time, a member of the organization and the one who provided the gun for the assassin.[30] That happened just one month before Eid Nowruz. I was in Uncle Sarrullah's house that day and was extremely sàddened by the news. Khanoom Amoo Maliheh, my uncle's wife, was crying. She would always get emotional hearing news as such.

"I know for sure Agha Joon is going to be very sad," I told my uncle.

I went to another room and put myself into the shoes of his children thinking, "God forbid what if something like this happens to my father or to my uncle?"

I went home that night and, sure enough, I found my father sad and emotional. My father's sorrow and the death of the prime minister had an emotional impact on me, and I couldn't get over it for weeks. I was only twelve years old and could not comprehend why some human beings kill other human beings for political gains. Frankly, I still don't understand why! Human beings are the only mammals in the world that kill mass amounts of their own kind. Why?!

I remember one day Mehran came to me and asked me to go see the school principal as soon as possible. I got worried that I might have done something wrong. I went to his office during the break. All the teachers were there; in those days, the teachers did not have their own offices. There was one big office with a number of chairs; during each break, teachers would go to that office to catch their breath, to socialize, and to have a snack. I was embarrassed seeing everybody there, especially Mr. Zamani and Mrs. Taheri. I seriously thought that I had done something wrong. Mrs. Taheri came to me and said, "I heard that you are doing well in Mr. Zamani's class. I am happy for you and proud of you." I was relieved. Then the principal asked Mr. Zamani to excuse me from class for a few minutes. After everybody left for class, the principal and his office assistant sat next to me and asked me if I could sing for them before an audience for *Jashn-e-Sadeh*, the Sadeh festivity.[31] I was surprised as to how the principal knew that I could sing.

---

30   Sandra Mackey, *The Iranians: Persia, Islam and the Soul of a Nation* (New York: Dutton, 1996), page 230.

31   *Jashn-e-Sadeh*, Sadeh festivity is an ancient Iranian tradition normally celebrated 50 days before Nowruz. Sadeh in Persian means "hundred" and refers to one hundred days (50 daytime plus 50 nighttime) left to the beginning of the New Year celebrated at the first day of spring on March 21 each year. Sadeh is a mid-winter festival that was celebrated with grandeur and magnificence in ancient Iran. It was a festivity to honor fire and to defeat the forces of darkness, frost, and cold.

"I have never sung before an audience," I said.

"We are going to have a band that you could practice with. I am sure that you will do fine," the principal said.

I was supposed to practice for at least a couple of weeks with the band to get ready for the program. I told the story to my parents. My mother was supportive; my father was not. My father always enjoyed listening to me singing, but he was adamantly against the idea of singing before a big audience. "I don't want my son to be a *motreb,* a streetwise singer, or musician," he told me.

"Do you call *Fakhteii, Banan, Molook Zarrabi, Iraj,* or *Golpa* a *motreb?*" I asked him. These people were classical Persian singers whom my father liked and respected.

"Son, not very many people can become singers like them," he said. "At this stage of your life you should concentrate on your studies. You have a good voice; it is in your genes. You didn't work hard for it. Try to work hard to become somebody for yourself and a useful person to society. Find a career other than singing; if, in your adulthood, your interest in singing outweighs your other career, you can choose singing as your profession and I will not stand in your way."

After that day, I went to my principal and mentioned the fact that my father was against the idea. He respected that, and I stopped going to the singing practice.

I was somewhat disappointed that I couldn't perform for the ceremony, but that was not going to deter me from my goal of doing well in my studies. I studied hard and my hard work paid off! I did very well in the first general tri-annual exam and was ranked fourth after Behrouz, Shamon, and Mehran, in a class of about forty or fifty. I made my parents very proud. After the first exam, Behrouz, Shamon, and I developed an excellent relationship. Mehran, being the captain of the class and from an upper-class family, did not want to mix with us. We always hung out together, studied together, and played sports together. Behrouz was a genius and a master in math and science subjects. Shamon was also a very smart kid. There was a soccer field near Behrouz's house that Shamon, Behrouz, and I used to play on that field with a bunch of other kids during some weekends.

One cold winter day, we were playing on that same dirt soccer field. I don't think Behrouz was playing that day, but Shamon was there, and he was playing for the opposite team. I was having the time of my life, maneuvering, dribbling, and scoring goals. Shamon, on the other side, was playing very well. During one of the maneuvers, I was tripped by one of Shamon's teammates, fell down on the ground, and passed out. When I regained consciousness, I found myself outside the field with Shamon on my side. He was trying to make sure that I was okay while everybody else was playing. He asked me if I wanted to continue playing. I was not feeling well and couldn't continue. Shamon also stopped playing in order to be with me. Before we left, he turned to his teammate and gently told him, "You hurt my friend. It was not necessary to play that rough." The guy came to me and apologized. We shook hands and said good-bye. I was limping and not quite balanced, so Shamon made sure to accompany me and to get me to my house safely. He paused every few minutes to make sure that I was all right.

Often I cry when I look back at those days. Shamon and I were from two different backgrounds; he was from a devout Jewish family, and I grew up in a Muslim family, yet religion did not come between us. We were good friends and enjoyed each other's companionship. In those days, despite the fact that some fanatics tried to cause friction between Jews and Muslims or Baha'is and Muslims and so on, the Shah's government was vehemently opposed to those kinds of vicious acts.

It is unfortunate that in the twenty-first century, there are still governments that, in the name of religion, are killing innocent human beings. It is sad that today there are still heads of governments who are using religion as a means of gaining more power and expanding their dictatorships. In Iran, the mullahs are using religion as a tool to label freedom fighters as blasphemers. They use religion as a tool to torture people, to stone people to death, and to execute people. It is daunting and reprehensible that some governments separate humans based on their religion and ethnicity and commit the most horrendous crimes against humanity.

In my humble opinion, religions are there to improve people's personal lives, to boost morale, to bring inner peace, joy, prosperity, and happiness. Religions must not be used as barriers between human beings. Religions must not be used to rule!

I believe in the following quotation about religion by Frank Sinatra:[32]

"Religion is a deeply personal thing in which man and God go it alone together, without the witch doctor in the middle."

In addition, I strongly believe in the following statement by Ralph Waldo Emerson:[33]

"The faith that stands on authority is not faith. The reliance on authority measures the decline of religion, the withdrawal of the soul."

This quotation has proven to be factual; it was experienced by the medieval people during the middle Ages in Europe and is a reality in contemporary Iran.

---

32   Frank Sinatra interview with *Playboy*, February 1963, *Random House Webster's Quotationary*, by Leonard Roy Frank (New York: Random House Reference, 1998), page 713.
33   Ralph Waldo Emerson, "The Over-Soul," from *Essays: First Series, 1841*, *Random House Webster's Quotationary*, by Leonard Roy Frank (New York: Random House Reference, 1998), page 712.

E L E V E N

I passed the sixth grade very successfully, and I was ranked among the top five in my class. I was getting ready to enter high school. The high schools in our district did not have a very good reputation. In the meantime, my Uncle Sarrullah, who owned a two-story house in a more upscale neighborhood, had rented the second floor of his house to the dean of Bamdad High School, Mr. Mohsen Bozorgmehr. The high school was located within walking distance from my uncle's house.

My uncle suggested to my father that I register at Bamdad High School. It was pretty far from our house; however, my uncle thought that a high school located in a good community was well worth the commute. The distance was an issue for me, and my father was reluctant to register me at that high school. My uncle, his wife, and my cousins Guity and Morteza suggested that I could stay with them and go to my house during the weekends and holidays. That was okay with me and my parents.

I finally registered at Bamdad High School. I was delighted to live at my uncle's house. I was particularly happy to hang out with my cousin Morteza. He had just finished high school. He was getting ready to go to America to pursue his college degree there. My other cousin Guity was a sophomore at Tehran University in medical school. Morteza and I had a great time together; we went to movies together, read storybooks together, listened to music, watched cartoons on their old black-and-white TV, played card games, and visited family and friends. He was an excellent chess and backgammon player and taught me how to play those games. I always looked up to him as an older brother and enjoyed being around him. We had a lot of fun together during the summer of 1964.

It was my first year at high school; I was living in my uncle's house, away from my parents, my brothers, my newly born sister, and my friends. I was particularly missing my infant sister, Afsaneh. My cousin Morteza was already gone and my other cousin Guity was always into books. I felt so lonely there. None of my friends from elementary school attended Bamdad High School. I was missing my good friends Behrouz and Shamon. The first few months at my uncle's house were somewhat depressing for me. What kept me there was my love for my uncle Surrullah and his wife, *Khanoom Amoo* Maliheh, not to mention my cousin Guity, whom I always loved like an older sister and admired for her perseverance and her accomplishments in academia. There was nothing to do there other than studying and doing homework. I decided to study hard. My goal was to achieve the highest rank in class. I wanted to make my father and my uncle proud. Back in those days, it was an honor to be among the top five in a class.

I did my assignments meticulously and religiously. I did very well on my first tri-annual exams. Nevertheless, no matter how hard I worked, I could not surpass one of my favorite classmates, Victor. He was good in all subjects. The only subject in which I could surpass him was my theology class, which he was exempted from attending because he was a Christian. Victor was a studious and hardworking student. He was also an excellent athlete; his specialty was track and field. Victor and I became good friends. We never let our academic competition come between us.

English became my favorite subject in seventh grade. I had a great teacher by the name of Mr. Jazayeri. He was short and tough but very personable. My first experience with him was not very pleasant; he used to give us writing assignments and graded them by going around to each desk the next period. The very first time he graded mine, he asked me whether it was my handwriting. "Yes, sir, it is." I said.

"Is this really your handwriting?" he repeated his question.

"It is my handwriting sir; God is my witness," I said.

He paused for a moment and turned to the class and said, "Some people think that God belongs to them and to them only; they can do whatever they please—they can lie, they can cheat, they can commit sins and can get away with their wrongdoings by swearing to God. What's sad is that some of our government officials and religious leaders are examples of such people. I have a problem with these kinds of people," he said.

I felt embarrassed and somewhat humiliated that day. After he calmed down, I told him, "Sir, I don't understand why you don't believe me. Do you want me to write a few sentences for you in your presence?"

"Yes, open your notebook and write: 'I will never swear to God in this class again,'" he said. I did that, and he liked my handwriting and said, "I believe you, but remember what I told you. Son, I was not suggesting that you were lying about your handwriting, but your phrase 'God is my witness' is nonsense." He made me feel a little bit better.

Not too long ago, here in the United States I was watching TV during a program saluting the movie star Richard Gere in which he made a speech by saying that he had a problem with people who thought God was exclusively on their side. This statement by Richard Gere reminded me of Mr. Jazayeri.

Mr. Jazayeri was a great teacher and a good person. He became my most favorite teacher that year. Most often, he would tell us stories about influential people and words of wisdom about life. I learned from some of my friends that not too long after the revolution, he died of a heart attack. God bless his soul. In the eleventh grade, he became our history teacher. We could easily read between his words that he was against the tyranny of the previous regime and against *akhondism (mullahism)* as well, although he was a true believer of Islam.

His statement about some government officials and religious leaders being liars applies more to the leaders in Iran today. Some so-called religious leaders who are also government officials lie through their teeth and have committed the most horrible crimes against the people of Iran for more than thirty-one years in the name of God and Islam.

Another pleasant and memorable day for me in the seventh grade was the rematch victory of Cassius Clay (who had become a Muslim and changed his name to Muhammad Ali) against Sonny Liston. While almost everybody in our class was rooting for Ali, opinions on the match were split. Some thought Sonny Liston would take revenge, while others predicted that Ali would win again. Ali's popularity soared in Iran after he became Muslim. He became everybody's hero after the rematch victory against Liston.

T W E L V E

I did very well in my seventh-grade. I remember one day my uncle Surrallah came up to me, gave me a pat on the back, and congratulated me for achieving the second rank among all seventh-graders. There were two classes of seventh grade, with forty to fifty students in each. I was curious as to how he came to know that; he later explained that he had heard it from Mr. Bozorgmehr. As I expected, I came second after Victor.

In the summer of 1966, I was torn between my family and my uncle's. I was attached to my uncle's family as much as my own. I went back and forth. I would have wished that both families lived together in the same household like some families in Iran back in those days. On one hand, I couldn't leave my uncle alone because his son was far away and he was considering me as his second son. On the other hand, I was missing my parents, brothers, and sisters. However, that summer I spent most of my time at my uncle's house while my mother along with my brothers and my little sister traveled to Taleghan.

My uncle's family and I did our own traveling to different parts of the central province of Tehran, mostly during the weekends. Some weekends Mr. Bozorgmehr's family accompanied us. Travelling to the city of Damavand, located under the highest point of Alborz Mountain (elevation: 5,610 meters or 18,406 feet) was especially enjoyable and memorable for me. That city is well known for its beautiful climate, the clear sky, hospitable people, and the dairy and meat products, and is located approximately seventy kilometers northeast of Tehran. The city is also well known for some of its therapeutic springs. We had a lot of fun traveling with Mr. Bozorgmehr. He was a great human being with a great sense of humor. He used to make everybody laugh.

Mr. Bozorgmehr was not only the dean of our high school, he took care of the school's accounting business, student transcripts, class scheduling, and so on. In addition, he had a reputation as a great algebra teacher. Mr. Bozorgmehr was going to be my algebra teacher; he was the only one who taught algebra to the eighth- and ninth-graders at Bamdad High School, so I wanted to do well in his class.

School started as usual in the fall of 1965, around September 22. I was particularly interested in knowing who our English teacher was going to be. I was hoping to see Mr. Jazayeri again as my English teacher, but Mr. Ashtari showed up the very first day of the class. I didn't like him at first, but he turned out to be a good teacher. I learned a great deal from him.

I was glad to see Victor as my classmate again, even though he was going to be my biggest competitor. I couldn't wait to start our algebra class. In our first day of algebra class, the tall, bald, charismatic, and a well-dressed man, showed up in our class. He was none other than our beloved Mr. Bozorgmehr. He was well known with his distinctive mustache and his strong voice. The very first day of class, he defined what algebra was, gave a historical background for the course, described the purpose of the course, and gave us the outline of the course. The rest of our teachers rarely did that. His teaching style was very different from the rest of my previous math teachers. The funny, upbeat, and loving Mohsen at home was a different person at school; he was a commanding high school dean, he hardly smiled, he was too serious, and was a disciplinarian. In class, however, he measured up to his good sense of humor to some extent; he often cracked jokes and made us laugh without any smile on his face, but we had only thirty seconds or so to finish our laughs. His lectures were thorough and organized. His exams were tough, but he had taught us how to tackle difficult problems. He was well liked by all the teachers, all the school officials, and students. Unlike most high school deans at that time, he hardly ever punished students physically; nevertheless, students would not dare violate the school's rules and regulations. He was also known as the best-dressed teacher at our high school. For what I am today, I am mostly indebted to him, as he made me interested in teaching. I truly adored and loved that man. I visited him many times during my visits to Iran until I found out that he died of a heart attack a few months before my visit to Iran in summer of 1997. I could not hide my emotions that day.

I remember the very first time I visited Mr. Bozorgmehr in his house, I noticed a picture of an old man hanging on the wall right above their TV stand. I asked him whether that old man was his biological father. He said, "Not my real father, but the father of the nation." I gave him a curious look. He then said, "If you really must know, I will tell you."

"Yes, I would like to know who that person is," I said.

"He is Dr. Mossadeq."

I was shocked that he dared hang the exiled prime minister's picture on the wall. That was the first time I saw a picture of Dr. Mossadeq. I was always curious as to who Dr. Mossadeq really was and how he looked like. I had heard people talking secretly about Dr. Mossadeq, and I had been warned not to mention his name in public. However, I never read anything about him and there was no mention of his name in our history classes whatsoever. Mr. Bozorgmehr gave me the impression that he didn't want to talk about him any further. Later on in my adulthood, the more I read about Mossedeq, the more convinced I became that we had had a better shot at achieving democracy under his leadership than under anybody else in the Iranian history.

Dr. Mossadeq was truly a remarkable politician, and a great person. He fought hard to nationalize Iranian oil, which was under the control of the British government, and he fought for democracy. If it wasn't for the coup d'état engineered by the CIA, which brought the Shah back to power, and the treasonous act of Ayatollah Kashani, who turned people against Mossadeq, the political equations in Iran, and perhaps in the whole Middle East, would be different today. It was daunting to me to learn that Kashani received money from the CIA for $10,000 to organize mobs against Dr. Mossadeq.[34] It is interesting to note that Kashani was a big supporter of Mossadeq at first, but later on turned against him because he was against Dr. Mossadeq's attempt to establish a secular and democratic government. It is also noteworthy to mention that Khomeini was not at all fond of Dr. Mossadeq and had always given Kashani credit as the key person for nationalization of the Iranian oil, and as the one who fought against the Shah and the British Imperialism.

Later on in early 1980, Kashani's son visited Israel to negotiate an arms deal and military cooperation with the Israeli government against Iraq, which resulted in Menachem Begin's[35] approval of the shipment of weapons as well as tires for Phantom fighter planes to Iran. Khomeini approved this arms deal provided that the source of the weaponry was not discussed and was kept secret.[36] Kashani's rhetoric against Britain and America, and then his secret dealings with them, and Khomeini's repeated rhetoric against Israel by denying its right to exist and then his secret dealings with the Israeli government, clearly depict the true picture and double-faced nature of these so-called religious leaders. Ayatollah Khomeini annihilated the true democratic movements of the Iranian people in 1979. Ayatollah Kashani was a key member to cause annihilation of the democratic movement in 1953.

---

34   Stephen Kinzer, *All the Shah's Men*, John Wiley and Sons Inc, 2008, page 178.
35   Menachem Begin, Prime Minister of Israel from 1977 to 1983.
36   Trita Parsi, *Treacherous Alliance, The Secret Dealings of Israel, Iran, and the U.S.*, Yale University Press / New Haven and London, 2007, page 95.

THIRTEEN

In spite of my hard work to beat Victor, again I came second after him. I made my father proud. He would embarrass me by bragging to friends and family for my perseverance in academics. Back then, there was nothing more important to me than making my parents happy.

In the summer of 1966, my sister Maasoomeh and her husband rented the two bedrooms downstairs from us. Part of the summer, I spent a lot of time with them during the daytime while my father was at work. The rest of my family had gone to Taleghan. I was proud of my sister, who, without any parental supervision and with only an elementary school education, managed to educate herself about Islam and had become a role model for the young girls in the northern small city of Shahsavar where she grew up. I had a great time with my brother-in-law, Mr. Momeni, and my sister. I also had fun spending some quality time with my father. In the meantime, I went to visit my uncle in his house quite often.

I was getting bored and felt useless staying around the house and doing nothing. The weather was getting hotter in Tehran, so my father and I decided to take a trip to Taleghan for a mini vacation. It was great to see everybody there, especially my little sister Afsaneh. Other than visiting the whole family, we enjoyed the pleasant climate. We stayed there for one week. My father had to go back to Tehran for work. I was getting ready to go with him but my mother, grandmother, uncles Mousa and Isa insisted that I stay. My father also suggested that there was more to do in Taleghan than in Tehran. I decided to stay. That summer we did a lot of hiking, camping, and mountain climbing with my friends and relatives. I also tutored my childhood friend Mohammad in math. He was getting prepared to retake the math exam. That was my very first experience of teaching. I found it enjoyable and very rewarding.

In the fall of 1966, when I started the ninth grade, I chose to stay at my parents' house most of the time and visited my uncle's quite often. Algebra, arithmetic, geometry, English, and physics were my favorite subjects. Mr. Bozorgmehr was again my algebra teacher; Mr. Zarsaz, my geometry teacher; Mr. Ashtari, my English teacher; and Dr. Shayesteh my physics and chemistry teacher. These guys impacted my life very positively. I aced algebra, English, arithmetic, chemistry, and physics without any difficulties, but did average in geometry and other subjects. Mr. Zarsaz had the reputation as the toughest math teacher, and Dr. Shayesteh as the most innovative one in Chemistry. Dr. Shayesteh also had a reputation among the students as the most flamboyant and the womanizer among all of our teachers. He was handsome and very popular in the neighboring girls' high schools, where he also taught. We thought that he could have been more successful money wise as a movie star than as a teacher. I learned so much from him. He made me interested in chemistry and particularly physics.

In that year, I associated with Farid, one of my classmates, and his family, who had rented an apartment in our neighborhood. He was the biggest fan of the Beatles and got me somewhat interested in them. He liked Iranian pop music and tried hard to get me interested in learning and singing pop and Western-style music as opposed to the traditional Persian music. Farid was an excellent ping-pong player and taught me how to play that game. This guy was so good at ping-pong that he once beat the Iranian national champion. Although Farid was an extremely intelligent person, he was not much into studies and was a mediocre student. He was superior to me in non-academic general knowledge such as social sciences, politics, world history, and in sports. However, I was a better student than he was. I used to somewhat tutor him in math, physics, chemistry, and English. He was also the biggest fan of Steve McQueen, and we saw a couple of his movies together—the *Magnificent Seven* and the *Great Escape*. Farid and I commuted to school most often. We were of more or less the same height but he was big and stocky, and I was skinny. The kids in the neighborhood called us Laurel and Hardy. Farid taught me that life was not all about academics; you need to educate yourself about the other aspects of life and be aware of what is going on around the world by reading books, newspapers, and magazines. I really enjoyed hanging out with Farid and learned a great deal from him.

I did not try to earn top ranks that year, but I passed all of my exams successfully. I knew that I did very well in all the math courses, so I chose mathematics as my major for the tenth grade. Back in those times, we had to choose a major after the ninth grade. We had three choices: mathematics, natural sciences, or Persian literature. My biggest rival, Victor, chose the natural sciences area. I was sad not to have him as a classmate, but I thought I was going to have less competition in the tenth grade. My good friend Farid also chose the natural sciences area.

FOURTEEN

About a month after the start of the tenth grade, on October 26, 1967, the country celebrated the coronation of the Shah on his forty-eighth birthday, with his wife, Empress Farrah, and their eldest son, Prince Reza, who was six years old at that time. The coronation ceremony lasted for one week, and it was broadcast all over the country. Several foreign guests as well as internal dignitaries were invited. The crowns were adorned with jewels. Anti-Shah activists and mullahs did not like it, and the Shah was criticized for spending too much money for the crowns and the coronation ceremonies.

In that year, I had Mr. Zarsas as the teacher for all of my math courses: algebra, geometry, and logarithmic arithmetic. I had   d an excellent relationship with him. According to Mr. Bozorgmehr, he was the most punctual and the most organized teacher at Bamdad High School. He was an excellent teacher, the most analytical and the most detailed person. He classified the homework problems into three categories: elementary, intermediate, and advanced. He expected everyone to be able to do the elementary and intermediate problems. He had a small pocket notebook that he used to assign the very challenging advanced problems. The advanced problems were difficult and time consuming, but I was so determined to solve them all. I enjoyed a great deal solving the advanced problems. Very seldom, other students were able to solve all of the assigned advanced problems. Sometimes Mr. Zarsas would ask the class, "Other than Habib, who else was able to solve all of the problems?"

Every time he reached into his pocket, the kids would tease me: "Here are special assignments for you, Habib."

Samuel was a better student than I was in most other subjects. He was an excellent student all right, but a feisty Jewish guy. He was a very nice person but sometimes would get into heated religious debates with other students.

67

I remember during the Asian Soccer Cup Tournament that was held in Tehran for the first time, Israel, and Iran reached the final game for the championship. The Israelis had won the previous Asian Cup in 1964. Unfortunately, the game was politicized by anti-Israeli elements, especially religious fanatics as the game of infidels against Muslim heroes." These kinds of propagandas were not promoted by the Shah's government, but mostly by the mullahs. The day before the game, Samuel, who was rooting for Israel and a bunch of other classmates, got into a big argument. It could have turned ugly had it not been for some of us mediating between them. I pulled Samuel aside and urged him, "Please put religion aside; what about your national pride?"

I want the Iranian team to win, those are the people who bring religion into this and I am tired of being insulted because I am Jewish." he replied. I realized that he had a good point there. It is to be mentioned that such incidents were isolated cases during the Shah's time. Muslims and Jews in Iran got along fine for the most part.

The final match took place the day before my final exam on religious studies, which was my weakest subject, and I was very much afraid of failing and repeating my fifth-grade drama all over again. An hour before the game started on May 18, 1968, the streets of Tehran were empty, many shops were closed, Amjadieh Stadium was overcrowded, and people had left work early to come home and watch the game on TV. My father, my three younger brothers, and I were glued to TV. My four-year old sister, Afsaneh, was playing in another room and making loud noises. We constantly yelled at the poor little girl to be quiet. My mother would yell back at us, "You guys be quiet; it's just a game, don't be crazy over it." She finally picked my little sister up and took her downstairs to the kitchen.

The Iranian national team only needed to tie the game in order to win the Asian Cup. It was an exciting and breathtaking game. The Israelis had three excellent players that Iranian media mentioned as players to watch: Visoker, their goalkeeper, who wouldn't easily budge; Spiegel, one of the best strikers of the tournament, and Spiegler, another offensive player who played very well with Spiegel. Their harmonious cooperation resulted in the first goal against Aziz Asli, the Iranian goalkeeper, at the fifty-sixth minute. The hard work of the best Asian defenders of the time—Mustafa Arab, Hassan Habibi (Team Captain), Jafar Kashani, and late Mehrab Shahroukhi—could not prevent this goal. This was the first and the only goal against the Iranians throughout the tournament.[37] One minute later, Fariborz Ismaeli was expelled from the game by the referee, which

---

37   Some details of the tournament were found through a Google search. I have chosen to mention the names of my favorite players.

brought disappointment to the spectators at the stadium and every one of us at home. At this moment, my father was having an anxiety attack, felt discomfort on his chest, and had a hard time breathing. I got scared and started rubbing his back, and Iraj called my mother for help. Luckily, it was not a major problem, and my father recovered quickly. Mother couldn't believe that much excitement, and kept saying, "It's just a game, it's just a game." She then yelled, "I am turning the TV off!"

We all yelled back, "No, you won't!" Despite playing ten against eleven, the Iranian players put tremendous pressure on Israelis. The hard work of all of the Iranian players, especially our striker Hossein Kalani, Akbar Eftekhari, and Homayoon Behzadi, paid off. Behzadi scored the equalizer at the seventy-fifth minute into the game. It was a controversial goal, and the Israelis disputed it. They argued back and forth with the Indian referee. The referee wouldn't change his mind. The game continued. Parviz Ghelichkhani, our midfielder and one of my all-time most favorite players, scored the second goal at the eighty-sixth minute to secure the championship of the Asian Cup for the first time. Iranian people poured onto the streets to celebrate the victory. It is worthy of mentioning that Parviz Ghelichkhani, one of the most valuable Iranian soccer players ever and the captain of the team for many years, is another hero of many Iranians. Like Takhti, he decided to take the side of the people rather than using his fame to his benefit. He was arrested in 1972 by the SAVAK and jailed for a couple of months for opposing the Shah's regime and he is now a political activist against the current regime, living in France.

The Iranian national team successfully defended the Asian Cup championship for the next twelve years before the revolution, and they were in command in most Asian tournaments. After the emergence of the Islamic Republic, the Iranian soccer team has never regained its championship title due to a lack of good management! This is just the tip of the iceberg about the nature of the "Islamic Republic" ever since it was established!

After the game, it dawned on me that I had to study for my final exam. I was too tired, too distracted, and had no motivation whatsoever to study my most boring subject. After the dinner, my father asked me to go to bed, get up very early morning, and study the most important parts of the book. I took his advice and focused mostly on the topics that our teacher stressed in class. I ended up doing very well in that subject.

Samuel, obviously, didn't show up for the exam because he was exempted from the theology class. After the exam, and after my teacher left, I made a plea to my classmates to not brag about the Iranian victory to Samuel and just let it go. The class took it well.

Although I was not much interested in religious studies at school, in my spare time I started reading religious books, and under the influence of my father, I became a practicing Muslim and a strong believer in Islamic values. I had repeatedly heard people whispering about Khomeini and wanted to read more about him and his religious philosophies, but because of censorship, there were no literature available at that time. Names like Elijah Muhammad and especially Malcolm X were often mentioned by the youths as revolutionary Muslims who were fighting for the rights of black Americans. Muhammad Ali had become a Muslim hero of the youth, not only for his punching power, but for refusing to go to Vietnam as well. I wanted to know more about these people, but no details were given anywhere. During the month of Ramadan, I did not miss daily prayer and fasted the whole month. During school lunch breaks, some of us who were fasting chose to go to a mosque near our school, the well-known Mosque *Masjed-e-Vali Asr*, to pray and to listen to the well-known clergyman, Mr. Kauffee. He was a good speaker, a good storyteller, and a funny person. Going to the mosque was a break from studies for us. It was a means for us to release tension. Back in those days, religion was about peace of mind, joy, humanity, prosperity, and getting closer to God. Unfortunately, the Islamic Republic changed all of that. Most well-known religious leaders in Iran today are also the most powerful political figures and the richest people in Iran.

My sad memory of that year was the sudden and mysterious death of *Pahlavan*, champion Takhti which happened on January 7, 1968. I actually heard the news about the death of Pahlavan Takhti and Dr. Mossadeq at the same time from Mr. Bozorgmehr. One early morning just before classes started, I happened to be in the main office of the teachers and administrators in the high school when I heard Mr. Bozorgmehr telling some teachers, "Last year it was Massodeq and this year Takhti." That day the mood of our high school was so sad. Many students were crying for the passing of their hero, Takhti. Because of censorship, I was not aware of Dr. Mossadeq's death (March 5, 1967) until that day, more than a year later. I cried for both of them, two of my heroes. Dr. Mossadeq was eighty-five when he died, but Takhti was only thirty-seven. They were both people's persons; Mossadeq, genuinely a people's politician, and Takhti, truly a people's champion.

I was not born when Dr. Mossadeq became a popular figure in Iran, but I grew up reading about Takhti in sports magazines and newspapers. He was an Olympic and world wrestling champion and the pride of Iranians. He was tough in sports arenas but soft at heart. I had read about his tireless humanitarian gestures and his chivalrous attitude. He had become an icon and a symbol of courage, generosity, honesty, and kindness. He was especially popular for not bowing to the Shah and his government. He could have easily aligned himself with the Shah's regime, made TV commercials, or played in movies to make himself rich. Instead, he chose to be on the side of the people. He assisted the needy people and helped many during the Boein Zahra earthquake. His death was a big loss for the Iranian people. Millions of people mourned his death. The media declared suicide as the cause of his death, while the rumor spread quickly that he was killed by the Shah's secret security police, SAVAK (*Sazman Amniat Va Attela'at Keshvar,* Security and Intelligence Agency of the country) for his anti-government views.

During the sermon at his memorial, many people told stories of Takhti's heroic and sportsmanship mannerism. The Russian champion Alexander Medvid, one of the all-time-best freestyle-wrestling champions of the world, described one story that stuck in my mind. He explained that prior to his match with Takhti, he had injured one of his legs. During the match, while Takhti was well aware of Alexander's injured leg, he never tried to take advantage of the injury in his favor and never touched that leg. Takhti ended up losing that match. He could have won the match but he chose to lose rather than hurting his opponent.

Personally, I am not sure what caused Takhti's death, but today many believe that the actual cause was suicide. What I am sure of is that if Takhti were alive today, he would again be on the side of the people against the tyrannical regime of the Islamic Republic.

FIFTEEN

In the eleventh grade, Mr. Zarsaz was my teacher for algebra and trigonometry. I had a very strong background in algebra, and had so much fun in that class. I was taking trigonometry for the first time and that subject became my favorite. I had no problem solving Mr. Zarsaz's challenging problems out of his "pocket notebook." Spatial geometry was my most difficult course. We had a very knowledgeable teacher for that subject, but almost the whole class had a hard time understanding him. Mr. Ghods was our English teacher. Students used to call him a "moving dictionary." He was a perfect gentleman and a great teacher. Mr. Jazayeri was my history teacher. I always enjoyed reading history books, but not as a course because we had to do a lot of memorization. Mr. Jazayeri made it interesting; instead of making us memorize too much, he required us to write essays and give presentations in class. This meant lots of work but less memorizing.

Speaking of history, in that year I occasionally visited one of my distant relatives, Hooshang, who had moved with his parents to Tehran from Northern Iran not too long ago. His mother was the sister of Yazdan Amoo, a cousin of my father. We used to call her *Khanoom Ammeh*, Lady Aunt. Hooshang's father, Mr. Molaei, was a retired security guard. They had rented a small room from Uncle Yazdan. They were poor financially but very rich at heart. I loved that family so much for their purity and sincerity. Every opportunity I got, I visited them, especially during the summer of 1968, before I started the eleventh grade. Mr. Molaei was full of stories and myths about the kings and legendary heroes of ancient Persia. His main hobby in his youth was to read *Shahnameh Ferdowsi*.[38] Every time I visited his

---

38   *Shahnameh* is a classical poetical work of one of the noblest Persian poets, Hakim Aboulghasem Ferdowsi (935-1020), and is the national epic and pride of Iran. It is a collection of stories about Persian legends. All the poetical stories in *Shahnameh* are about ancient Iran before the Islamic conquest of Persia by the Arabs in the seventh century. What is fascinating about this masterpiece is that Ferdowsi used only Persian words in the entire book. It is worth noting that after the Arab invasion of Iran, the Persian language adopted numerous

house, he would tell us stories while Khanoom Ammeh was cooking her delicious northern dish. He was an enthusiastic and animated storyteller. One of the stories that he told us and I liked very much was about Cyrus the Great.

Story has it that Astiages; the brutal King of the Mede Dynasty had several bad dreams about his daughter's pregnancy. He consulted one of his dream interpreters who told him, "Your daughter will deliver a boy who not only will seize your land but the whole continent of Asia." His daughter Mandana was married to Cambyses, the king of Pars, a small part of the Mede Dynasty. When Cyrus was born, he was delivered to a shepherd who was ordered to destroy the little boy. The shepherd and his wife decided not to kill the little boy but raise him. They raised him in a village away from the king's royal court. When Cyrus was ten, Astiages found out that Cyrus was still alive. He was outraged but was assured by his magi that Cyrus was not going to be a threat to his throne. After consulting with his magi, he sent Cyrus to his biological parents. When he reached adulthood, he became very popular as a courageous, wise, and a strong willed young man. His popularity grew beyond the borders. He was made aware of his grandfather's brutal ruling. Cyrus mobilized a big army, advanced to the capital of Mede, and defeated his grandfather's army decisively. Cyrus took his grandfather captive but never allowed anybody to harm him. Astiages died in captivity. He then founded the greatest and the most powerful Persian Dynasty of *Hakhamaneshian*, Achaemenids.

Cyrus the Great was the first leader who formed the centralized government at his Capital in *Pasargad,* Pasargadae,[39] along with smaller governments administered by governors or the so-called "satraps." Cyrus left many legacies in the history of humankind. He was known as one of the most honest leaders of all time, a generous, kind, noble, and a magnanimous king. He is mentioned in history as one of the best military strategists of all the military leaders and attributed his success to "Diversity in counsel, unity in command.[40]" It is also a historical fact that the first human rights establishment was instituted by Cyrus. Although he was a Zoroastrian, he treated all the other religions with dignity and utmost respect. Iran was a haven for all the religions under his reign.

Arabic vocabularies. Ferdowsi tried to revive the Persian language through his poems. Although Ferdowsi talks about so many heroes in his book, Persians believe that he himself was the main hero. It took him more than thirty years of hard work to finish *Shahnameh.*

39 *Pasargad,* Pasargadae is located in the Fars Province, near the city of Shiraz. Pasargad was the capital of the Cyrus the Great and also his last resting place. The most important monument in Pasargad is undoubtedly the tomb of Cyrus the Great. It has seven broad steps leading to the sepulcher, which measures 534 meters in length by 531meters in width and has a low and narrow entrance.

40 Garvin, David; Roberto, Michael (September, 2001). "What You Don't Know About Making Decisions". Havard Business Review, 79 (8): pp. 108-16.

Unfortunately, before the revolution, some Islamic and leftist opposition groups openly and unfairly criticized some of the most celebrated pre-Islamic Persian kings as tyrannical figures in Iranian history, most notably, King Cyrus and King Darius.[41] After the 1979 revolution, many mullahs started bashing all the kings, especially King Cyrus, King Darius, Reza Shah, and Muhammad Reza Shah. They condemned the monarchy as the most corrupt way of ruling. However, when Reza Shah ended the shameful ruling of the Qajar dynasty in 1921, he offered to abolish the monarchy and replace it with republicanism, the very same group of people, the mullahs criticized him and resisted the idea. They condemned republicanism as ungodly and believed that monarchy was the correct way of ruling. Reza Shah then founded the Pahlavi dynasty and became the first Pahlavi king.

After the revolution, it was sad and insulting to hear the name-calling and unjustified allegations against some of our finest historical figures. For example, the infamous clergyman Mullah Khalkhali (1926 – 2003), known in the West as "the hanging judge," wrote a book calling Cyrus a tyrant, a corrupt king, and a homosexual. On the contrary, history has judged that King Cyrus was none of those. Khalkhali called for the destruction of Cyrus's tomb and all of the historic sites in Persepolis.[42] In fact, he went there with a bunch of thugs to carry out his evil desire but was faced with the biggest resistance by the brave people of Shiraz and was forced to get out of the city. Khalkhali was a mad man who enjoyed executing people without trial. It was unfortunate and shameful that such a crazy man was chosen as the supreme judge of the then "Revolutionary Court." The leader and the founder of the Islamic Republic, Ayatollah Khomeini, appointed him for this post.

The man who hatefully talked about Cyrus in many of his speeches is remembered by a vast number of Iranians as one of the most hated persons in Iran.

---

41   King Darius (550BCE – 486BCE), Darius I, known as Darius the Great was the third king of the Achaemenid Empire. When he rose to power, there were rebellions everywhere in Iran. He quelled his opposition decisively. He then expanded his empire to include Egypt and part of Greece. The Persian Empire reached its peak under king Darius. It is believed that king Darius was the first Persian king who organized his empire by dividing it into several provinces and designating governors to govern the provinces. Throughout his empire, Darius focused on the infrastructure of the country. The well-known cliff-faced Behistun Inscription (known as katibeh Bisotune in Iran), located near the city of Kermanshah in western Iran was carved during the reign of king Darius.

42   Persepolis was chosen as the capital of the Persia during the Achaemenid dynasty. It is located approximately sixty kilometers northeast of Shiraz in the Fars province and approximately 47 miles away from Pasargad. Persepolis is also known as *Takht-e-Jamshid*, Throne of Jamshid. The French Archeologist Andre Godard believed that Cyrus the Great chose the site of Perspolis but Darius the Great built the terrace and the great palaces. The UNESCO declared the citadel of Persepolis a World Heritage Site in 1979. Persepolis is also one of the eighty treasures featured on "Around the World in 80 Treasures," a BBC documentary presented by Dan Cruickshank and Husain Gholami.

History has named Cyrus "Cyrus the Great." Today Cyrus is in the heart of the Persian history and a vast majority of Iranian people.

The Islamic Republic was against Persian customs and traditions from the first day it was established. At one point, its leaders brought up the idea of abolishing *Chahar-Shanbeh Souri* (see footnote 21) and *Nowruz*. Ayatollah Morteza Mottahari (1920 – 1979), who was one of the most important disciples of Khomeini, a well-known theologian, and an ideologue of the Islamic Republic, disrespectfully, called the Iranian traditionalists "donkeys." There were even rumors that they wanted to change the official language of the Persians to Arabic. In fact, Mottahari, in his book: *"ketaab Nour, Malakout Quran,"* (The Book of Brightness, The Spirit of Quran) states: "Restoring the ancient Persian words means turning away from the teachings of the Quran." He continues: "Making so much noise and propaganda to glorify Ferdowsi, building a tomb and holding a festival in his honor and inviting foreigners from different countries to revive 'Mystical Shahnameh' is against the Quran." He then calls Ferdowsi a harmful and despicable person.

I have no idea as to the relationship between the restoration of Persian words and the texts of the Quran. I do know that Ferdosi in none of his poems shows any disrespect to the Quran. Nor do I have any idea why Mottahari interprets Ferdowsi's use of only Persian words in his poems, and his patriotism for Iran as being anti-Islamic or a challenge to the Holy Scriptures. Such a statement amounts to character assassination and, in essence, a character assassination against other good people, is against Islam, and against the teachings of the Quran.

They wanted to topple the statue of Ferdowsi, the most patriotic poet and historic hero of Iranians. But they knew better—they would have dug their own graves had they insisted on implementing such actions.

However, they succeeded in interfering with deeply personal affairs and personal choices of the people. For instance, certain Persian music was not allowed. They would randomly stop cars to see if people were carrying cassettes or CDs of those types of music. They temporarily succeeded in banning the naming of the newborns with certain pure Persian names, but all Arabic names were allowed. The founders of the Islamic Republic and some present rulers of the regime have had absolutely no pride in being Iranian; they have not been proud of the rich, glorious, joyous, and peaceful Persian culture and traditions.

Going back to Mr. Molaei, I also enjoyed his story about Kaveh Ahangar,[43] another ancient heroic champion in Iranian history who revolted against the most

---

43   The word *ahangar* means blacksmith. It is believed that when Kaveh met Zahak for the first time, he took off his leather apron and put it on the tip of a spear and raised it as a symbol of resistance and unity known as "Derafsh-e-Kaviani." This flag was later decorated with precious jewels and became the symbol of

tyrannical and most demonic ruler in Iran, Zahak.[44] There is a myth that Zahak was a friend of the devil and that both sides of Zahak's shoulder were kissed by the devil and from each side of the shoulder had grown a dangerously spiteful snake. The Devil tells Zahak, "If the snakes die, you will die." He then advises Zahak, "The only way that the snakes will survive is that you drink the blood of at least one young Iranian every day." Zahak's men go on a rampage of hunting and killing so many innocent young lives in order to keep bloodthirsty Zahak alive. That angered so many Iranians, especially Kaveh, who had lost eighteen of his sons to Zahak's vicious killing spree. Kaveh organized an army of Iranians to revolt against Zahak. Along the way, he met a young man by the name of Feraydoon,[45] who had mobilized a separate army to conquer Zahak. Kaveh and Feraydoon with their unified armies moved toward Zahak's capital and together they triumphed against Zahak and destroyed his evil empire. Zahak was captured and imprisoned in a cave in Alborz Mountain until he died. Feraydoon became the king, and legends have it that he ruled Iran for five hundred years.

The anniversary of the day Zahak's empire was destroyed and celebrated by Iranians as *Jashn-e-Mehregan*, Mehregan Festivity. However, there are different beliefs as to the beginning of Mehregan festivity.[46] After the revolution, some of the Persian celebrations, such as *Mehregan, Saddeh*, and *Tirgan*, were demoted and no longer celebrated. As mentioned before, the mullahs would have banned three

Persian independence, resistance, and resilience, as well as the revolutionary symbol of the masses in their fight against foreign invaders. By the late Sassanid era (224–651), Kaveh's Derafš-e Kāvīāni had emerged as the standard of the Persian Sassanid dynasts. It was thus also representative of the Persian Sassanid state— Ērānshāhr, the "Kingdom of Iran"— and may so be considered to have been the first "national flag" of Iran.

44   Zahak is mentioned in Shahnameh as an Arab king. In some stories he was mentioned as being from Saudi Arabia. Other stories have it that he was from Babylonia (today's Iraq). In Avesta he is mentioned as Azhi Dahaka. Zahak was the son of Mardas, an Arab ruler in Iran. Stories have it that Zahak killed his father in order to earn the kingdom.

45   Fereydun was the son of Abtin, one of descendants of Jamshid. His mother's name was Faranak. According to a poetic myth in Shahnameh, Zahak dreamed that somebody by the name of Fereydun had risen to power and destroyed his empire. The next morning he ordered his soldiers to look for Fereydun and kill anybody by that name. Faranak immediately sent her son to a farmer in a town in Northern Iran called Larijan. The farmer took a good care of the little boy for a while. The farmer had an unusually beautiful cow whose every hair was of a different color. Zahak was made aware of the unusual cow and personally went to Larijan in search of the cow. Faranak found out about this and took her son and left him with an old man who lived in a small cottage in a mountain. Once Fereydun reached the age of sixteen, he started searching for his mother. He finally found her. She explained why she had to send him away. Fereydun became extremely angry and sought revenge.

46   The different beliefs of the origination of Mehregan Festivity are: the day angels helped Fereydun and Kaveh to defeat Zahak, the day God gave light to the earth, the day God created the Sun, the day God created Adam and Eve. Some historians believe that the word Mehregan comes from the month of Mehr (currently, 7th month of the Iranian calendar) used to be the first month of the Persian calendar during Achaemenid empire and Persians celebrated that month as the beginning month of the New Year.

other celebrations *Chahar-Shanbeh Souri, Nowruz,* and *Sizdeh-Bedar,*[47] if they had their choice.

Under the influence of some of my classmates who labeled the Shah as cruel and some, unfairly, as "Zahak," I became curious as to whether Mr. Molaei, by telling us these kinds of stories, was implying that the Shah was as cruel as Astyages (Aztiac, as he would call it) or Zahak. I asked him that question once and his response was, "On the contrary, I am trying to convey a message that the Shah is not one of those types and he is a good man but surrounded by some bad people."

Hooshang Molaei's house (rather, Amoo Yazdan's house) was very close to my aunt's, Khale Saffieh. I often visited my aunt and my cousins. Like Mr. Molaei, Aunt Saffieh's husband, Ghadir, whom we called Ghadir Daei, was also a security guard. Ghadi Daei was tall, tough, charismatic, and a disciplinarian father. He wanted the best for his kids. He always stressed on education as the key to success. He would often get disgruntled with his kids if they did not study enough. If they made bad grades, he would get mad. When he was mad, he would become appalling and frightening. In spite of his rough personality, however, there was a soft, kind, and fatherly side to him that would make him so likable. His security region was often shifted near our house during which he would visit us quite often. He was always very nice to me and used to call me *shah pesar,* a term Persians use for a dutiful and responsible boy.

One day as I was coming back from high school, I stopped at a newspaper and magazine stand to scan through the headlines. Checking newspaper articles at newsstands on my way home was one of my habits. I read on the first page of one of the prominent daily newspapers that a security guard was stabbed to death by a robber. I usually wouldn't read the crime columns of the newspapers, but this was written big and boldly. When I got home, I was tired and hungry. My brothers were watching TV but there was no sign of my mother and my little sister. My brothers didn't know where they were. I went to the kitchen in search of food but couldn't find anything to eat. I thought my mother had gone shopping for dinner. I waited for a while; nobody showed up. I asked our tenant, an old lady living with her weird son downstairs, whether she knew where my mother was. She said, "Your mother left the house furiously with a lady this morning."

---

47   Sizdeh Bedar is another Persian celebration that occurs on the thirteenth day of the New Year (thirteenth day of the first month, Farvardin) as the word sizdeh suggests. On this day Persians get out of their house and celebrate the day outdoor. Some people interpret Sizdeh Bedar as having jubilant and lucky day on the thirteenth (the unlucky number) day of the year. Some historians trace Sizdeh Bedar back to the king Jamshid of Pishdadian Dynasty (6000 B.C.) who had considered a day of outdoor celebration with his people.

"Furiously? Why?" I asked.

"I don't know. She didn't tell me anything," she said.

I became curious and started worrying. Finally, after hours of waiting, my mother showed up. She looked sad, disturbed, and daunted. I asked my mother what was going on. She kept saying, "Nothing." I insisted. She said, "Ghadir had an accident."

Persians have the habit of hiding unpleasant news from their loved ones. I became more curious and thought that maybe the newspaper article was about Ghadir. Maybe the unthinkable had happened to Ghadir.

I turned to my mother and asked, "Was Ghadir Daei stabbed to death?"

She burst out crying and said, "How did you know that?"

"I read it in the paper."

It turned out that the lady who picked up my mother in the morning was Amoo Yazdan's wife. Ghadir Daei was working the night shift; he noticed a suspicious-looking person wandering around in the middle of the night. He followed the man and ordered him to stop. He refused. Ghadir ran after him, caught up with him, and apprehended him. As he was attempting to handcuff the man, Ghadir was stabbed numerous times by this person—every inch of his body. By the time the police squad came to the rescue, it was too late. Ghadir was already dead. However, the police chased the murderer and found him in a garden hiding behind a tree. To the best of my recollections, the killer did not want to turn himself in; he was killed by the police during the shootout that morning.

We heard several stories regarding the killer's motives. One was that the killer was on his way to his own house to kill his wife. Another was that he had already robbed a house and was on his way to rob another. Another story was that he had lost his job as a military sergeant and was extremely enraged. Another story that caught my attention was a rumor that spread among some people including my classmates was that the killer was an anti-government guerilla fighter or a freedom fighter. I found that to be baseless and far from truth. I argued with some of those people telling them that the killer was just a cold-blooded murderer, not a free-dom fighter. It is a disgrace to all freedom fighters to call this killer, a freedom fighter."

In those days, due to the displeasure of the majority of people over the Shah's ruling, every disaster that happened in the country, the people would blame it on the Shah's government. Even the occurrence of an earthquake in a secluded area would be blamed on the Shah's regime; some people would likely spread the rumor that perhaps the military had done some underground missile test. This horrible news haunted me for months. Such crimes rarely happened in Iran back in those days. I had a great deal of respect for Ghadir Daei. He was a good man and did not deserve to die so viciously and unexpectedly. I was extremely saddened for my aunt and cousins. I did not go to his funeral and was reluctant to see my aunt and my cousins for a long while because I did not want to be reminded of Ghadir Daei's terrifying death.

SIXTEEN

Isuccessfully passed the eleventh grade among top three in my class. One of my most memorable moments before the start of the twelfth grade was to watch Apollo 11 land on the moon on July 20, 1969. The names of the American astronauts,[48] Neil Armstrong, Edwin Aldrin, and Michael Collins, surfaced in the Iranian media for weeks. It was just incredible to watch humans walk on the moon for the first time. This was not only the goal of the American government as expressed by the visionary President John F. Kennedy, but the desire and anticipation of the whole world to see that moment in human history.

I remember one day, after the moon landing success by the American astronauts, my father, while reading *Daneshmand* (*Scientist*) magazine said, "Why is there war, while you can capture the moon?" He continued, saying, "No doubt, America is one of the greatest nations and the most powerful country in the world. Its people are smart and very innovative, and yet its government is fighting one of the poorest countries in the world, Vietnam. Why?" He always condemned the war in Vietnam. He then praised the Shah as a peaceful leader and admired him for trying to find a peaceful solution for the dispute over Bahrain,[49] and for

---

48   Neil Armstrong, the mission commander, and Edwin Aldrin, the lunar module pilot, landed on the moon while Michael Collins, command module pilot, orbited above the moon.

49   Bahrain Island used to be a part of Persian Empire until 1521 when Portuguese occupied the Island. The Safavid king, Shah Abbas drove Portuguese out of Bahrain and Persian Gulf in 1602. The Island was ruled by Persians intermittently until 1783. Then an Arab tribal family, the *Khalifs* (the Caliphs), ruled the island until 1861 when it became the British protectorate. In 1950s and 60s the island went through a series of demonstration by the people of Bahrain demanding greater participation in the government. In late 1960s they demanded independence from the British. In 1970, Iran laid claim on the island but the Bahraini people insisted on independence. The Shah respected the demand of the people for the total independence and withdrew his claim. In 1971 after British withdrew from Persian Gulf, Bahrain became independent.

81

not engaging in a war against Iraq for its aggression[50] against Iran, and for taking a neutral position in the Arab-Israeli war. I often disagreed with my father regarding the Shah and his policies.

In the meantime, within that year, the media in Iran were the messengers of turmoil in the neighboring countries and different parts of the world. The unpleasant news were being reported and broadcast on a daily basis—the Arab-Israeli conflict, the Vietnam War, the coup d'état in Iraq that brought Ahmed Al Takriti and Saddam Hussein to power, the military coup in Pakistan led by General Yahya Khan that ousted General Ayoub Khan, the student demonstrations in Turkey, and the unrest in Eastern Europe. Perhaps the intention of the media was to convey a message to all Iranians that Iran was the most stable country in the region and at peace with the world while other countries were in chaos. These kinds of propagandas by the media had a positive impact on ordinary Iranians and worked for a while. It worked because the government was profiting from oil and, consequently, the economy was better and inflation was low. The Shah and Prime Minister Hoveida were successful in keeping inflation low for years. The economic reforms continued because of the appointment of Hooshang Ansari, the former Iranian ambassador to the United States, as the minister of economy, who brought some new ideas. For a period, the Shah and his economic team focused on the infrastructure of the country such as building roads, bridges, amusement parks, movie theaters, and more. It was interesting to note that they built a movie theater in the holy city of Qom for the first time in late 1969. There was a lot of resistance to building that movie theater by the religious leaders.

The automobile industries were advancing; in addition to Paykan,[51] more luxury cars such as Arya and Shahin[52] were introduced. The government built

---

50   The souring relations between Iran and Iraq over the dispute of the waterway of *Arvand Rūd*, or Shatt-Al-Arab started in the early 1930s. The two countries accused one another of border violations. A treaty was signed by both parties in 1937 that extended Iranian sovereignty to the Thalweg alongside the city of Abadan which basically confirmed the 1913 treaty. The dispute started again when the Baath government led by Ahmed Hassan-Al-Bakr (president) and Saddam Hussein (vice president) took over in a coup against President Abdul Rahman Arif on July 17, 1968. They demanded the full control of the waterway, whereas the Shah was simply asking half and half as established in the 1937 Tehran treaty. The Iraqi aggressions instigated decisive reactions by the Shah which finally brought the two governments to the negotiating table. On June 13, 1975, a peace treaty was signed between Iran and Iraq over the border waterway. The negotiation occurred in Algeria and the treaty was named the Algiers Accord. According to the Algiers peace accord, *thalweg* (the median course of the waterway) was designated as the border. In return the Shah agreed to cease his support of the Kurdish insurgents against the Iraqi government.
51   Paykan was the first automobile that was manufactured in Iran in 1968. The design of Paykan was based on the 1967 British car, Hillman Hunter. Paykan was first introduced by the then well-known millionaire investor Mahmoud Khayami. It was a popular car in Iran from late 1960s to late 1990s.
52   From 1967 to 1971, Rambler automobiles, a brand of American Motors Corporations (AMC), were assembled in Iran and were offered in two trim levels as Aria (sometimes spelled "Arya") and Shahin. The Arya

petrochemical factories in Abadan and elsewhere. Many other industrial contracts with European companies, American companies, and the former Soviet Union were signed. Also, a few hospitals and institutions for advanced education were built. The country needed more medical doctors, professors, economists, engineers, technologists, and so on. The youth were more optimistic about their future, and parents were more concerned about the higher education of their children than ever before. There were more incentives for the youth to pursue Bachelor of Science degrees and beyond. However, not enough universities existed to accommodate the needs of the young people in Iran. To enter the universities and advanced colleges, we had to take the ever-challenging university entrance exam or the so-called "Konkoor." This exam was extremely difficult and required a lot of concentration and hard work. Twelfth grade, the last year in high school, was more focused on the chosen concentration areas—mathematics, natural studies (including biology and anatomy), or Persian literature. After the 1979 revolution, the educational system went through a series of changes. The current high school system in Iran consists of four different branches: math and physics, experimental sciences, socioeconomics, and literature and culture.

In the twelfth grade, I had a good friend by the name of Niazi whom I used to walk to school with. He was a good student, had a great personality, and a good sense of humor. However, there was something strange about him. He never wanted to study with me, never invited me to his house, and always declined my invitations. A few weeks before the start of our final twelfth grade exams, as we were walking together, I asked Niazi, to join us, a bunch of classmates and me, to study for the finals. He ignored me and kept on talking about the usual stuff—school subjects, teachers, or girls. I paused for a few moments and then turned to him and asked, "Why are you acting so strange?" He ignored me again. Although I am not a pushy person, I demanded an answer.

He finally opened up and said, "Habib, I am a Baha'i." I was very surprised to hear that. I was speechless.

He turned to me and said, "Are you disappointed?"

"Yes I am," I said. I paused and then said, "Not because you are a Baha'i, because you hid this from me for such a long time, because I thought you were more open minded than this." I continued, saying, "Who do you think I am?—a

---

was a more luxurious version that came with a three-speed automatic transmission, while Shahin was the base model with a manual transmission. They were assembled under the license of AMC by Pars Khodro starting in 1967and then at the Iran Jeep Company plant in Tehran. The production ended in early 1974, and the Iran Jeep Company changed its name to Iran General Motors, producing selected Opel Rekord, Chevrolet Nova and Pickup, Buick Skylark, and Cadillac Seville model from 1974 until 1987 (Google search).

fanatic, a phony person who cares about your origin, your religion, or your race? I respect you because you are a good human being. I happen to be born in a Muslim family, and I am sure if I were born in a Baha'i family, I would have been a Baha'i, too."

Unfortunately, many Baha'is and Jews back in those days hid their identities, not because they were concerned with the government, but because they were fearful of bigots. Religious bigotry was not allowed in the shah's government, but it seems to be a mandate in the Islamic Republic and it is being promoted by the current regime in Iran. Some of those bigots are now the heads of the government—Ahmadinejad, the appointed president, is an obvious example. He was an anti-Baha'i activist in his young age.

Niazi and I became even closer as friends. I did invite him again to my house, but he didn't feel comfortable to go to people's houses, and I respected that. We met occasionally at school and strategized how to prepare for the final exams and, more importantly, for the konkoor.

After the final exams, a number of my friends attended konkoor preparation classes, but I couldn't afford going to those classes. Niazi and another friend attended the preparation classes; they were nice enough to bring me their notes every day.

We took the highly competitive university entrance exam, the konkoor, which was a common nationwide exam. It was a dream for many young people to pass the exam. I had no idea how I did on my exam. I didn't have much hope of passing. Back then we had to select only ten majors in colleges or universities of our choice. If passed, they would admit us in one of those majors based on our scores. I was interested in engineering in the colleges and universities in Tehran only, so my choices were limited. Niazi had already taken the entrance exam at the then Pahlavi University in Shiraz and passed it and was admitted in the economics department. Pahlavi University was renamed as Shiraz University after the revolution.

About three weeks after taking the exam, Niazi came to our alley looking for me. I was talking to a bunch of friends there. I was surprised to see him in our alley. I asked him what brought him over. "I just came to visit," he said. We talked about different issues. He then asked, "Habib, what was your konkoor ID number?" I thought that was a strange question. I didn't have it on me, so I went home and I got it. I showed it to him. He compared it with the number he had written on a piece of paper and then shook my hand and said, "Congratulations, my friend, you passed the entrance exam." That was really great news to me, because I had not done much studying for the exam and didn't expect to pass it that year. I asked him whether he was sure about that. He said that the names were posted somewhere at the University of Tehran, and continued, saying, "I saw your name, and then immediately jotted down your ID number to make sure that it was you."

I thought it was very clever of Niazi to ask my number first before giving me the news, as my first and last names are not unique. My brother Iraj was there listening to us. He gave me a big kiss and lifted me off the ground, put me on his shoulder, and announced the news to the whole neighborhood. My mother joined us in the alley. She was very happy. All the neighbors shook my hand and congratulated me.

Niazi made my day. He really made me happy. I was proud of him for being so unselfish and so thoughtful. That evening my mother gave my father the tidings of my success. He was happy and had tears in his eyes. I told my father about Niazi. He said, "This is what humanity is all about; this is how you judge your friends, not by their race or religion, by what they are as a human."

Later on through newspaper announcements, I learned that I was admitted to the then Iran College of Science and Technology in Mechanical Engineering Department.

SEVENTEEN

After passing the konkoor, we moved from the southwest of Tehran to farther north. Shortly after, I went to Taleghan and had a couple of weeks of relaxing time there. I spent the rest of the summer playing soccer, hanging out with my cousins Ghobad and Khosro, or reading some books until school started.

The college system in Iran back in those days was more or less a duplicate of the American system. The first semester in college in the fall of 1970 was pretty fun for me. The college that I was attending is located east of Tehran in the city of Narmak, which is a suburb of Tehran. The distance from our house to the university was very far. I had to catch three different buses to reach my destination. Because of terrible traffic situation in Tehran, commuting was unbearable. Sometimes, it would take me a couple of hours to get home from the college. A good portion of my daily life was spent on the buses.

It was costly to pay for college expenses. I didn't want to be a burden on my father, so the second semester I decided to work as a tutor to high school students. After school, I would go to people's houses to tutor their kids, mainly math and physics. I made enough money to buy books, to pay for transportation, to buy food at school, and to buy groceries sometimes. My father often insisted on giving me money, but I wouldn't take it. I felt that he had other obligations and four other kids to take care of.

Life was tough in my college years. I would leave early in the morning and would come back home late in the evening, no sooner than 10 at night. Most of my time was spent commuting, working, and occasionally studying. That had become a boring routine for me. We did not have much incentive to focus on our studies because of political, socioeconomic, and future uncertainty in Iran. The universities back in those days were on strike most of the time. For some general education courses, I didn't even know who my teachers were until the day of the final exam. Most of us didn't bother to attend those classes, and most teachers wouldn't take attendance. I didn't have much time to socialize other than getting together with my cousins sometimes and going to the movies with them once in a blue moon. I found a good friend at the college—my Azari[53] friend, Nima—whom I could trust. Back in those days, we were warned to beware of some students and perhaps some professors at college who could be members of the SAVAK.

Nima and I got along great. Both of us were from blue-collar-type families, and we were both interested in the same kinds of music, movies, and sports. We were both proud of the success of Iranian soccer teams in Asia and impressed with the mastery of some of the Iranian wrestling and weightlifting champions in the world. We both cheered Muhammad Ali for whipping Jerry Quarry and were saddened for his loss to Joe Frazier.

I remember that I was at my uncle's house when I watched Muhammad Ali's fight against his tough opponent Frazier. It was very early morning on March 8, 1971; my uncle Sarrullah was not much into watching sports, but he knew that I was a Muhammad Ali fan, so he woke me up to watch the match. He stayed awake to keep me company. It was a spectacular match—fifteen rounds of excitement, but not a pleasant ending for me. I was so sad that Muhammad Ali lost, and I couldn't hide it. My uncle looked at me, gave me a big smile, and said, "A good champion is the one who learns from each loss and turns it into a victory in the next match. Like a boxing match, life is a challenge; you win some, you lose some. Winning in life is not for granted. If you cry for a loss and don't learn from it, you are not a true champion." I always benefitted from my uncle's words of wisdom. I learned from him that "One must learn to earn." His words would give me hopes and energy. I went to school and found my friend Nima. He was sad for Muhammad Ali's loss as well. We talked about the match for a while. We often talked about politics in Iran and were concerned about the future of Iran.

Although the Shah's government enjoyed the boom in the oil industry, most of the revenues from oil went to a very small sector of the population, such as high-ranking military officers, some of the *bazaari* merchants, some ruthless members of the SAVAK, and some government executives. Unlike the late sixties, the middle class and working class Iranians had tough times financially. Nima and I were the children of those types of families who were struggling to make ends meet.

---

53   People from Azarbaijan or Azerbaijan are called Azari or Azeri. Iranian Azarbaijan is located in the northwest of Iran and is comprised of East Azarbaijan, West Azarbaijan, Zanjan, and Ardabil provinces. It shares a border with the Republic of Azerbaijan, Armenia, Turkey, and Iraq. The Republic of Azerbaijan and Iranian Azarbaijan were both part of Iran. The current Republic of Azerbaijan was acquired by the former Soviet Union from Persia through the Gulistan Treaty in 1813 and the Turkamanchai Treaty in 1828.

Most of the news in the media in those days were about wars in other countries, the bloodbath in Iraq, or turmoil in some of the neighboring countries. Some headlines were about domestic and international celebrities, or the glorification of the royal family. Such news angered many Shia clerics and their followers. Also, we watched and read about the SAVAK's bolstering of the arrest and killing of "terrorists." In reality, they were arresting, killing, and torturing anti-regime activists.

A former high-ranking military official and the first chief of the SAVAK, General Teimoor Bakhtiar (1914 – August 1970), who later on turned against the Shah and became his longtime foe, lived in exile in Iraq. He was murdered in that year. One of his "new advisers," who, actually, was a member of the SAVAK killed the General. They showed members of the Shah's opposition groups on TV confessing to be Communists or belonging to "Islamic terrorist" groups or to "Islamic Marxist" organizations or to Maoist groups. The youth, especially the college students, would consider such news and confessions as government propagandas to scare people.

Summer times were more relaxing for me. I had more time to go to the movies or to read books. I took summer courses only once. I started reading books by Sadegh Hedayat (1903-1951), who was well known as a powerful but somewhat gloomy writer. He was also known as Iran's foremost modern writer. His specialties in writing were prose fiction and short stories. In addition to writing a substantial number of short stories and novels, he published two historical dramas, a play, a travelogue, and a number of other books. He was the first contemporary Persian writer who brought Persian literature into the international mainstream.

Some people, and especially some parents, believed that Sadegh's writings would make his readers suicidal. Before attending college, I remember one day our high school principal, who had lost one of his sons to suicide, gave an emotional speech advising us against reading the books by Sadegh Hedayat. He claimed that his son committed suicide after reading a few of Sadegh Hedayat's books. Sadegh ended his life by committing suicide (gassing himself) as well.

However, I liked Sadegh Hedayat because he understood the pain and sufferings that Iranians were going through and blamed most of the problems on two elements: the monarchy and the clergy. He believed that these two powerful elements were the causes for the destruction of the nation's true identities. Although I was really affected by Shadegh's writings, they could not change my attitude, my feelings, and my optimism for life. My preference was to read the books, which conveyed the messages of hope, peace, prosperity, and love for life. I still enjoy reading such books. Those days most college students were concerned about the political environment in Iran. They all hoped for a brighter future under a democratic society. That was what they were striving for. Thus, books and essays that dealt with political situations in Iran and the authors who wrote such books were popular.

I started reading some underground books by Jalal Al-e-Ahmad (1923 - 1969). Jalal was another excellent writer who also was a big critic of the Shah's regime and did not believe in clergy in spite of the fact that his father and his elder brother were both Islamic clerics. They tried to influence Jalal to become a clergyman as well, but he refused and described the clergy as "a snare in the shape of a cloak and an *aba*."[54] Jalal believed that the Shah was rushing the Iranian society toward westernization, and he strongly condemned it. Like Sadegh, Jalal also believed that Iranians were in danger of losing their noble identity. He blamed it on the *Gharbzadegi*,[55] Westernization. In the book *Gharbzadegi,* Jalal says, "A West-stricken man who is a member of the ruling establishment of the country has no place to stand. He is like a dust particle floating in space, or a string floating on water. He has severed his ties with the essence of the society, culture, and custom. He is not a bond between the old and the new. He is something unrelated to the past and someone with no understanding of the future."[56] In my opinion, this statement by Jalal was true for many elements of the Shah's regime but I don't think his statement can be accepted as a rule of thumb.

As a Western-educated person, I learned very valuable lessons about life from my teachers in the United States, my peers, my American friends, and my students. I respect the American culture and customs. However, I do not advocate the injection of Western culture and Western customs into the culture of Iran. I strongly believe that each nation has its own unique culture and characteristics, and nobody can take that away from the people of that nation. To the Shah's credit, he tried to preserve our true Persian identity but he ignored the will of a vast majority. For example, building casinos and nightclubs, promoting Western-style entertainment, throwing lavish Hollywood-style parties, allowing R- and somewhat X-rated movies, allowing provocative plays and dances on the stages,[57] and things of this nature were against the will of the majority and against the Islamic values. On the other hand, the leaders of the Islamic Republic, ever since they

---

54   Al-i Ahmad, Jalal, A biography by Iraj Bashiri, University of Minesota. From Wikipedia.

55   *Gharbzadegi* is the title of one of Jalal Al-e-Ahmad's books.

56   Quoted in the book by Sandra Mackey, "The Iranians: Persia, Islam, and the Soul of a Nation," page 216. Originally quoted in R.K. Ramazani, "Intellectual Trends in the Politics and History of the Mussadiq Era," *in Musaddiq, Iranian Nationalism and Oil,* ed. James A. Bill and William R. Louis (London: J. B. Tauris, 1988), page 318.

57   Brazilian dancers performed sex acts on the stage at Shiraz Art Festival in 1978. This festival, founded by Empress Farah, had become an annual event.

took power, have tried to do away with Persian customs and tried to decimate our true identity by imposing their own version of "Islamic Sharia Law." As a result of such fallacies by both regimes, the Shah's regime is out, and the Islamic Republic is on its way out. Iranians want to remain as Persians. Through my dealings with so many Iranians from all walks of life, I came t know that most Iranians do not want an Islamic regime, they do not need mullahs to tell them what kind of government or religion to pick, and they do not want an absolute monarchy either. Today what Iranians want is freedom and democracy, for which they have been fighting for almost a century. It is a matter of time until the Iranians will get rid of the Islamic republic and we hope that we will not be dictated to ever again. I would like to emphasize that I am not against Islam; I am against the Islamic Republic and religious-based governments.

Jalal also believed that clerics and intellectuals should work hand in hand in order to be triumphant in their struggle for freedom. I share Jalal's view as long as they work under the umbrella of democracy to establish a secular government.

Samad Behrangi[58] (1939 – 1968) was another Iranian writer admired by many, especially by the youth. Samad's books were banned by the Shah's regime for his Socialist and Communist views. His underground books and essays were distributed hand to hand between the students. I first read his essay on "Investigation into the Educational Problems in Iran," in which he was critical of the whole educational system and government-sponsored textbooks. He believed that the educational system in Iran was discriminatory against the poor and the villagers since they could not understand Western terminologies and methodologies.

Samad's book, *The Little Black Fish* is an internationally well-known children's book, but was considered to be a symbolic political fiction by the Shah's government and not appropriate for children. I read *The Little Black Fish* when I was a freshman. The story begins with an old fish who gathered twelve thousand of her children and grandchildren together to tell them the tale of a little black fish. She lived in a little home behind a black rock in a tiny stream under a moss-covered ceiling with her mother. She wanted to be free, to explore the bigger world, and to find the sea. The story narrates the adventures, the beauty, and the dangers that she experienced along her path to the sea. She used a dagger to destroy her enemies.

---

58   Samad Behrangi was born in Tabriz on June 24, 1939 to a lower-class Azeri family. He finished his elementary and high school education in Tabriz and received a B.A. in English from Tabriz University. In addition to his well-known children's book, *The Little Black Fish*, Samad wrote several pedagogical essays. He also translated several Azeri stories from Azeri language to Farsi. He was found drowned in Aras River in Azarbaijan in September of 1968. The Shah's government especially SAVAK was blamed for Samad's death. However, Hamzeh Farhadi one of Samad's friend who accompanied him at the time of his death narrated that his death was just a swimming accident.

After reading *The Little Black Fish*, I felt that I wanted to be free and to explore the world. I felt that there was a lot more to learn than we were being taught. Samad's idea of achieving the ultimate goal of freedom was to fight by means of "armed struggle." Some opposition groups, such as Mujahedin-e-Khalgh (MEK) and People's Fedaiian Guerillas followed Samad's doctrine to fight the tyranny. It is, however, a different era now, and I don't think armed struggle is the answer for this era. I don't think armed struggle was effective back then. I believe that we can achieve democracy through education, and education only. I also believe that most people in Iran were not politically educated enough to realize the undemocratic nature of the religious type governments. History has witnessed that these types of governments are incapable of establishing democracy and bringing prosperity to people. The Islamic Republic was indeed the worst alternative. People of Iran today are experiencing the savagery of the current regime, one of the most despotic regimes ever.

EIGHTEEN

During the summers, every opportunity I got, I went to Taleghan. I loved going to that village. I enjoyed the environment and the purity of the country people, but it was frustrating to see not much being done by the government in terms of modernization and infrastructures in the countryside and the rural areas. There was no electricity, no agricultural development, no health clinics, no proper irrigation system, and no adequate school systems. There were no incentives given to the private sectors to make advancements in the countryside. Most people who owned houses in the villages used them for summer vacations only. During the rest of the seasons, those houses were empty. The native people who could not afford living in big cities were doomed. While the government benefitted so much from oil during the golden years of high oil prices, the resources going into the villages were minimal or virtually nonexistent. However, millions of dollars were spent on the beautification of northern Tehran and some major cities in Iran. A lot of money was spent on casinos, tall buildings, entertainment centers, boutiques, and so on. Nevertheless, in the south of Tehran, many people lived in slums with contaminated water, especially in a well-known rural area, *Hallabi Abad*. The kids and elderly were dying of malnutrition. Those places are in a much worse situation under Ahmadinejad's ruling.

The first year in college made me understand more about the sociopolitical and socioeconomic environments in Iran. Reading Samad's essays and his books and getting familiarized with the views of Sadegh and Jalal and the intelligentsia in Iran made me interested in reading more about the situations in the country.

I had heard about Ayatollah Mahmoud Taleghani and his anti-Shah views. I wanted to read his books or his articles, but none was publically available. Unlike Kashani, who deserted Dr. Mossadeq, Ayatollah Taleghani stood by the former prime minister all the way. Ayatollah Taleghani had a close association with Jalal-e-Al-e-Ahmad. They were both from Taleghan and supporters of Dr. Mossadeq. They both supported democracy in Iran, and they were both anti-government activists. After the successful but unpopular restoration of the CIA-engineered coup on August 18, 1953, Taleghani made speeches in some mosques in Tehran about religious values and the importance of political awareness of people. Mehdi Bazargan, a well-known critic of the Shah and a professor in the Mechanical Engineering Department at the University of Tehran, was a fan of Ayatollah Taleghani and a big supporter of Dr. Mossadeq. He encouraged students to attend Taleghani's lecture series. Ayatollah Taleghani was well-respected by all the students, secularists, Islamists, and leftists. The students used to call him *Pedar*, father Taleghani. The triangle of Taleghani, Al-e-Ahmad, and Bazargan[59] attracted many intellectuals and students to the series of talks. All three of them were imprisoned by the Shah's regime for several years. The talk series took place before my time, but I got to know about these scholars through some of my fellow classmates.

The sixteenth day of the month of *Azar* (December 6) of each year was and still is known by the people of Iran as "National Student Day." It goes back to December 6, 1953, when the then vice president of the United States, Richard Nixon, made a trip to Tehran at the invitation of the Shah. Nixon's trip fueled anti-American sentiments in most universities in Iran. Students at the University of Tehran staged a big demonstration against Nixon and the Shah. Police attacked the protestors, and three of the demonstrators—Azar Shariat Razavi, Ahmad Ghandchi, and Mustafa Bozorgnia—were killed. Iranian students have been commemorating National Student Day annually ever since.

My very first exposure to the strike by students happened in the early morning of December 6, 1970, in my freshman year. I went to get something to eat at the little snack place in our school when I noticed a different mood in students. Most classes were literally empty, especially the junior and senior level classes. I asked one of my classmates if he knew what was going on. He explained that it was the "student day" but didn't know the details. At lunchtime at the dining center, students were beating their spoons on the plates and chanting anti-regime slogans demanding the release of the political prisoners and the release of Father Taleghani.

In my sophomore year in the fall semester 1971, students protested the celebration of the 2,500[th] anniversary of the Persian kingship, and the demonstration escalated on December 6. Students opposed the Shah's excessive expenditures for

---

59   For more details, one can refer to the book by Roy Mottahedeh, *The Mantle of the Prophet, Religion and Politics in Iran*, published by One World Oxford, 1985, 2000, 2009, pages 324-326.

the ceremony. They believed that the country's assets went to waste and could have been spent on feeding the starving citizens and on the creation of more jobs and infrastructure.

The celebration took place on October 12, 1971, and continued for five days. Several weeks before the ceremony, there were riots all over Iran. Shops, banks, movie theaters, and some government buildings were attacked, and *bazaaries* (people who work in Bazaar, plural of Bazzari) were on strike. My parents warned me to be extra careful—not to get into a clash with police, and not to say anything against the ceremony to jeopardize my future. A few days before the ceremony, the rioting masterminds threatened to attack Persepolis, the location where the ceremony was supposed to take place. The security was extremely tight and luckily, the events ended with no incidents.

The ancient city of Persepolis hosted many leaders and dignitaries from across the world. Among the invitees were the emperors, kings, former kings, presidents, prime ministers, and so on. Dictators of the time, Emperor Haile Selassie of Ethiopia, President Ferdinand Marcos of the Philippines, his shoe-loving wife, Imelda, and their beautiful daughter, President Ceausescu of Romania, King Hussein of Jordan, and King Juan Carlos of Spain, were all there. We were surprised to see the Ethiopian Emperor Haile Selassie bringing a couple of his dogs. There were some jokes about that. Many youths in Iran and some of my fellow classmates were infatuated with the daughter of Ferdinand Marcos. Also, the deposed king of Greece, Constantine, was there and stayed in Iran for a while even after the ceremony. Students were making fun of him as the "king of no land."

In addition, Nikolai Podgorny, the leader of the then Soviet Union, and the Chinese representative were there. It was astonishing to see the Soviet leader and Mao's replacement at the ceremony, as the Shah was among the strongest critics of Communist nations and especially Soviet Union and China. Among the absentees were Queen Elizabeth, President Nixon, and Georges Pompidou, French president at the time. Prince Phillip came in place of the queen, Vice President Spiro Agnew came in place of President Nixon, and Prime Minister Jacques Chablan-Delmas came in place of President Pompidou of France.

One of the most notable, historic, and proud moments of the ceremony was the famous declaration made by the Shah during the ceremony in Pasargadae before the tomb of Cyrus the Great: "Cyrus, sleep peacefully, for we are awake." He was in tears at that moment. This statement by the Shah sparked many jokes thereafter.

The ceremony was unpopular by the measure of most Iranians, nevertheless very spectacular. A vast majority of Iranians who were proud of their heritage enjoyed watching the horsemen and chariots representing every dynasty since 559 BC in Iran.[60] Such an elaborate festivity amused even the Shah's biggest critics. Most fanatics, mullahs, and radical Muslims in Iran, on the other hand, have never been proud of the magnificent Iranian heritage and Iranian history.

Students and opposition groups criticized the Shah for not using Persian designers and Persian accessories to decorate the tents for guests. Everything was French; even the chefs, the foods, and dinnerware were French. Iranian students were angry about that, and Khomeini supporters, mainly the bazaaries, used this opportunity to slam the Shah. American journalist, television reporter, and author, Ms. Barbara Walters, in her memoir,[61] explains:

> "Instead of keeping the theme ethnic and Persian, which would probably have been very charming and even meaningful, little in the tent city, was Persian. It was wall-to-wall French."

She also added:

> "The lavishness and the emphasis on Western taste turned out to be a major mistake, though no one knew at the time just how he was westernizing Iran, the Shia mullahs in Iran were slamming him for his infidel efforts. Ayatollah Khomeini, who would later lead the Islamic revolution, was already pronouncing the festivities an 'evil celebration' and, from his exile in Iraq, warning the Shah that even darker future, God forbid, lies ahead of you."

It was estimated that the cost of the ceremony was about $300 million while the government announced that it was about $16 million. Part of the $300 million was spent on infrastructure leading to the ceremony, but most, in the eyes of the opposition, was spent unwisely. The Shah's intention for the ceremony was to showcase Iran's glorious times before the Arab invasion, which Iranians are proud of, and also to institute a national symbol of kingship for the future of Iran. Nevertheless, the ceremony caused the mullahs to be more hostile toward the Shah and separated him further from people.

In that particular year, in addition to learning more and more about the sociopolitical situations in Iran, I heard and read so much about crises in other countries. For example, I read about the Vietnam War. I had read that Vietnam, for much of

---

60   Dynasties before Arab invasion included Achaemenid, Parthian, and Sassanid; dynasties after the Arab invasion included Tahirid, Safarid, Samaniad, Seljuk, Safavid, Qajar, and Pahlavi.

61   Barbara Walters, *Barbara Walters Audition* (New York, Alfred A. Knopf, Publisher, 2008), pages 201 and 202.

its existence, was under the control of mostly foreign forces: Chinese, Japanese, French, and then Americans. The more I read about Vietnam, the more I became sympathetic towards the Vietnamese people. On one hand, the Vietcong were portrait by the Iranian media as "evil Communists" who betrayed South Vietnam by helping the North; on the other hand, I was hearing from some friends, especially my Kurdish friend, Farid that the Vietcong were trying to unite the North and South. Anti-Shah activists considered Ho Chi Minh, the leader of North Vietnam, as a liberator and a hero, while the media pictured him as "the bad guy." Ho Chi Minh's life, his defiance against the French government, his fight for his country's independence against the French and Japanese, and then his longest battle with the United States for unification of North and South fascinated many student activists in those days, even though some of us were against Communist influences in Iran.

I read about Che Guevara, another heroic figure of the time, who was fighting against "imperialism" in Latin American countries. I admired Martin Luther King, the leader of the black American civil rights movement, Nelson Mandela, the anti-apartheid activist, and Gholam-Reza Takhti, the most well known hero of Iranian youths. These names, however, were underground names, and we could not publicly talk about them.

I often visited Farid and his family, who had already moved to a new house near my previous high school. One of Farid's distant cousins was a political science student at the University of Tehran. He had recently moved from the university dormitory to live with Farid's family in a small room. He had lived in the Kurdish town of Ilam most of his life until he was admitted at Tehran University. He was a nice guy and a fun person to talk to. Kurdish people were mostly opposed to the Shah's regime. Farid's cousin used to get together with a bunch of his classmates to study and discuss politics. Farid and I joined them a few times. They were too knowledgeable for Farid and me. Political terminologies they were using were Greek to us. It was obvious that those guys were mostly strong supporters of Dr. Mossadeq. Although they all admired Khomeini for his struggle against the Shah's government, they mostly believed that any Islamic establishment in Iran would be detrimental to democratic movements. Those guys were mostly praiseworthy of Ayatollah Taleghani as a more democratic thinker and a more knowledgeable person than Khomeini. I learned a lot from that group, and was eager to learn even more, but as a precautionary measure, I chose not to get too close to them.

A few weeks later, I paid another visit to my friend Farid. He was not in a good mood; I asked him, "What is going on?"

"They arrested my cousin and the rest of his friends," Farid said. "They have interrogated me and the rest of my family; luckily, they let us go."

After hearing this, while I felt so sad for those guys, I started panicking and thinking, "What if one of these guys reveals my name under torture?" I had heard so much about the brutality of SAVAK—I was scared. I was especially concerned that if they arrested me, my father would have a heart attack. However, I started becoming more resentful of the government for arresting people just for their antagonistic views. I felt bitter about the government for persecuting the students, for imprisonment of democracy seekers, for torturing the dissidents, and for executing the political prisoners.

A few days later, I paid a visit to Hooshang Molaei. We decided to go see a movie. I suggested the movie *Gaav*, The Cow. Hooshang would hardly say no to me. I had seen the movie before when it first appeared on the cinema screen in late 1969 or early 1970 when I was still in high school. I was not politically mature enough to understand the movie; it didn't seem interesting to me, and I did not understand why the movie had received so much publicity and was so controversial. However, the second time around, having read books and essays by Samad Behrangi, and others, I understood the political connotation of the movie. The movie was directed by the renowned Iranian movie director Dariush Mehrjui, based on the story written by the well-known Persian writer Gholamhossein Saedi.[62] This movie was very different from any other Persian or foreign movies that I had seen before. The movie was a symbolic political drama about a villager, *Hassan*, played by the powerful Iranian actor, Ezzatolah Entezami who became

---

62   Gholamhossein Saedi was born on January 4, 1936 in Tabriz, Iran to a poor family. When he was only 5 years old, Tabriz was invaded by the Soviet Union, his whole family fled to a small village. He became interested in the culture of the rural areas and in his early youth, he started reading books at very young age and became fascinated with writings of Anton Chekhov, the Russian writer. In 1945, the province of Azerbaijan became an autonomous socialist republic. Azari became the official language in Azerbaijan. The autonomy lasted for only one year when the Shah managed to force the Soviet troops out of Iran with the help of American government. In 1949, at the age of 13, he helped editing three magazines: Faryad, So'ud, and Javanan-e Azerbaijan, all of which anti-government publications. He wrote his first short stories in 1950. After the 1953 CIA coup d'état against the democratically elected Prime Minister Dr. Mossadeq, he and his younger brother were arrested and imprisoned in Tabriz for being activists of the Communist Tudeh Party. After being released from prison, he continued his sociopolitical activities against the government. He then moved to Tehran in early 1960s where he became acquainted with well-known writers; Jalal-e Al-e Ahmad, Simin Daneshvar, Ahmad Shamlou, a renowned lyric poet, and others. In the late 1960s, SAVAK started cracking down on the anti-government critics and they imposed harsh censorship on the writers. Saedi and other writers founded Kanun-e Nevisandegan-e Iran ("Association of Iran Writers"). They staged demonstrations against censorship, which did not go anywhere and resulted in more crackdowns. In spite of a ban on his books and articles, Saedi continued writing his anti-government articles. In 1974 he was imprisoned in the notorious Evin prison and tortured by the SAVAK. After the revolution, he joined the National democratic Front, a left wing opposition group, supporters of Dr. Mossadeq's doctrine, in opposition to Khomeini's right wing stance of Velayat-e-Faqih. In 1982, after his friend Saeed Soltanpour, a revolutionary leader and a writer, was executed by Khomeini's regime, he fled to Paris. He died in Paris on November 23, 1985, after a long battle with depression and alcoholism. He was buried in the Pere Lachaise Cemetery near Sadeq Hedayat.

obsessively attached to his cow—his only earthly possession. Owning a cow in that primitive village was a luxury. Hassan left the village temporarily, and his cow died while he was gone. On his return, the villagers who knew how much Hassan was attached to his cow hid the truth from him by telling him that his cow ran away. Hassan knew that the villagers were lying to him. He was convinced that his cow wouldn't run away. He was in denial and total disbelief.

Hassan went insane to the extent that he thought he was a cow himself. He started acting like a cow, sleeping in the cowshed, eating hay, and sounding like a cow. His mental state deteriorated. He became frightened of people. He, "the cow," called his master, "Hassan," for help. He was afraid that the Blouries, the looting bandits from another village were after him. The elders in the community, led by Eslam (played by another good actor, Ali Nassirian), got together, and decided to take him to a hospital. Hassan was not cooperating; they tied him with rope and dragged him out of his house. Hassan was resisting. Eslam ran out of patience and, to the dismay of other villagers, started treating Hassan like an animal, and beating him with a stick. Agitated Hassan broke loose and escaped. He ran away to seek his ultimate freedom—death.

In this movie, Entezami stunned the audience. He mesmerized people with his act. Director Dariush Mehrjui brilliantly depicted the life of most villagers in Iran, which was dominated by poverty, lack of education, superstitious religious rituals, and naiveté. He unveiled the politics behind hiding the facts from such societies—most village communities in Iran during the Shah's regime.

After seeing the movie, Hooshang and I were speechless. We walked for a while and then Hooshang turned to me and asked me whether I liked the movie or not. "I sure did," I said.

"You college boys like the weirdest movies," he said, "but this Entezami guy—he sure can act." We both laughed and said good-bye to each other and left.

I decided to go to my uncle Sarrullah's house. I was walking and daydreaming, thinking about different scenes in the movie. I stood by the first newsstand and as usual started checking all the important highlights when suddenly someone grabbed my hand. I thought it was one of my friends messing with me. Then someone else grabbed my other hand. I turned to my left and right; neither of them looked familiar. I felt troubled and resisted them. A third person stood by my face and calmly said, "We are SAVAK investigators and you must come with us."

"Why? I haven't done anything," I said. They were hurting me by grabbing my hand so hard. I told them to get away from me. They pushed me to the wall of a nearby pharmacy. One of them grabbed me by my neck and asked me not to raise my voice. He was much stronger than I was. I could not move. I felt a tremendous pressure on my throat and couldn't breathe for a moment. After he let go of my neck, I started coughing. They took me to a van. There was another guy behind the wheel waiting for us. They pushed me to the back seat of the van with two guys sitting on my right.

"We know who you are," one of them said. At this point, I got so scared, thinking that they might have found out that I was a friend of Farid's cousin.

I asked them, "Where are you guys taking me?"

"We are taking you to SAVAK headquarters," one of them said. I was scared and chose not to say a word after that. I did not want them to notice my fear. The driver and the guy in the front seat (the leader of the group) whispered to each other for a few minutes. Then the group leader asked me for identification. I had my student ID with me. They looked at my ID carefully and asked me a few questions, and then they stopped the van and asked me to leave.

"You mean I am free to leave?" I said.

"We apologize for mixing you up with someone else," the group leader said. For the long while that I was inside the van, I felt tortured not knowing what was going to happen to me next, and I was so frightened that my father would definitely have heart attack. My release was a big relief! I was happy that nothing drastic happened to me. I was happy that I was free.

Today, under the ruling of the Islamic Republic, when young people are arrested for political reasons, whether they are found "guilty" or not, many of them end up being tortured to death or raped to death—boys or girls. Although I hated SAVAK and what it stood for, at least they had the decency to apologize to me after the men found out that they were mistaken. Most agents of "intelligence services" under the Islamic Republic have no humanistic feelings whatsoever.

NINETEEN

In the middle of the fall semester 1971, I was getting tired of the long-distance commute. I was mentally tired, and couldn't comprehend why some people in northern Tehran were so well off financially, while most other people were poor, and a substantial number of people in the south were starving to death. I felt that there was so much injustice in Iran. I felt that I was overworked with teaching at a couple of high schools and tutoring at least three hours a day and not being compensated enough. I felt hopeless, as I was not sure what the future would hold for me. I disassociated myself from most of my friends and had no motivation to study. I stopped going to school. I went around searching for better-paying jobs. I went to the mechanic shops, to heating and cooling companies, to engineering drafting companies, and to some small engineering firms, and talked to managers about possible employment; almost all of them laughed at me. The responses were pretty much the same: "Go finish your degree first. If you are lucky, you might be able to find a job then." I was disappointed and went into further isolation. I decided to drop out of school. In spite of being warned that my name might be reported to the government and I might jeopardize my return, I went to school one day and dropped all of my courses.

I was teaching at a girls' high school in the south of the well-known *Amirieh* Street. I was also teaching at my former high school (*Bamdad*) under the mentorship of Dean Bozorgmehr. I was teaching algebra in both high schools. I adopted the same teaching style as Mr. Bozorgmehr and was using mostly his notes that I had saved from eighth and ninth grades. I had a much easier time teaching at *Bamdad* High School; students under the commanding deanship of Mr. Bozorgmehr were well behaved and very attentive. Teaching at the girls' high school, however, was different. They were very rowdy. I was the youngest teacher they had, and they wouldn't take me seriously in the beginning. Once they found out that I was for

101

real and they got used to my teaching style, they started liking me, and soon I became one of their most popular teachers.

In the meantime, I was tutoring a number of students. I was making decent money and helping my family a bit. Most often, after receiving my salary, I would go to my father's work place for lunch and would take him to his favorite restaurant, *Chelo Kababi Javan*. Very seldom would he go to the restaurant. His most favorite place to eat was home with his family but I always insisted. It was a joy for me to treat my father after his hard labor at work. He was proud of me for being so independent and always thought of me as being more mature and responsible than most kids my age. I was not sure if that was true, but I was sure of one thing, I did not want to be a burden on my father's back financially. I am not sure if he would have been proud of me, had he known that I had dropped out of school. I kept that a secret and hid it away from my family for years. I did not register in the spring semester either.

I was attracted to one of the girls in that high school; she was attractive, smart, polite, and very classy. She was always well-dressed but very conservatively. The age difference between us was just a few years. I was approaching 20 and she was probably 17. Before I began teaching at the girls' high school, I set a standard for myself that I would never start a relationship with a girl for as long as she was my student, including the ones I was tutoring. As a teacher, I set other standards: I would never play favoritism, never tutor students attending my classes for money, and I would try my best to teach my students the way I wanted to be taught. Classes were coming to an end; I wanted to keep her in mind for a future relationship. After the school was completely over and grades were submitted, I decided to find out more about her.

To make long story short, through the help of a friend, we found out where she lived—in a somewhat religious part of Tehran. Therefore, I didn't have any choice but getting my mother involved. My mother went to her house and found out that her father had been killed in an automobile accident and she was raised by her mother. She also found out that the girl was engaged to be married to a man twice her age. According to her mother, the girl did not have any choice. He was the son of a rich and influential religious bazzari merchant. Apparently, the marriage arrangement was made before the father died.

My mother came home and told me all the details. I asked her, "How did she react when she found out that I was interested in her?"

"She was in shock and disbelief," my mother said. She couldn't even guess it was me. She told my mother that I was too young. In response, my mother told her, "I think you are too young to marry a guy twice your age."

I was disappointed that I couldn't develop a relationship with the girl I liked, but it was a fact of life, and life must go on. A similar situation happened to a friend of mine at the university during the summer of 1972 when I decided to register for summer classes. He was madly in love with a girl who was attending the same university. To the best of my recollection, my friend was majoring in industrial engineering and she was in civil engineering. They started with friendship at first and gradually developed romantic relationship. However, the girl's parents wouldn't approve of the relationship because they had made pre-arranged marriage with a rich English professor who had proposed to her. She was not happy with the arrangement but her family insisted that she would be better off marrying the English professor. My friend then became obsessed with her and wouldn't take no for an answer. This obsession caused the souring of the relationship. In spite of the fact that they loved each other, she couldn't handle the pressure from both sides.

He approached me one day and wanted to talk to me desperately. He told me that he couldn't imagine life without her and that he was thinking of ending his life. I gave him a long speech trying to convince him that suicide was a selfish and a stupid thought that will have bad consequences on his family members. I continued saying, "The reason why she left you for the English teacher was probably because she saw a weak person with a low self-esteem. You need to be strong. You should stay away from her and give her time to think. Let destiny play its role. You never know, she might come back to you. If she doesn't, then deal with it and go on with your life. There will be other girls in your life." I said that and we separated.

About a year later, I saw him on the campus one day. He was excited. He gave me a big hug and said, "Habib, I took your advice and it worked. I stayed away from her for a while. She broke up with the English teacher and came back to me, and we are now engaged to be married." He really made my day, and I was very happy for him. I was glad that unlike mine, his love story had a good ending.

TWENTY

Early in 1972, a new wave of student demonstration erupted in protest against the visit by President Nixon and his wife to Tehran. Street fighting between anti-regime forces and the police had intensified in those days. One day just before the final exams, I went to school to visit with my friend Nima. After searching for him for a while, I found him at the cafeteria around lunchtime, sitting and talking to a bunch of students. Once he saw me, he paused for a few seconds, got up, and greeted me with hugs and kisses.

"I haven't seen you for a while, where have you been?" he asked.

"I was tired of school and decided to work for a while," I said. I joined the crowd; they were talking about the situation at school and criticizing how bad the food was at the cafeteria. One of the fellows talked about the arrival of *Arastoo* (Aristotle) Onassis in Tehran, the then richest man in the world, and criticized the Shah for associating himself with the rich, and ignoring the poor.

The Iranian wrestling team had just won the Asian wrestling tournament, so we chatted about that. We then noticed students beating their spoons on the table—that was a tradition at our college and many other colleges and universities in Iran in protest against the regime. Nima asked me to get out before the police and SAVAK arrived at the scene. I asked Nima what was going on. He said that the protest was in response to President Nixon's upcoming visit to Iran. We got out of the cafeteria and noticed security forces everywhere with their batons in hand. "The police are like mad dogs these days; just don't pay any attention to them," Nima said. He then escorted me to the university gate and asked me if I would come back to school in the fall. I told him that I would most likely be back in the summer.

In late July or early August 1972, on a very hot day, I was eating my lunch at a sandwich parlor outside the university; next to me there was a seemingly senior student eating his lunch as well. He asked me whether I knew anything about the latest crimes of the SAVAK in *Siahkal*. I had no clue what he was talking about. Back in those days, in the university environment, we had no idea who we were talking to, whether the person was genuine or a member of the SAVAK. We were warned not to talk to strangers. At any rate, I turned to the guy and said, "I don't know what *Siahkal* is and what crimes you are talking about." He started talking and educating me about the situation in *Siahkal*. I interrupted him and told him, "I don't mean to be rude, but after a hard workday in the lab and a heavy meal on this hot day, I am extremely tired and out of energy. The last thing I need is a lecture. I need to find a place to take a nap."

"That is a good idea. I could use a nap myself. Just come with me, I know a quiet place we can take a nap without being disturbed," he said.

He then took me to the university mosque in a small room with a ceiling fan. There were other students, each taking a nap at every corner of the mosque. We finished our nap and the guy continued his lecture about *Siahkal,* and mentioned that *Mohammad Safari Ashtiani* was killed in a battle against the government forces in *Siahkal*. "I am sorry, but I don't even know who this person is and where *Siahkal* is located," I said.

"Siahkal is a jungle located in northern Iran, the Gillan province, where People's Fedaiian Guerillas[63] have been fighting against the regime to liberate Iran. Safari Ashtiani was the commander of guerrilla fighters," he said. The words "guerrillas" and "Fedaiian" were Communist terms and scary to use, so I had to cut him off and leave. I was not rude to him; I politely expressed my lack of interest in the subject. I did not know the person well enough to carry on a conversation with. Years later, when I came to the United States, I learned more about the Siahkal Group.

Fall semester 1972 started, and I was concerned about my status at school and whether or not I was going to be interrogated by the university authorities or by the SAVAK for missing the school for one academic year. I did register for the classes, and luckily, nobody questioned me for my absence. In the meantime, that semester, I was teaching at *Bamdad* High School and another boys' high school in the well-known district of *Sarcheshmeh* near the bazaar and close to the center of Tehran called *Dabirestan-e-Badr*, Badr High School. My house, my college, and these two high schools were situated at four different locations in Tehran, making

---

63   The Organization of Iranian People's Fedaiian Guerillas (OIPFG) was founded by Mohammad Safari Ashtiani and Ali Akbar Safaei Farahani on February 8, 1971. This organization was an active Marxist-Leninist group in Iran until the fall of the Shah.

commuting tiresome and very difficult for me. However, I managed to take my courses in such a way that there would not be any conflict.

Teaching at Bamdad High School was again a breeze for me, as the kids there were well- behaved and well-disciplined. The people in the district of Sarcheshmeh were known as mischievous and roguish. That district was also known for its friendly and chivalrous people. The Badr High School was located in a very long alley with old houses. Some of the houses were probably four or five hundred years old with authentic all wood entrance doors. All kinds of people used to live in that alley—rich, middle class, and poor. The alley was somewhat historic but not a tourist site. Badr High School was located in the rundown part of the alley and was known as a high school for mostly streetwise kids. It was not my choice to go there. I was sent there by the ministry of education, but going to Bamdad High School was my choice. I was one of Mr. Bozorgmehr's favorite math teachers.

At Badr High School, I was put in charge of teaching a math subject for non-math-major tenth-graders, in a class of about fifty. The very first day I attended the class, I noticed a bunch of noisy, undisciplined, and out-of-control kids. Most students in the class were well built and bigger than I was. I was not much older than the students—some of them were probably my age. I had been told that most of the students in that class had been repeating the class for several years in a row. I stood by the blackboard while the captain of the class was cracking jokes for the class. He then turned to me and said, "Why don't you sit down?"

"I am all right; I am just listening to your jokes," I said. "Just let me know when you are done with your jokes, so I can start the first lesson."

"You are the teacher!" he exclaimed. "Sorry, I thought you were one of the students."

Everybody was laughing and whispering in class, "He is the teacher!"

I really had a hard time teaching that class; those guys didn't care about studies, particularly about math, and had no respect for teachers. Controlling the students and getting them to settle down was an impossible task. Several of their teachers had given up and left. I used to get very frustrated with that class and didn't know what to do. I could have easily left. The money school paid me was not much. I would have made more money tutoring three or four students instead of going to that class, but I didn't want to give up.

The nice thing about that school was that it was pretty close to my father's work place. The class hours ended around lunchtime, and I often visited my father and we had lunch together. One day during lunchtime, my father noticed that I looked preoccupied and depressed. He asked me, "Son, what is going on with you?"

"I am having a hard time with my students at Badr High School," I said.

"Don't get yourself so miserable over this, you are not an employee of that high school, you can quit if you want."

"I am not a quitter father; I will find a way to make it work."

In order to ease the situation between the students, and me, I came up with a plan; I went to the classroom and gave them a little pep talk. "Friends, I am on a mission to teach you this subject whether you like it or not. If your intention is to make me quit as you did to some of your former teachers, let me tell you, I am not going to do that. You will quit before I do. You will quit acting so childish, you will quit talking in class, you will quit being disrespectful to your teacher, and you will start taking me and this subject very seriously." Then I continued, saying, "I am a student like you, not much older than you guys, and I am not out to get you. I care about my students, and you can trust me. Here is what we are going to do; I will teach you math for the first half of each period, and for the rest of the period I will go from one chair to another to talk to each of you individually to find out why you lack enthusiasm and why you act the way you do. I want to get to know everyone and to answer any questions you may have for me, but you have to promise to be quiet and attentive during my lecture. Is that a deal?" Everyone said yes.

The next day when I went to class, they all rose at the same time.[64] I found them extremely polite and quiet. I was surprised. I lectured them for half of the period. I asked if there were any questions; a few of them politely raised their hands and asked their questions without being yelled at by others to "shut up." Then I assigned some homework and encouraged them to work collaboratively like a team without disturbing others. Working like a team was something new for the students—that was not something teachers would do in the past. I wanted them to learn from each other, and I found that to be very effective. Then I started talking to them on a one-on-one basis while the rest of the students were doing their homework. I found out a lot about them. One of them complained how badly he was treated at home by constantly being told that he was a bum and that he was not going to amount to anything. In fact, quite a big number of them told me more or less the same thing. I asked them why they were being treated this way, and one of the students said, "Because I don't want to be a doctor or a lawyer or an engineer. I just want to be a carpenter."

Another student said, "I want to be a blacksmith."

---

64   It was a tradition in Iran that students used to rise for their teacher to show their respect when he or she entered the classroom.

"I want to be a mechanic," another said. These kinds of jobs were considered low by the measure of most parents in Iran those days. I had another student who told me that his father wanted him to become a theologian, an idea he hated.

Unfortunately, most Iranian families, especially middle class families, back in those days expected too much of their sons or daughters. They dictated to their kids what to do and what to become. Most parents never tried to encourage the particular talent of their kids unless it was what they wanted. For example, if the kid wanted to be a musician, a carpenter, or a blacksmith, the parents would bring up an excuse such as "that is not a job," or "that is un-Islamic," or "that is not a good career," and things of that sort. In my opinion, these kinds of attitudes by the parents stemmed from the dictatorial nature of the society and the lack of democracy. The people of Iran have been dictated to by their government, by their employers, by their teachers, and by their parents. Dictatorship, unfortunately, has been the way of life in Iran for generations.

Life was tough for many of my students in that rough neighborhood. In the meantime, many *bazaaries* and some mullahs lived in that alley. They were well off financially. The children of bazaaries didn't need college education to follow in their fathers' footsteps. I had a few of those guys in my class. However, most of my students were from low-income and blue-collar families. I remember one of my students told me that he had lost his father to cancer and that after school he had to work in two different places—intense, hard-labor jobs he had to do to help his family. He cried for his younger sister, who had to work as a house cleaner at people's houses along with her mother. He mentioned that a few times his employer had beaten him up for not working hard enough. He also mentioned that he had been mugged and beaten up by robbers after leaving his job, usually around midnight. He had vowed to work hard to get his little brother through school. "I don't want my little brother to go through the same troubles as I am going through." He said. The story of his life and his love and compassion for his family made me cry. There were many similar stories. I also learned from some of the students that a few of their former classmates were in jail for opium and other drug-smuggling charges.

I sympathized with my students. I cried for them; I cried with them; I gave them a lot of encouragement, and I tried to comfort them as much as I could. They realized that I was one of them and that I really cared for them. I became their favorite teacher, even though I was teaching their least favorite subject. I was proud of myself for making a dramatic change in the attitude of the rowdiest and most disturbed class within a period of less than three months. It was a joy for me to go to that class for the rest of the academic year.

One day the dean of the high school came up to me and complimented me for the way I handled those guys and asked me, "What did you do to these guys to make them so well mannered in a math class?"

"I didn't do anything spectacular; I just cared for them. I showed them compassion, love, and respect, things that were missing in their lives," I said.

After the final exam, these guys stood outside the classroom waiting for me. They expressed their love and gratitude to me. They were appreciative. They complimented me, pleaded with me to come back in the fall. I was speechless and had tears in my eyes. I was sad and felt that I was leaving my brothers behind. A few days later, I went back to school to submit the grades. Unfortunately, I did not see any of my students, but the high school principal was there. He was thankful for my efforts and said, "I have never seen such enthusiasm by students for their teacher in this high school." It was rewarding for me to hear those words from the high school principal. I felt so good that my hard work, dedication, and my love and respect for my students paid off. I received even more love and respect back from them. The Great Zoroaster, the Persian Prophet said, "The happiest person in life is the one who tries to bring happiness to other people's lives."

TWENTY-ONE

I paid more attention to my studies in my junior and senior years. Three of my professors stood taller than the others did. They were Professor Forootan, Dr. Dailamian, and Dr. Aslani. They each had a positive impact in my life, and I have pleasant memories of them.

Professor Forootan was kind, funny, caring, and a hands-on type professor. He was a good teacher and had excellent handwriting, which made it easier for us to follow his lecture on the board. I took two courses with him, Strength of Materials and Theory of Machines. He liked my handwriting and the way I wrote my notes and hired me as his assistant. My job was to translate problems from some English-written engineering textbooks into Farsi and to solve those problems. My English was not so good at that time, but translation of engineering problems was not a difficult task. However, some of the problems were difficult to solve and they were time consuming. I worked hard not only because professor Forootan paid me but also because I liked Professor Forootan and learned so much from him. Nima and I thought that he looked somewhat like Einstein. Professor Forootan was kind and influential. When he talked, everybody listened. Students had a great deal of respect for him and rarely did they miss his classes.[65]

He had made a copy of his office key for me. He gave me permission to use his office any time I felt like it. I had my own little desk in his office. One day while we were working together around lunchtime, he asked me, "Son, have you had your lunch yet?"

"No sir I haven't," I replied.

"I am going to treat you to lunch today," he said.

The student-dining center and the dining center for faculty and staff were different. It was my first time going to the faculty-dining center. The food and

---

65   Back in those days, because of political unrest and uncertainty, students missed classes quite often.

the environment there were much better. During lunch, we heard the familiar spoon-beating sound from the student-dining center. They were chanting anti-government slogans. He turned to me and asked, "Son, what do you think? Do you think the students are right?"

"I don't know the answer to that question?" I said. "What do you think, sir?"

"I think students are always right when they demonstrate against their government, but they don't always know what they want. If they knew what they wanted and if they had become united for one cause, we would have been a democratic state by now." He continued, "Instead of fighting for democracy and freedom, some want an Islamic establishment, some want a Communist government, others want only the Shah gone, and so on."

I was flattered that he called me "son" and trusted me enough to talk to me about politics. Professor Forootan was correct. During the seventies, if we knew what we wanted, if we were united for establishment of a democratic and secular government, we would not allow dictatorship and the rise of another dictator in Iran.

Professor Dailamian was another good teacher that I admired. I took the Advanced Dynamics and the Vibration course with him. He was thorough and tough but a kind man. He was soft spoken and a gentleman. He was a serious teacher and not very friendly on campus, but I found him very relaxed and friendly off campus.

One evening after the class, four of us were walking towards the main exit door. Professor Dailamian drove his car past us, and after a few feet; he pressed on the brakes, backed up, and stopped in front of us. He rolled his window down and asked us if we needed a ride. He said that he could take us to one of the main bus stations in *Maidan-e Seyed Khandan* (Seyed Khandan square), located a few miles from the campus. Many of us used to catch a bus to get to the main bus stop. Because of traffic congestion in Tehran, especially during early evening times, the bus ride was not very pleasant. We were surprised by the kind gesture of our professor offering us a ride. Back in those days, professors in Iran, for political reasons, usually kept a distance from their students.

One of my fellow classmates in our advanced dynamics class by the name of Farshad, who was walking with us, whispered to me, "I am not going to get a ride from this Jewish guy."

I was appalled by such a stupid statement and said to him, "We'll talk about this later." Three of us got in the car, and we all found the serious professor Dailamian very friendly and nice to talk to.

I remember that he asked us each, "Why do you want to become an engineer?"

One fellow said, "I want to help my father in his mechanic shop by bringing more scientific flavor to his designs."

Another fellow said, "I want to make money, date a lot of women, and have fun."

I said, "I want to be an engineering educator like you."

His response to the first guy was, "Good, I like the idea." To the second guy, he responded, "You are in the wrong field; maybe you should switch to an art or architecture major." To me, he said, "You will not be a rich person." He then asked us, "Do you know what engineering is all about?" We each expressed our own opinion.

I then asked him, "How do you define engineering?"

"Engineering is a science that applies math and physics to design and manufacture machines, structures, buildings, roads, aircraft, and other necessities of life," he said. "Engineering is about precision, self-discipline, integrity, and honesty."

As an engineer, and engineering educator, I came to realize that professor Dailamian's definition of engineering was absolutely correct and made perfect sense.

Professor Dailamian took us farther and beyond *Maidan-e Seyed Khandan*. We thanked him and got out of the car somewhere in a more upscale neighborhood in northern Tehran. These guys suggested grabbing a bite to eat before going home. We found a little sandwich shop and had our dinner there. After dinner, these guys suggested that we go to a disco. I reluctantly accepted. We went to a well-known night club called, Chattanooga. The place was packed with young boys and girls. I felt tensed there from the first moment we went there. My friends each ordered a bottle of Persian beer, *Shams* and I ordered just a soda. One of them asked me why I didn't order a beer, "I don't drink alcoholic beverages," I said.

"Habib, you need to cool down, relax a bit, and enjoy your life," he said.

We met an American acquaintance of one of the guys with his Persian girlfriend. I started practicing my English on the American guy. He said, "Don't bother, I can speak Farsi." We laughed. These guys were drinking, talking loud, and dancing. The music was too loud, and the smoke of the cigarettes polluted the air. That place was not very entertaining for me, and I felt that I didn't fit in. I slowly and quietly sneaked out. That was my very first time going to a Persian nightclub in Iran, and my very last.

Just before our next class period, I ran into Farshad. He asked me whether I had a good time with the Jewish professor and whether or not I bribed him for a better grade. I asked him, "If you have a problem with this person because he is Jewish, why did you take a course with him?"

"He is a good teacher," he said.

"Then, shut up and have some respect for your professor," I said. He then gave me a lecture about Jewish people being infidel and labeled them as enemies of Islam and mostly agents of SAVAK. "Do you have any proof that Dr. Dailamian is an agent of SAVAK?" I asked.

"I don't have to have any proof; I just don't trust him."

"You know, this discussion is not going anywhere; I don't agree with you at all."

A few days later, Farshad and I met again, he said, "Habib, I thought about what I said the other day and realized that I was wrong." Farshad and I became close friends thereafter and we studied together often.

One of my all-time-best teachers in Iran was none other than Dr. Aslani, a distant relative of mine. He was kind, charismatic, respectable, and personable. Dr. Aslani was a full time professor at another engineering school in Tehran and taught at our school as an adjunct professor. He quickly gained a reputation as a great professor and became very popular with students. I had heard about him from my friends, some of whom asked me whether we were related. I took two design courses with him.

Dr. Aslani's classes met in the evenings, yet his classes were not boring at all. Most often, he gave me a ride home after class. During my interaction with him, I found him to be brutally honest, ethical, and a true gentleman. He had a great deal of respect for his students and genuinely cared whether we understood the subjects or not. Dr. Aslani's philosophy was, "If you want to succeed in life, strive to be the best and don't settle for less." His advice to me was, "If you want to be an engineer, try to be the best, and don't settle for becoming a mediocre engineer just to get by. If you want to be an academician, don't settle for less than a PhD." The universities in Iran did not offer a PhD during the seventies, and I had no desire to leave Iran because I thought it was going to be costly. However, as I approached closer to graduation, I became more serious about pursuing higher-level education. Dr. Aslani was my biggest patron in pursuing a PhD. For that and other valuable lessons that I learned from him, I am indebted to him.

TWENTY-TWO

In the seventies, the Shah pursued the purchase of the most sophisticated weapons from the United States in order to strengthen the defense and military capabilities of Iran's armed forces against the "aggression" by the Soviet Union and some Arab neighbors. That was the main purpose of President Nixon's visit to Iran in 1972. During that visit, President Nixon made a firm commitment to the Shah to sell the laser-guided bomb and fighter planes F-14 and F-15. Nixon and Kissinger's strategies were to equip Iran with the state-of-the-art military technologies in order to counter the Soviets' presence in the region. Iran, therefore, became the police of the region.[66]

The first government showdown of its policing of the region was the military intervention in Dhofar, Oman. This intervention occurred at the request of Oman's Sultan Qaboos to suppress the anti-government uprising in Dhofar.[67] The Iranian military dispatched forces to that region. The pro-government media justified this intervention as fighting against evil Communist insurgents. The opposition groups called it "a military show-off," "a war against Omani freedom fighters," and things of this sort. The young Iranian soldiers didn't know what they were fighting for, and Iranian students demonstrated against the Shah's military buildup and the senseless war in Dhofar.

Farshad and I discussed the war in Dhofar occasionally, and we both condemned it. One day Farshad jokingly mentioned to me, "If we don't work hard and don't finish our studies on time, we might end up in Dhofar."

In my absence and without my knowledge, Farshad showed up at our doorstep one evening and rang the bell. My mother opened the door, and he asked if I was at home. "Habib is not at home," my mother said. He asked if he could

---

66   Robert Graham, *Iran, The illusion of power, 1978*, Croom Helm Ltd, London. Revised Edition 1979, pages 173-175.
67   Ibid, page 180.

come in and wait for me in my room. "I am sorry, I don't know you well enough to let you in. You are more than welcome to come in when Habib is here." He then left. She told me the story at dinnertime. I got a little upset and told her that she should have let him in. Agha joon agreed with me. My mother argued and said, "It is not safe to let strangers enter your house in this day and age, especially if you have a college student in the house. He could be a SAVAK agent."

"Oh mother, you don't know what you are talking about," I said.

I saw Farshad the next day and I apologized to him for my mother's behavior. A few days later, as Farshad and I were walking on campus together, we ran into a former classmate, who turned to Farshad and said, "Hey, Farshad, if I were you, I wouldn't bother studying. You are going to have a government job, and who knows, you might even become the prime minister one day." Then he turned to me and said, "Hey, Habib, watch your back. Associating with this guy might be costly."

"What was that all about?!" I exclaimed.

"This guy hates my guts, and I have no idea what he is talking about," Farshad said. Surprisingly, a couple of days later, Nima told me to be extra careful and watch my mouth when hanging out with Farshad.

On October 1, 1973, SAVAK announced that they arrested a group of twelve Marxist anarchists on charges of attempting to kidnap the Shah's son, crowned Prince Reza. Khosro Golsorkhi, the well-known journalist and poet, Keramat-tollah Daneshian, another poet, writer, and journalist, and Reza Allameh Zadeh, a filmmaker, were among them. Their trial started in early January 1974 and was broadcast live on Iranian national TV. None of the arrestees was affiliated with the military, and yet their trial was held in a military court! Rumor spread among students that the official Iranian court refused to hold a trial for a crime that didn't happen and there was no legitimate evidence against the arrestees. It was surprising to people that the accused were given the opportunity to defend themselves. Live broadcasting of the trial of anti-government activists was unprecedented until that day.

The first few days, some of the accused made confessions implicating the group leaders, admitted wrongdoing, and asked for forgiveness and clemency. Golsorkhy defended himself at his trial. He claimed that he was a Marxist-Leninist, but sought social justice in Islam for the first time, and then became a socialist. He mentioned that he was wrongly accused and imprisoned for a crime that didn't even happen. He mentioned that he was tortured to the extent that he urinated blood. He told the military judge that he was not bargaining for his own life, but defending the oppressed people of Iran. He stated that he admired Imam Hussein, the revered martyr of Shia Muslims, for his struggle against Yazid's tyranny (see footnote 28). He then blasted the Shah's land reform as being a corrupt practice and not a true reform. At this point, he was interrupted by the military judge and was reminded that he should only defend himself. Golsorkhi turned to the judge and rephrased his statement, "I am not defending myself; I am defending my people. If I am not at liberty to speak freely, I will sit down."

By broadcasting the trial, the Shah's regime expected the defendants to confess and ask for leniency. Most of them did, but Golsorkhy and Daneshian did not. They were both sentenced to death. The bravery of these two and their defiance against the regime made them instant heroes. Although they were both Communists, they spoke of Islam respectfully. They gained the respect of everybody: young and old, leftists, and clergies. University and high school students went on strike and demonstrated against the military court's decision.

A few days after the executions, students in our college staged a big demonstration and chanted sharp slogans against the Shah and the regime. The demonstrations turned ugly. Students broke the windows, classroom doors, and the blackboards. Police attacked the students violently. I was caught between mobs of demonstrators and the police and received a baton on my back that made me have hard time breathing for a while and hurt for days.

Another member of the group who defended himself courageously was Reza Allameh Zadeh. He was an artist and a filmmaker. Empress Farah was an advocate and promoter of art, so the court gave him clemency. He got a lighter sentence, life in prison. Incidentally, Allameh Zadeh and his wife had rented a room on the second floor of a house right next to ours a few months before the trial. To the best of my recollection, they did not stay in that house very long. My family and I were shocked to see him on TV during the televised court session. After watching the trial of Allameh Zadeh, my mother started getting worried. She started putting pictures of the Shah, Empress Farah, and Prince Reza everywhere. She then, in my absence, went through all of my books, papers, and essays, and with the help of my brothers she burned all the suspicious ones.

It wasn't too long after the trial that our house was stormed by the agents of SAVAK. They asked for me. Luckily, I wasn't at home. They searched through all of my books and everywhere in the house in the hopes of finding government-banned books and anti-government articles and essays. They couldn't find anything. My mother was scared but composed and kept her cool. They looked at the pictures of the Shah and the royal family and left. That evening, my mother told me the whole story but kept it from my father. He would have been furious. Had it not been for my mother's wit, her quick thinking, her sharp instinct, and her prudence, I am not sure where I would be today. I would probably have been jailed for a few years, to say the least. It is unlikely that I would have ended up coming to the United States.

My mother strongly believed that my classmate, Farshad, had a lot to do with SAVAK's suspicion and persecution of me. She also assumed that having Allameh Zadeh as a neighbor at one point, might have contributed to SAVAK's suspicion of me and their storming of our house. I am not sure if Farshad, or being the neighbor of Allameh Zadeh had anything to do with this, but I am sure that when it comes to protecting loved ones, mothers will never go wrong.

The regime's intention by showcasing the trial was to intimidate the opposition and to rally support and empathy for the peacock throne and against the "terrorist" intention of the group. That was an enormous mistake. The trial did not scare the opposition, nor did it rally any support for the Shah. Moreover, the execution of Golsorkhi and Daneshian was a drastic mistake by the Shah's regime. To this day, I don't think there were any legitimate and lawful reasons behind their execution for a crime that didn't occur. The Shah had the power to pardon them or at least order lighter sentencing than execution, but he didn't. That disturbed me personally, and a lot of other people across the whole country as well.

One day, after a long day at school, I decided to visit my father at his workplace. It was mid-afternoon. It was always a joy seeing his kind face and fatherly smile. I was hungry. I asked him whether he had any leftover from lunch. He said no.

"Son, why don't you eat your lunch around lunchtime?" he asked.

"I just didn't have time to eat," I said. "I will get something to eat and go to my tutoring, and will go home afterward."

I walked to Naderi Street, a block away from my father's workplace; there were a couple of great sandwich shops there. One of them was well known for its hamburgers. I had a hamburger, a small bowl of pinto beans, and a Coca-Cola. The food was great. After lunch, I decided to go for a long walk and check out the shopping centers in a famous valley known as *Koucheh Berlan*, Berlin Valley. The valley was jam-packed with people as usual. I passed through the valley into the *Lal-e-Zarno* Street—a narrow street with many comedy clubs, live play theaters, and movie theaters. One of the movie theatres was showing the movie *Spartacus* with my favorite movie star, Kirk Douglas. I always wanted to see that movie when it first came out in the early sixties, but I was too young to go by myself, and I never had the opportunity to go with someone else. Unfortunately, I was supposed to tutor one of my students, but I had the urge to see that movie. I decided to give my student a call and cancel our appointment. Luckily, I found a two-Rial[68] coin in my pocket and found a telephone kiosk. There were too many people waiting to make a phone call. I patiently waited until the last person finished. I made my phone call, and by the time I got to the movie, I had missed a few minutes of the movie.

The movie was fascinating. I was always interested in the historical movies. It was spectacular to see all the great movie stars, Kirk Douglas, Peter Ustinov, Laurence Olivier, and Tony Curtis together in one film. I was inspired by the charisma of a slave who became a gladiator, a hero, an icon, and the leader of the slaves and the oppressed people. The part that intrigued me the most was the scene when in response to the Roman Army General's demand to identify Spartacus, every captured member of the slave army proclaimed, "I am Spartacus." That scene made me cry and affected me for weeks. After seeing that movie, I thought maybe we needed a Spartacus to get rid of the tyranny in Iran. Unfortunately, we ended up picking not a Spartacus, but another tyrant.

---

68   We needed a two-Rial coin to place a phone call at that time. One Iranian Rial was equivalent to approximately 1.43 cents in the early seventies. Now each Iranian Rial is almost equivalent to 0.0001cent! This is what Islamic Republic has done to our currency.

TWENTY-THREE

During my academic year 1974-75, a sort of cold war over oil prices started between Iran and the United States. Among all the oil-producing countries, Iran, in particular, was blamed for boosting the price of oil and lowering oil production. As a result, the American Senate offered to halt military aid to Iran.[69] On the other hand, the controversy over the Watergate scandal, which ultimately led to resignation of President Nixon, dominated the media in Iran. Also, Iraqi aggression on the Iran-Iraq border, in spite of the hah's attempts to end the crisis through diplomatic means, continued and subsequently forced Iran to retaliate militarily against Iraqi forces. The Iranian government helped Iraqi Kurdish rebels led by General Mustafa Barzani to escalate the war with the new Baath government of Iraq led by Ahmed Hassan-Al-Bakr and Saddam Hussein. Saddam never again attacked Iranian border cities for as long as the Shah was in power, and ultimately was forced to sign the 1975 treaty (see footnote 50).

The Shah's war of words with the United States intensified. He made several news conferences in Iran and other countries, naming the American administration "the blue-eyed arrogant." In his news conferences and speeches to the nation, the Shah declared victory against foreign aggression, bragged about his military capabilities, and announced that no country in the world would dare attack Iran.

In the meantime, Iranians won second place in the Asian Olympics,[70] earning thirty six gold medals, twenty eight silver, and seventeen bronze after the Japanese. The games were hosted by Iran, and it was for the first time that the Chinese athletes were allowed to participate in any international games. They

---

69   Translated from the *Rouz Shomar-e-tarikh-e-Iran az mashrouteh ta enghelab-e-eslami, Jeld-e Dovom*, Chronology of Iran (1896-1979), Vol. 2 by Bagher Agheli, *Nashr-e Goftar*, 1995, *Chronology of Iran (1896-1979)*, page 287.

70   These games started on the twenty-fifth of Shahrivar 1353 (September 15, 1974) in Tehran.

came third. This achievement by the Iranian sportsmen has never been repeated after the 1979 revolution.

The combination of all of the aforementioned news brought a lot of publicity and notoriety to Iran and the Shah. Iran had emerged as one of the strongest Asian countries and one of the richest countries in the world. Iran lent money to many Asian and European countries. Many trade and economical treaties were signed between Iran and international communities. One of the largest sources of natural gas in the world was discovered in Kangan, a county of Bushehr Province on June of 1974. Iran exported natural gas to Germany, Russia, India, and many other countries. The Shah and his wealth minister, Jamshid Amoozegar, were the key persons and deciding factors behind setting OPEC's oil prices. They had a way of convincing other OPEC members of boosting the oil prices and reducing the production of oil in early seventies, which resulted in the shortage of oil and the oil crisis of the mid-seventies in the West. That upset most of the Western countries, especially the United States.

In spite of the oil boom, Iran was still a consumer and not much of a producer. Too much military spending by the government, price gouging and profiteering by the bazaar's merchants and tradesmen, and not producing enough, had caused inflation. The Iranian people enjoyed prosperity, peace, and low inflation, under the Shah's government for a long time, but high inflation during the mid to late seventies started taking a toll on the Shah's regime internally. The gap between the middle class and the rich widened. The poor became poorer and rich became very wealthy. Not much was being done for the people in the rural areas and the villagers. Despite an increase in inflation, the Iranian currency was still strong against the dollar.

In addition, the Shah's fight against profiteers in the bazaar caused him more enemies and eventually cost him his throne. One of the biggest problems we have had in Iran, and still have, is the bazaar sect in the country. During the Shah's reign, bazzaries mobilized many naïve and uneducated Iranian people against the Shah. In the Shah's defense, he was anti-profiteering and did not have tolerance for overcharging and swindling. The bazaar merchants supported the mullahs on their struggle against the Shah's regime. During the Shah's rule, prices of the basic necessities such as food and gas were pretty much the same everywhere in the country. Since the revolution, the bazaar merchants have been completely in control of setting prices any which way they wish. Furthermore, the food prices differ from one store to another. The Islamic Republic has not been doing anything about it. There is absolutely no control over the prices, nor is there any control over the inflation. Unfortunately, during the recent uprising in Iran, the bazaar merchants opted not to take the side of the people and stayed silent.

Early in 1975, just before Eid Nowruz, the Shah surprised everyone by out-lawing all the political parties in Iran and declaring a single-party system. The new party was named *Rastakhiz* (Resurrection). Shortly after the single party dec-laration, the Shah made a speech before all the parliamentarians and heads of all the parties, *Iran-e-novin, Mardom, Pan-Iranist*, and more. He announced, "The era of political hypocrisy is over, and anybody who opposes the constitution, the mon-archy, and the Sixth Bahman Revolution (White Revolution, January 25, 1962) will be put either in jail, or can get out of Iran."[71] The main goals of the party were to unite all the Shah's loyalists, to monopolize all the political activities, to create a bond between the Shah and the nation, to fight against the profiteering and bazaar influences, and to force the opposition groups, especially bazaaries, to either join the party or face isolation.

The party mandated that every Iranian had to join. Membership dues were required of only the bazaaries, all merchants, and those of the highly paid class of people, not of the ordinary people, and not of the students. Students were not happy about the creation of the single-party system. We believed that the Shah's intention of changing the system of government to a single-party system was to expand his authority and to further suppress the freedom of speech and freedom of press, but we didn't have any choice. We had to join.

During the summer of 1975, the Rastakhiz party recruited university students from across the country to participate in the so called, *"Ordoy-e Omran-e melli,"* "Nationwide Reconstruction Camps," in order to fulfill some of the missions of the party. They were recruited to check out shop prices in the shopping plazas and in the bazaars and report those who overcharged people. They were also recruited to go to the primitive villages, or to the rural areas, to find out people's needs, demands, and deficiencies in those areas and report them to the government.

Nima and I decided that we didn't want to be a part of watchdog spies for the government, so we chose to help people in the rural areas. We were drafted to go to the city of *Astara,* a town in the northern province of *Gilan* at the border of the then Soviet Union and now the Azerbaijan Republic. Astara is a very pretty beach city located on the shores of the Caspian Sea.

We had students from every university in Iran in our camp. The first few days, they took us on a tour of the whole city and the neighboring towns, such as the beautiful city of Talesh and the port city of Bandar-e Pahlavi (now Bandar-e Anzali).

---

71   Translated from the *Chronology of Iran (1896-1979),* by Bagher Agheli, page 294.

We then started working during the daytime. Nima and I were put in charge of a district with some rundown villages. We talked to many people in that district, including the village council. The local language of the people of Astara is Turkish. Some of the old people of that district couldn't speak Farsi. Nima quickly became very popular in that district because he was a Turk himself and used his Turkish communication skills and his good looks to charm everyone, especially the young girls. Some of those village girls didn't have much education, but they were absolutely gorgeous. That was the case for most girls in Astara. The people of Astara, however, were mostly highly educated and politically well informed—they were mostly anti-government and, under the influence of the neighboring Soviet Union. They mostly leaned towards socialism and advocated a Russian-style Communist government. Inside the camp, we were cautioned by the camp organizers not to start political debates especially with people outside the camp.

I took my job very seriously. I wrote down every problem and every complaint people had. In the evenings, we got together to crack jokes, sing, and socialize. Often we would get together with a bunch of guys in the camp to go to the beach for a walk, or to eat grilled trout or salmon, or to drink. I didn't drink alcoholic beverages, and neither did Nima but a few of the campers drank on Thursday evenings and celebrated for hours. They were entertaining and funny but never disturbed anybody.

Some weekends, starting from early Thursdays and ending Friday evenings, the camp organizers would either take us on field trips or we were free to go visit our family and friends. Astara was pretty far from Tehran, so visiting our families in a day and a half was out of the question for Nima and me. One weekend, I made a suggestion to Nima to go to Rasht (approximately 160 km from Astara), to visit my sister, Maasoomeh, whose husband was relocated on duty to that town. The city of Rasht was not very far from Astara. My sister was surprised to see me. My brother-in-law, Mr. Momeni, and my little nephew, Mohammad greeted us warmly. That evening, Nima and I left the house for a walk around town. Near my sister's house, we noticed a couple of guys talking and laughing. One of them from behind looked very curvy and caught the attention of both Nima and me. When we got closer, we both noticed an angelic face, absolutely gorgeous, but dressed like a boy and had a boyish hair cut but it was a girl. She noticed that we were both looking at her. With her low and girlish voice, she turned to us and said, "What are you looking at?"

"We were just admiring your beauty," Nima said.

"You want a piece of me, come and get it you, bastards," she yelled. "Come on, you bastards."

"Just don't pay any attention to her," I told Nima. Soon we were surrounded by a bunch of guys who asked the girl whether we hurt her or not. I told Nima to keep his cool and not say a word. Then she came to us and started pushing Nima and challenged him to a fight.

"We apologize if we were disrespectful to you. We are just visitors in this town; we have no intention to fight anybody, so please leave us alone and let us go," I said.

They finally calmed down, and she told us to leave the town, and never come back. We started walking a long distance before reaching downtown Rasht. We checked out some shopping centers, walked around some more, and decided to head back towards my sister's house. As we were walking on the street, a taxi driver stopped by and asked whether we needed a cab. "No thanks." We kept on walking. As we were trying to keep away from a puddle of water in front of us, a taxi at a high rate of speed ran over the puddle and dirty water splashed all over both of us. "You coward, you bastard, stop if you have the guts," we both yelled. The driver pressed on the brake and backed up toward us.

"You stay away, I am going to handle this guy," Nima said.

He parked the car by the side of the street and was walking toward us, but we noticed a bunch of other guys joining him. "Oh boy, we are going to be dead meat," we said. We recognized the taxi driver—he was the one we met in downtown. Luckily, one older and apparently well-respected shop owner, who had witnessed everything, intervened and asked the taxi driver and his friends to back off.

The cab driver with his Rashti accent yelled, "These *Tehrani* people (people from Tehran) make fun of everybody from other cities, and they think they own the whole country. We need to teach them a lesson." We did not dare say a word.

"They are our guests and we should treat them with respect. After all, you were the one who splashed dirty water on them, so back off," the shop owner said. They left. We thanked the shop owner and left.

We walked back, and as we were approaching my sister's house, we ran into the girl again. She came to us with a couple of guys and said, "You guys are back again? Didn't I tell you not to come back?"

"Listen, my sister's house is in the neighborhood. We are staying at her house tonight and we'll leave tomorrow and will never come back to this town again," I said.

"Who is your sister?" She asked.

"Mrs. Momeni," I said.

"Maasoomeh Khanoom is your sister!" she exclaimed.

"Yes, she is," I said.

"Why didn't you say so? Everybody loves and respects the Momeni family," she said. "I apologize for the inconvenience that I caused you guys."

We were so glad to have come back to my sister's house in one piece. I told the whole story to my sister, and she laughed and said, "This girl thinks that she is actually a boy."

My sister then told us to freshen up and do our *namaz,* prayer, until dinner was ready. We went to our room. Nima whispered in my ear, "I don't know how to pray—I don't know the words. Do we have to do that?"

"My sister is a very strict Muslim and this is a rule in her house; do your prayers before you eat. Just do what I do," I said. Nima copied every move I made. My nephew also was in the same room with us. He pretended to pray, he was funny and made us chuckle occasionally. Then he would laugh loudly. Luckily, my brother-in-law was praying in another room.

Upon my request, my sister had made her well-known northern dish—eggplants stuffed with smashed walnuts mixed with special northern greens, smeared in pomegranate sauce, and topped with tomatoes. In addition, she had made her special seafood dish (fish stuffed with marinated fish eggs, cooked on a grill). Nima couldn't stop eating. He kept saying, "This food is out of this world."

We left the city of Rasht on Friday afternoon. It is worth mentioning that the people of Rasht are mostly very liberal, very intelligent, and highly educated. We had the misfortune of meeting the wrong people in downtown Rasht.

Another weekend, early Thursday morning, the camp leaders took us to the city of Sar-Ein.[72] The town of Sar-Ein is well known for its hot springs. These hot springs are very rich in various minerals and are used by the visitors from across the country for therapeutic purposes. We went inside one of the springs and stayed in the hot boiling water for about an hour. At the end of the one-hour period, I had a hard time breathing. The combination of the heat and especially the crowd made it hard to breathe for Nima and me. We had already arranged with the camp organizers that we would separate from the rest to go visit Nima's uncle in a village near Ardabil. We took a bus to a small town in Ardabil—that was as far as ground vehicles could go. From that town on, we had to walk.

It was around noontime and we were very hungry. We found a little restaurant in that town. It served only three kinds of food: Persian omelets; *abgoosht,*[73] and local bread, butter, cheese, and honey. Nima asked me what I wanted, "Abgoosht,"

---

72 Sar-Ein is a small town located at the foot of Sabalan Mountain and is twenty-eight kilometers north of the well-known city of Ardabil (now Province of Ardabil). Sar-Ein is well-known for its various hot springs and is highly visited by tourists, mostly domestic.

73 Abgoosht is a traditional Persian food, made from lamb meat (leg of lamb preferably), white beans, onions, potatoes, and chickpeas boiled in water with lots of turmeric, salt and pepper, and dried lime.

I said. The waiter in the restaurant didn't speak Farsi much, so Nima had to order for both of us in Turkish.

He took the order and came back a few minutes later and said, "We don't have abgoosht."

We then asked, "How about omelet?"

Then again, after a few minutes he came back and said, "No omelet either." We didn't have any other choice but ordering, bread, butter, cheese, and honey. We were hoping that he wouldn't come back with a "no" answer because we were both extremely hungry and there were no other restaurants around. Luckily, he came back with a plate full. I never thought that I was going to enjoy bread and butter, cheese, and honey for lunch, but everything was local and natural. That food was different and really delicious.

After lunch, we walked to a nearby village. It was somewhat hot, and we were sweating. We found a spring with very clean and cold water. We drank a little bit of water. A few feet from the spring, we noticed a medium size natural water pond. The water in the pond was very clean but cold. Nima suggested swimming for a few minutes. "Not in this cold water," I said.

"Don't worry; once you come in, you are not going to feel the cold," Nima said. He was right. I didn't feel the cold at all. After swimming for a little while, Nima suggested that we go back to the spring and drink some more water because we would have a long walk ahead of us.

"How long are we talking about?" I asked.

"Probably a couple of hours," Nima said.

Nima was not kidding; the walk was long. He was, however, wrong about his duration estimate—it was longer than a couple of hours—three or four hours more likely. We walked in the middle of nowhere—just desert, no other towns, no trees, and no water. We saw snakes, lizards, and other reptiles, but no sign of any human beings. It was sunny and hot—we were both somewhat dehydrated by the time we finally got there. That village looked very backward and not very clean. I did not notice any green grass, nor did we notice any trees. The houses were all made of clay. Luckily, we didn't have to walk any farther; his uncle's house was at the edge of the village.

Nima knocked on the all-wood and dilapidated door. A little boy opened the door. We were directed to the guest room. It was a big room, meticulously clean, with nice carpets on the floor, all handmade by the local villagers, clay but clean walls, decorated with all kinds of antique accessories, small carpets, swords, guns and deer horns. I was absolutely amazed that in such a rundown house, you would find such a clean and gorgeously decorated room.

There was no electricity, but they brought us cold water and cold watermelon. They kept everything cool in the small basement of the house. Nima and his uncle spoke Turkish for a while, and then they shifted the conversation to Farsi so I could understand. Nima's uncle was a serious person, but jokingly asked me if I had ever walked such a long distance before.

"I would have sent a couple of horses, had I known you guys were coming," he said.

All we did for the rest of the afternoon was chat. No ladies and no kids showed up in that room except when Nima's uncle wanted something. Nima's uncle sat on his exclusive mat on the floor, leaning against carpeted back cushions in a corner of the room like a king, ordering tea or fruits or food. We were really tired and hungry when dinner served. I don't remember exactly what we had for dinner, but the same kind of breads, butter, honey and cheese as we had in the restaurant were there. I only remember that we enjoyed the dinner. Shortly after dinner, we went to sleep on very clean sleep wares.

The village was flat and not very pretty, but it was a memorable night for me, even though the wolf howl and snoring by Nima and his uncle were annoying. I was pleased with the hospitality there. We left right after the breakfast. We followed the same path back to the bus station to Sar-Ein and from there to Astara. We stayed in Astara for another week or two and departed back to Tehran to get ready to start a new academic year—my last year in college.

TWENTY-FOUR

In the fall of 1975, I was taking my toughest courses and teaching at two high schools: Bamdad and the well-known girls' high school, Azar. As usual, it was a breeze teaching at my former high school, but at Azar High School, I had to deal with a bunch of naughty girls—rowdy, but mostly beautiful and smart and from a more upscale part of Tehran.

I was looking forward to finishing my bachelor's degree. I tried not to pay much attention to politics but focus mainly on my studies. My immediate goal was to finish my degree, then serve the two-year military duties, and worry about a career thereafter.

The Shah had made an announcement in early September during an interview with the well-known and well-respected Egyptian journalist Mohamed Hassanein Heikal that he was going to pull his army out of Oman. A couple of months later, Sultan Qaboos declared a complete victory against Dhofar insurgents after ten years of fighting. I was relieved that even if they arrested me for political reasons and forced me to discontinue my studies, I would not be drafted to go to the unpopular war in Dhofar.

A big incident in the fall of 1975 was the raid on the OPEC meeting in Vienna, Austria by a team of six people led by Carlos. They killed three people and took more than sixty hostages; among them were the well-known Dr. Jamshid Amoozegar of Iran and Sheik Ahmed Zaki Yamani of Saudi Arabia. First, they demanded a newsflash, which was written in French to be read on the radio and TV every two hours. The newsflash was about "extolling the virtues of Palestinian struggles." Then they demanded a bus, an airplane, and three flight attendants to be at their disposal. They threatened that if their demands were not met by a certain hour, they would kill the hostages one by one. Quickly a rumor surfaced in Iran that Amoozegar was going to be the first one to be killed. The government of Iran was quick to blame the Austrian authorities for not taking precautionary measures against terrorist attacks. The radio and TV in Iran broadcast the event as special breaking news every hour or so. Most people in Iran were worried about the fate of their wealth minister.

Although Dr. Amoozegar was an unpopular government authority in the eyes of the opposition groups in our university, most condemned Carlos for his terrorist act while some called him a hero. It was hard for me to understand the mentality of a handful of my classmates who rooted for Carlos and his men, and wished for the execution of Dr. Amoozegar. It was hard for me to digest why some people took the side of a terrorist group against one of their own fellow citizens. They argued that Amoozegar was a part of tyranny and guilty of bringing corruption and bureaucracy.

"If that is the case, why not prove it and show evidences that he caused corruption? Demand that he be brought to justice inside the country instead of being killed by a terrorist group in a foreign land," I said to one of my classmates. "If the system is under question, let's fight the system, not the individuals. Violence, terror, and killing individuals are not the answers." That was my philosophy back then, and that is my philosophy now. That's how Martin Luther King fought racism in America, that is how Mahatma Gandhi prevailed in India, and that is how Nelson Mandela destroyed apartheid in South Africa.

I was glad that those classmates of mine did not get their wish and Amoozegar and the rest of the hostages were eventually freed. It was hard for me to comprehend why some opposition groups chose violence and guerilla attacks as the only viable methods to fight the tyranny.

Unfortunately, most leftist groups back then promoted guerrilla attacks and violence as the only method to fight dictatorship. On the other hand, Islamic groups, mostly inspired by Khomeini, promoted hate against the system and mainly the Shah. Unfortunately, Khomeini succeeded. Most Iranians fell for Khomeini's hateful remarks and they got what they asked for—a hateful government. People of Iran today, and especially the youth, realize that violence is not the answer. Hence, they have chosen peaceful means to demonstrate against the tyrants of the "Islamic Republic." Their peaceful protests are being responded to violently, but these waves of young freedom fighters are not giving up—they have damaged the credibility of the current regime thus far and they will eventually break the backbone of the darkest dictatorship of the time.

In the mid-seventies, the Shah made several speeches on looking into other sources of energy, especially nuclear energy, in addition to oil. He was actually encouraged by the U.S. government to expand Iran's non-oil energy base.[74] Stanford Research Institute had conducted research on the future energy needs of Iran and concluded that by 1990 Iran would need an electrical capacity of about twenty thousand megawatts. The U.S. government suggested that Iran would need several nuclear reactors to acquire the electrical capacity that the Stanford Research Institute had proposed. The Shah, under the influence of the U.S. government, started making contracts with many Western countries to build nuclear reactors in Iran. He contracted with West Germany to construct two Siemens twelve-hundred-megawatt nuclear reactors in Bushehr.[75] He signed two nuclear cooperation treaties with the British in early fall 1975. In addition, in 1975, MIT signed a contract with the Atomic Energy Organization of Iran (AEOI) to train Iranian nuclear engineering students to become practical nuclear engineers. Iran contracted with the Indian government to do nuclear cooperation. Moreover, the Iranians collaborated with the French to construct the Nuclear Technology Center in Isfahan. This center now operates four small nuclear research reactors, all purchased from China. In addition to China, the current Iranian government has collaborated with the Russian government under president Putin for the most part.

Because of the Shah's ambitions to expand research in the field of atomic energy and to make many nuclear reactors in Iran, most engineering students, including some of my classmates, became interested in being hired by the AEOI. Students were given incentives through government-sponsored scholarships to study nuclear engineering or nuclear physics abroad. Back then, the foreign countries volunteered to cooperate with Iran on building nuclear reactors because they felt that they were dealing with a civilized government and they trusted the Shah.

The subject of nuclear engineering, which was a very hot topic in Iran back in those days, has never been appealing to me, and I never had any desire to work for the government. I never wanted to learn anything about nuclear energy, and the thoughts of what nuclear weapons could do to humankind and the images of Hiroshima were so horrifying to me that I became impassive and apathetic toward the subject.

The semester was ending. It was a very busy semester for me—teaching and trying to finish my courses successfully. I was taking the second design course with Dr. Aslani that semester, and he constantly encouraged me to continue pursuing

---

74   Drs. Etemad and Meshkati, "The U.S.-Iran Nuclear Dispute: Dr. Mohamed El Baradei's Mission Possible to Iran," *Iran News*, July 13, 2003.

75   Bushehr, a major city and one of Iran's chief ports, is located four hundred kilometers south of Tehran in southeastern Iran on the Persian Gulf. It is the main seaport of Iran and the capital of the Bushehr province. The Bushehr Nuclear Power Plant is located twelve kilometers from the city of Bushehr. Russian government helped Iran with this power plant.

higher education, preferably in the United States. Because of my financial situation, going to the United States was not a possibility for me and pursuing higher education was not on top of my priority list. My immediate plan was to get ready to fulfill my military duties.

Hard work paid off. I did well on the final exams as well as my teaching job. My students were mostly praiseworthy of my teaching and the superiors at the two high schools were happy with me. I received gifts from many of my students as well as verbal and written appreciations. However, the best reward I received from my students was when they said, "I learned so much from you." The fact of the matter is that I learned so much from them. I also learned so much from many of my good teachers, and so many of them inspired me. I never forget those who made a difference in my life.

Just after my graduation, my cousin Khosro stopped by our house one day for a visit. He asked me, "What is next for you?"

"I am going to serve in the military and then I will probably teach," I said.

"Teaching at high schools," he exclaimed. "You can do a lot better with your engineering degree than teaching at high schools! You can make a lot more money working as an engineer than as a teacher." Those days, engineers used to make good money. Although the country was going through economical turmoil and unemployment was rising, it was not too difficult for engineers to find good-paying jobs.

My response to Khosro's remark was, "There is a lot more joy in teaching than money can buy."

"Have you thought about continuing your education abroad?" Khosro asked.

"That is not an option for me because I can't afford it," I said.

"Why don't you at least take the English exam?" Back in those days, it was required to pass an English exam of those who were interested in continuing studies abroad before going for military services. Those who finished military services didn't have to take the English exam. The English exam was tough but not as bad as TOEFL test.

I figured that it was not going to cost me much to take the test, and it was not going to hurt even if I failed it. I took the exam a few weeks later. There was not much emphasis on learning English at our university, and I had ceased practicing my English after high school. I didn't have any hopes of passing it, but surprisingly, I did. That shifted the direction of my life. When my father found out that I passed the English test, he suggested that leaving the country might be a better alternative for me than going into the military. His rationale was that if I were to go into the military, I might get myself into trouble with the government.

In that particular year, the infamous Sabeti, the head of the SAVAK, appeared on TV occasionally and announced the arrest and the apprehension of the opposition leaders, as usual some of them confessed to wrongdoing. As mentioned before, SAVAK's intention was to terrorize people and to show that the government did not have any tolerance for opposition. Prior to my taking the English exam, one day during a breaking news flash on TV, Sabeti announced that nine dissidents were executed for being belligerent against the rest of the detainees and for trying to instigate a fight with the security officers. Among them was Bijan Jazani, whom I had heard so much about—about his love for his country, his heroic manners, and his fight for freedom. I had heard that he was a strong and influential person and that he was well respected in the prison and inspired many of the prisoners including some of the prison guards. He was not anything as Sabeti described him to be. That announcement by Sabeti angered me so much that I shouted at the top of my lungs, "You SAVAK-i bastards, you murderers." My parents, my sister Molood, and I were watching TV that day. The rest of the kids were not present. My father yelled at me to calm down and be quiet, or get out of this room. I did not expect the harsh reaction from my father; I immediately went to my room, put on my clothes, and was about to leave the house but I couldn't find my shoes. My sister Molood hid them from me. I left the house dressed up but barefooted. I walked almost half a mile to catch a bus; she was running to catch up with me.

She begged me, "Please, Habib, come back, you might get yourself killed today." I did not pay any attention to her until she started crying. I was a wimp when I saw tears shedding from the eyes of a family member, especially a lady—I still am. I paused; I gave my sister a hug and walked back toward the house with her. At the door, my parents were standing and waiting for me. My father and I apologized to each other.

That incident had made my parents wary, worried, and concerned. My father never wanted to see us leave his sight, but one day he came to me and said, "I seriously want you to plan on leaving the country. I'd rather you leave than be jailed or killed."

"I don't want to be a financial burden on you," I said.

"Not to worry. I have saved up all the money you have given me and I am planning on selling this house and moving to a quieter place, a bigger but less expensive house," he said.

Selling the house was not acceptable to me but my father made me convinced that he was going to do that regardless. We sold our house in Tehran and moved to the town of Fardis.[76] I applied for a passport. It was a lengthy process getting a passport back then in Iran, it still is. I had to wait for it for a few months. The day I went to receive my passport, the officer asked me the purpose of my travel, and I explained, "Study abroad." He advised me to beware of the Iranian Student Confederation in Europe or in the United States. The next step for me was to get admission from an accredited university. Not only did we have to get admission from a university, but from an English learning center as well. Back then, many private agencies and dealers started building connections with foreign universities. They would facilitate the admission process for the young people who were interested in pursuing higher education abroad. It was a lucrative business. I went to a consulting firm owned by a person in a wheelchair known as "Mr. Ironside," named after the character on the popular American TV series of the time, played by Raymond Burr, shown on Iranian TV as well.

Mr. Ironside got me admission at the University of Dallas in the master's of business administration program (MBA program), and an admission at English Language Services (ELS) in the same city—Irving, Texas. There was a rumor that ELS classes were administered and run by the mafia and Mr. Ironside was a mafia member. There was no authenticity to that claim.

Next, I had to get an F-1 visa (student visa) to enter the United States. That was a painful process. We had to stand in line—a big line of people—at the American Embassy in Tehran for hours waiting to be interviewed. People often would sleep overnight in order to be in the front of the line. Most often people wouldn't get their visa on the first attempt. I was lucky; the counselor who interviewed me was a nice person. He approved my visa on the very first attempt. The next step was to purchase a ticket. My father bought the ticket from the company he was working at with a little discount. Unfortunately, due to the loss of my first passport, I do not know the exact date of my departure, but I am sure I entered the United States sometime in late October 1976.

All of these lengthy and painful steps and processes aside, the thoughts of change, leaving my loved ones behind, leaving my beloved land, leaving my friends, and entering a new world, made me extremely depressed. I was having nightmares and anxiety attacks. I was having fevers and night sweats. I was young and inexperienced and did not know how to manage depression. I had lost so much weight and became too skinny.

A few weeks before I left the country, during a weekend, we had company at our house for lunch, a distant relative, his wife, and their two children. One of their kids was a seven or eight-year-old boy. My brothers and I were talking

---

76   Fardis is a suburb of the city of Karaj situated about twenty-four kilometers northeast of Tehran.

in the TV room. This chubby little boy approached us and said, "You guys look like athletes." He pointed at my brother Iraj and said, "You look like you are a wrestler," and it was true—Iraj was a good wrestler, and won several trophies during his high school years. He turned to my brother Nasser and said, "You are tall. You must be a volleyball or a basketball player." He then turned to my youngest brother Ahmad and said, "You look like you are a football (soccer) player." He left.

My brother Iraj called him back and said, "Hey, what about Habib? You didn't mention anything about him."

He looked at me, rolled his eyeballs up and down a few times, and said, "Habib, you must be a good chess player!" Everybody laughed. The fact of the matter was that I wasn't even a good chess player. My brother Nasser used to beat me most of the time.

I was very worried about my grandmother, Jaan Jaan Naneh. That year she had chosen to stay in Taleghan. I wanted to see her so badly. It was in my priority list to visit her and to say good-bye to her. The weather was very cold in Tehran and it had snowed in Taleghan. My parents were adamantly opposed to my going to Taleghan because the roads were icy and dangerous. A few days before my departure, my brother-in-law Mehdi and I secretly made a plan to leave one early morning in his car and come back the same day. Unfortunately, the plan did not work. I was so sad that I could not see my grandmother's angelic, Mother-Teresa-like face one more time. I never saw her again.

COMING TO AMERICA

PART II

ONE

It was late October 1976, I packed my suitcases and we left for the airport. My parents, brothers, sisters, my uncle Sarrullah, my cousin Morteza, and my uncles Isa and Mousa accompanied me to *Foroodgah Mehrabad,* Mehrabad Airport. It was hard for me to say good-bye to my family. My father was extremely emotional, my mother could not stop crying, and my uncles were in tears. My cousin Morteza, who had completed his education in the United States, kept whispering in my ears to be strong. My toughest moment was to face my father. I was hoping that my grandmother Jaan Jaan Naneh would be there. I hugged my uncles Isa and Mousa and begged them to take care of her until I came back. My youngest sister, Afsaneh, eleven years old at the time, was crying hysterically.

My uncle Sarrullah said the prayers into my ear and told me, "Remember, Habib, *nabordeh randge gandge moyassar nemishavad."* This Persian expression means, "The one who does not feel the pain does not gain the treasure," which is equivalent to the American expression "no pain, no gain."

Finally, we boarded the airplane, a Pan Am Airlines, Boeing 747. I could not believe it; I was flying thousands of miles away from my family, friends, and my motherland—the land that I adored. I was extremely emotional and started crying. I did not have any appetite and hardly ate on the plane. A nice middle-aged Persian gentleman was sitting next to me; he gave me a tissue and said, "If you don't like the airplane food, I have some Persian food in my handbag; would you like to have some?"

"No, sir, thanks," I said.

"What is wrong?"

"I cannot imagine being so far away from my loved ones."

"Is this your first time flying out of Iran?"

"Yes, sir, it is." We introduced ourselves. I don't remember what his name was, but he introduced himself as a doctor working in one of the hospitals in Tehran.

"Where are you going?" he asked.

"To Dallas, Texas."

"What are you going to be doing there?"

"I will be studying."

"Studying what?"

"My admission is in MBA. I am hoping to switch to mechanical engineering, but I have to take English first."

"My son is also interested in engineering."

"Where is your son?" I asked.

"Kentucky," he said, if I am not mistaking. "He has been in America for only one year and I have already spent so much money on his education."

"How much money, sir? If you don't mind me asking."

He gave me a figure that was outrageous to me and I couldn't believe it. "Is it really that expensive to live there?" I asked.

"It is expensive to live in America."

"If it is going to be that expensive, I will go back," I said.

After getting me so worked up and so worried, the man changed his tone and sounded more positive and optimistic. "Listen America is known as the Land of Opportunity; just follow your dreams, you can conquer all of your obstacles in life," he said.

We finally landed at JFK Airport. After going through the passport check and customs, I boarded another airplane, Braniff Airway, for departure to my final destination, Dallas, Texas. My English was very rusty and I was surprised how patient and courteous people and the airline crew were to me. "What a smooth ride and what friendly people," I thought to myself.

It was late in the evening when we finally landed at Dallas Fort Worth airport. I felt confused, lost, and didn't know what to do next. A taxi driver approached me and asked me where I was going. I said, "University of Dallas in Irving."

He grabbed a couple of my suitcases and said, "I can take you, let's go."

With my broken English, I told him, "Please put my suitcases down and first tell me how much you are going to charge me." He gave me a figure that was too much for me. As I was going back and forth with the taxi driver, I was approached by a fellow who asked me whether I was from Iran. "Yes, I am," I said.

"*Salam haleh shoma chetoreh?* Hello, how are you?" he asked.

I was so glad to find someone who spoke my language. "I am fine, how are you?" I responded.

He introduced himself as Javad and asked me where I was going. I said, "University of Dallas in Irving."

"Don't be fooled by these taxi drivers, it would cost too much from Fort Worth to Irving," he said. "I am here to pick up a friend who is also coming back from Tehran."

Javad was a nice guy and knew his way around. His friend finally showed up. The very first thing he said was, "I need to contact my family back home?"

"You mean we can actually call oversees via public phone?" I asked.

"Yes, you can either put some coins into the public phone or call collect," Javad replied. "It is expensive, but you can."

Javad's friend managed to call his family collect, and he showed me how to make a collect call. We did not have a telephone at home, so I decided to try my father at his workplace. The telephone operator, whom I knew well, picked up the phone. Her office and the kitchen that my father was in charge of, shared a common sliding window. It was late in the evening in Fort Worth and early morning in Iran. I was not sure whether she was going to accept the collect call or not. She accepted. She was very courteous, and called my father, *"Karim agha*, Mr. Karim, you have an important phone call."

My father picked up the phone. *"Agha Joon* Salam," I said.

"Habib, Pesar? Is that you?"

"Yes, this is me. I just wanted to let you know that I got here safe and sound," I was full of tears when I was talking to him.

His voice was trembling. *"Khoda ra shokr, Khoda ra shokr*, Thank God, Thank God," he said.

"I will write you as soon as I get settled in and try to call you once in a while. *Khoda hafez, Agha Joon*," I said.

"Khoda hafez, Pesar, Good-Bye Son. May God be with you."

We got in the car, and Javad's friend and I had too many bags and suitcases. We could hardly fit them all inside the car. We proceeded to leave the airport. I could not hide my emotions and could hardly talk. Javad noticed the sadness on my face and said, "Life in America is so fast; you cannot be too dependent emotionally. We won't succeed if we let our emotions get in the way of our goals. I thought Javad was very mature for a young man in his probably mid 20s. I regretted that I did not ask for his contact information.

Javad and his friend dropped me off at the lobby of the University Center at the University of Dallas. It was very late in the evening and school was closed.

Javad suggested that I sleep on a couch in the University Center until morning, he then left. I was dead tired, hungry, and didn't know what to do. I opened one of the bags and got something to munch on. I fell asleep on one of the couches there. It was very early in the morning when I was woken up by a security officer; I didn't understand a word he said. I only understood that he didn't want me to sleep there. It was after midnight, and I was half sleep. I asked him, "Where do you want me to go, sir?"

"Just follow me," he said.

I guess he felt sorry for me and directed me to a vacant room with a couch. I thanked him, and I slept there soundly for a while. I had a dream that my mother, my brother Iraj, my sister Afsaneh and I were stranded on a deserted island. A helicopter came to our rescue, but unfortunately, the helicopter could carry only one person. As I was being lifted by the helicopter and moving away, my mother was crying and begging me not to leave them there. I felt so bad that I betrayed my family; I suddenly woke up and found myself on the floor. I had no idea where I was; I thought I was still in Iran. It was cold in that room and I was shivering. I got up and started looking for the heater to turn on when all of a sudden I realized how far away I was from home and that I was in a different world.

I was too tired and the room was too cold. I opened one of the suitcases, grabbed my winter coat to get warm, and decided to go back to sleep. It was probably around 8:00 or 8:30 in the morning when I woke up. I didn't know how to catch a cab to take me to a nearby hotel. I didn't know how the transit system worked in that town, and I didn't know who to turn to. "What am I going to do now? Where am I going to go? How am I going to carry these heavy suitcases?" I felt useless, helpless, homeless, and hopeless. I wanted to kick myself in the behind for putting myself in that situation. Then I thought, "Yes, I do deserve a kick in my behind for being so pessimistic and thinking so negatively." My father was always encouraging us to be optimistic and have a positive outlook on life.

"Get up and do something," I told myself.

I went back to the lobby of the student center and saw a few people there. Some were watching TV, some were reading books, and some were relaxing. I also noticed some machines leaning against the wall, people were putting coins, and getting drinks and snacks. I was hungry and became curious as to how those machines worked. I had never seen such machines back home. I approached one of the guys there and, with my rusty English, asked him how those machines worked. He gently explained that I needed to put coins in order to get food out. I didn't have coins.

The guy was very friendly, so I decided to sit down with him and ask him for some guidance. I tried to explain my situation to him, but I don't think he understood me. I pulled my papers out and showed him my immigration papers and all the letters that I received from the university. He took me to the resident advisor of one of the dormitories at University of Dallas. The advisor took me to my room. I was so relieved to have found a place to put my suitcases. I was very hungry, so I opened one of the suitcases to find some food. All I found was pistachios. I decided to take a bag of the pistachios to give it to the guy at the vending machines as a token of appreciation for helping me. I was told that pistachios were very rare in the United States back in those days.

I went back to the lobby of the University Center, but I could not find the guy. I looked around and noticed that he was in the game room playing billiards with another person. I went to him and said, "Hello, I brought you some pistachios, and I hope you like them."

"Oh, I love pistachios, thank you," he said. "Do you want to play pool?"

I had no idea by playing pool he meant playing billiards. I replied, "You mean billiards," I said.

"Yes, I mean billiards. Do you want to play?"

"No, I am not good at this game. I am too hungry to play a game anyway."

"Did you find any coins to get some snacks?"

"No, I only have travelers' checks; I'll go to my room and find something."

I said good-bye to him, and as I was leaving the lobby to go to my room, I heard him calling me, "Hey, come back here, I've got an idea; follow me."

He took me to the dining room, got me some food, and asked me to sit down and eat. I was surprised of his kind gesture.

"Listen, I will pay you for this," I said.

"Don't mention it."

All along, I had been told that Americans were not as hospitable as Iranians were, and were not as friendly. "Here is a guy who hardly knows me; not only did he help me find my room, he fed me too." I muttered to myself. Out of my ordeal with this person, the good news was that he changed my image about American people and left me with a good impression, but the bad news was that I could never find him to thank him after that day.

I remember the day I went to one of the banks in Irving to deposit my money, I was greeted by the branch manager and was so pleased with the way I was treated there. The branch manager expressed his pleasure to do business with many Iranians and praised the Shah as a strong leader and Iran as a great country. He also praised the American government for having established good economic and political ties with the Iranians. That was the perception of many Americans about Iran and Iranians back in those days.

T W O

A couple of days later, I went for a walk around the campus. I found the campus to be very pretty and peaceful. As I was walking and thinking, I noticed a couple of guys sitting down on the grass and speaking in Farsi. I approached them and said hello and introduced myself. One of them introduced himself as Reza. I talked to Reza for a long time and we became very good friends.

A few days later, Reza introduced me to another person, also named Reza. I used to call him Reza T to distinguish him from the first Reza. He had come to the United States a few days before I did. He was stocky and well built. He was a big fan of sports and especially soccer and freestyle wrestling, as I was. He was an athletic person himself. When we were first introduced, he told me, "You look familiar, and I am pretty sure that I have seen you before."

He lived in the east of Tehran and I lived in the west. We did not attend the same high school, nor did we attend the same university. He held a bachelor's degree in physical education and his goal was to finish a master's degree in PE and work in the athletic department at my previous university.

Reza T was married with a child at that time. It turned out that Reza T's in-laws lived very close to my parents' house, and I knew his brother-in-law very well. In fact, Reza T's wife and my sister were good friends. His brother-in-law was also quite an athlete and was known as a "macho" in our neighborhood.

The next day, we went to the English Center, ELS. Reza had already registered in English classes. Reza T and I had to take the English placement exam to determine our levels. We took the test; I was placed in Level 3, and Reza T, whose English was better than mine, was placed in Level 8. Each level was one month long and very expensive. I was hoping to have been placed at a higher level than Level 3, because we were warned by the authorities at ELS that we had to finish all twelve levels of English classes before moving on to the community colleges or universities. Reza T noticed that I was a little upset; he came up to me and tried to make me feel better by telling me that he had taken a lot more English classes back home than I did.

Reza T, having coached soccer and wrestling teams, was full of pep talks. What I liked about him was that he was a very positive person. Reza T and I got along fine. In fact, all three of us got along great. Both Reza and Reza T were both very honest and had great sense of humor. We were more or less of the same age, we had common interests, and we clicked pretty well together.

One day Reza approached both Reza T and me and suggested that we find an apartment and stay together. Later on, he introduced a much younger person by the name of Saman and asked if it was okay to have Saman live with us, too. We didn't mind, so we started looking for a reasonable, two-bedroom apartment. We couldn't find one, but found a one-bedroom apartment instead. If my memory serves me correctly, the apartment complex was called Carl Road Apartments, located on Carl Road near the University of Dallas.

All four of us were crammed into a small semi-furnished apartment with a small kitchen, a small living room, and a small bedroom with a twin-size bed. We decided that Saman, being the youngest, should sleep on the bed, Reza T on the couch, and Reza and I on the floor. It was not very pleasant to sleep on the floor. The weather was very cold, and we really had a hard time warming the room. The expenses, however, were low as we shared the rent, utilities, and the food.

None of us was a good cook and we hardly ate out. Reza and I cooked most of the time. Most often, we ate Persian omelets with bread—they were cheap and easy to make. Occasionally we would buy a whole chicken, stuff it with an onion, some potatoes, celery, and tomatoes, add salt, pepper, and turmeric and put it in the oven until cooked. Reza T and Saman were in charge of washing the dishes but they hardly ever did that, so Reza and I would end up doing the dishes as well.

Life was a routine; it was not a whole lot of fun, especially waiting in line to go to the bathroom in the morning. However, we had a good time during the weekends when we would go for a walk, or do laundry, or buy groceries. Also, I used to write letters to different schools inquiring about their admission requirements. I sent letters to numerous engineering schools all over the country.

None of us had a driver's license yet. I couldn't drive anyway. Reza T had a very rich friend who was an engineering student at the Southern Methodist University. He used to hang out with him very often and hardly ever did any of his English homework. I was doing most of his homework on top of my own, especially the writing part. Saman was hardly ever at home; he came home to eat and to sleep. Reza was much more serious about learning. Reza T's friend took us for a ride and a quick tour of the city of Dallas and the SMU campus a few times. He suggested that SMU had a good reputation in engineering and a strong graduate program, and that I should apply there. I asked him about the tuition, I think he said around $130 per credit hour. That was a lot of money back then, and there was no way I could afford that.

Reza and Saman didn't get along very well. They constantly argued. The tension between them climaxed when Saman came home drunk one late evening. He could hardly stand on his feet. He went straight to bed. He woke us up couple of times feeling sick and miserable from drinking too much. The next day Reza asked Saman to leave and he did. Things got better after Saman left. We shared the responsibilities equally and had a lot of fun together. I only wished that Reza T wouldn't dump his English homework on me.

Some other Iranians who lived in the same apartment complex would join us sometimes, especially Friday evenings. We would eat together, crack jokes, talk about serious matters, sing songs together, watch TV, impersonate Persian actors and TV personalities, and drink. The very first beer I drank was Coors! I enjoyed Coors beer and it became my favorite. I was comfortable hanging out with those guys. We were a responsible bunch and always made sure not to disturb our neighbors.

I found another good friend in my English class in the fourth level. His name was Payam. He was funny and very friendly. He came to the United States to pursue a master's degree in computer science. Payam was infatuated with a very pretty girl from Chile in our English class. He was always full of jokes, and each morning just before the start of the class, he would either crack a joke or say something funny about the Chilean girl.

Payam and his roommate, Bahram, lived in a fancy two-bedroom apartment at the Lexington Apartments. They attended the same university back home, the same department, graduated in the same year, and came to the United States together. They each spoke Farsi with a distinctive and funny accent; they were from two different parts of Iran. Reza and I used to get a kick out of them talking to each other, especially when they were arguing.

Reza T, Reza, and I stayed in that tiny apartment for almost two months. We really enjoyed each other's company, but we couldn't stay there any longer. The English classes were too expensive, and we had to search for suitable colleges or universities before the start of spring semester. We all came to the United States on student visas and had to be full-time students or else we would be in trouble with immigration. Reza T was already admitted into the graduate program in PE at the University of New Mexico. Reza got an admission to a community college somewhere in Texas. They both left for their destinations. I moved to Payam's apartment temporarily. Payam, Bahram, and I were in the same boat; we all had admissions in MBA at the University of Dallas. Attending the University of Dallas was our last resort because first, the tuition was high, and, secondly, none of us was interested in an MBA degree.

It was after the Thanksgiving break and time was running out; we had to get a graduate admission somewhere in the United States.

One evening, Bahram introduced us to another student by the name of Abdi. He lived in the same apartment complex. Abdi held a bachelor's degree in agricultural engineering. He came to the United States to pursue a master's degree. He told us that he was already admitted at a university in southern Texas called Texas A&I University (now a branch of Texas A&M), located in Kingsville, Texas. He proceeded to say that the Agricultural Department at Texas A&I was seeking more graduate students and its requirements were much more relaxed. Moreover, the tuition at that school and the cost of living in Kingsville were reasonable, more so than any other places. Payam, Bahram, and I decided to take a trip to Kingsville early next morning. At this time, Bahram's girlfriend showed up to take him to dinner. "Here we go again. He is going to come back late, drunk, and to wake me up as usual. This guy spends all of his father's money on women," Payam said.

He then told Bahram, "Make sure to come back early so we can go to bed early and get up early."

"Oh, yes," Bahram said.

"I have heard that before," Payam said.

At this point, Abdi got up and left for his apartment, Bahram left with his girlfriend, and Payam and I stayed in our apartment. We fixed dinner and chatted a little bit. Payam went to his bedroom, and, as I was getting ready to sleep on the living room couch, the telephone rang. I answered the phone; it was Bahram. "You guys go without me," he said.

We got up early, had some breakfast in a hurry, got our passports and copies of our transcripts, and left for Kingsville in Payam's car. Although the trip was long and tiresome, we really had a good time. We listened to music on our way, stopped for gas, and paused to stretch. We stopped to have lunch at McDonald's. We had a McDonald in Iran during the Shah but I never had a chance to eat there. That was my very first time at McDonald's. "What is good here?" I asked Payam.

"Everything is good in here," he said.

I looked at the menu and all the foods sounded Greek to me. Payam ordered a Big Mac with a Coke and French fries. I ordered the same; it was delicious. I became hooked on Big Mac for a long time.

By the time we arrived in Kingsville, it was mid-afternoon. At first, I went to the graduate program coordinator of the Mechanical Engineering Department and asked for admissions information. He asked for TOEFL and GRE scores. I did not have either one. I asked for conditional admission, he adamantly refused. Then I went to the graduate program coordinator of the Agricultural Engineering department, and Abdi was right; that department had much easier standards. Neither TOEFL nor GRE was required. I was admitted into their graduate program. The only condition that the program imposed on me was to take a few undergraduate courses, but not too many. I immediately went to the registrar's office, filled out all the proper forms, paid the registration fees, and completed the registration procedures. Payam got a conditional admission into the Computer Science Department. We were both happy that our trip was fruitful and productive. We decided to head back to Dallas. We stopped a couple of times for dinner and gas. It was late in the evening and we still had quite a long way before getting to Dallas. We were both tired. I noticed that Payam was dozing off! I suggested that we pull over and rest a little bit, but Payam insisted that he was okay. I started singing loudly. That got Payam's attention, "You didn't tell me you could sing."

It was late, after midnight, when we got home. Luckily, Bahram was not home for Payam to start an argument. I slept like a log that night. We decided to stay in Dallas for the Christmas break and leave for Kingsville a few days before our classes.

THREE

One day, right after the Christmas break and just before New Year's Eve, I got a surprise telephone call from a guy named Ehsan. He was a good friend and the former classmate of one of my relatives in Iran. He was residing in Houston, Texas. We knew of each other but had never met before. After introducing himself, he asked me if I had any plans for the holidays. I said no, and he responded, "How would you like to come here and spend a few days with us?"

"That would be a great idea, but I don't have transportation, and I don't know where in Houston you live," I responded.

"Don't worry about it; I will come to pick you up tomorrow," he said.

He showed up the next day. I packed some clothes and my shower bag and we drove toward Houston. We got there within a few hours. Ehsan was from a rich family in Iran. I expected to enter to a big and luxurious apartment; it was big all right, but far from luxurious. It was a three-bedroom apartment with a big living room. There was no furniture in the living room other than a couch leaning against a wall. Ehsan took me to one of the bedrooms and showed me the closet to put my stuff in. I thought that was going to be my bedroom. We fixed something quick for dinner. I took a shower, and as I was getting ready to go to bed, Ehsan gave me a sleeping bag and directed me to the living room to sleep somewhere there. I was just about to get comfortable in my sleeping bag when somebody rang the doorbell; it was one of Ehsan's friends. He went right to the couch and slept on it. Then again, I heard someone trying to unlock the door; it was one of Ehsan's roommates. Then the third roommate showed up. Finally, after sometime, I fell asleep. I woke up early in the morning, and noticed a guy sleeping to my left, another to my right, another near the kitchen, a seemingly pretty girl by the couch, and so on. There were so many people sleeping in the living room, one could not walk without stepping on someone. Those people were not living there but they were visitors like me who used to go there very often.

I couldn't go back to sleep, and there was no room to sit. I couldn't go outside because I was wearing my pajamas, and the bedroom where I left my clothes was closed. I noticed a paper lying on the kitchen counter. I slowly crawled my way in between people to reach the paper. The paper was full of anti-Shah and anti-American slogans naming the Shah as a puppet of America and America as an imperialistic country, and so on.

I wondered what was going on. "Have I entered a branch of the Iranian student confederation that I was warned about? Have I been trapped by the radical Iranian Communists that I was told to keep away from?" I was questioning and thinking to myself. It was obvious that those people were not part of a radical Muslim group.

I was getting bored and a little worried. I decided to find a way to get out of the apartment and go for a walk. I slowly walked to the bedroom and quietly opened the bedroom door, went to the closet, and grabbed my shirt and pants. On my way out of the bedroom, Ehsan asked me where I was going. "Oh, I am sorry to wake you; I am going for a walk," I said.

"No problem," he said. I was so relieved that I finally got out of that apartment. I walked for about an hour or so just to kill time. By the time I came back, everybody was awake. Ehsan introduced me to everyone. The person who caught my eyes the most was a beautiful girl; the one who slept near the couch. She introduced herself and very warmly said, "Welcome to America." That evening Ehsan drove me to the campus of the University of Houston. I asked Ehsan about the girl, "What a surprise to see a beautiful girl among all those guys!"

"We don't look at her as a sex object; she is one of the comrades," Ehsan said. "I want
you to hang around until the start of the meeting."

I thought Ehsan was taking me on a tour of the campus. I became curious, "What did he mean by comrades, what meeting is he talking about?" I muttered. So I asked, "What meeting?"

"There is a meeting of the Iranian student organization here which will begin shortly, and I have to get everything ready for the meeting," he said.

"Is there anything I can do to help?"

"Yes, you can help me get some pamphlets and books out of my car and carry them here."

We went to the car; he opened the trunk of his car, and there were a couple of boxes full of pamphlets, newspapers, and books. I carried one and he carried the other. At this point, a couple of other people who were carrying a number of books joined us. We set the papers and the books on the tables outside the auditorium where the meeting was supposed to take place. One by one, people were coming and they all gathered inside the auditorium. The meeting started with the national anthem, the Pledge of Allegiance, and some slogans. There were different speakers. After each speech, people in the audience would gather in groups and discuss their points of view, and some would challenge the speakers for a one-on-one debate. From the pamphlets, newsletters, books, and the speeches, one could easily conclude that those people or students were not favoring Islamic ideology, but Communism. They were loyalists and supporters of different Communist parties or Communist organizations.

In those days, there were many active Iranian opposition groups in the United States and Europe under the auspices of the World Confederation of Iranian Students and Scholars. They were the members of many different groups: the Toufan Marxist-Leninist organization, the Toudeh Party, the Revolutionary Maoist group, the Supporters of the National Front, the Partisans of the Fedaein Guerillas of the People of Iran, the Mujahedin-e-Khalgh organization, and an active Muslim group led by Ibrahim Yazdi, a professor at the Baylor University in Texas at the time. Ibrahim Yazdi and his followers were supporters of Khomeini. Each of these groups claimed that they could lead a revolution in Iran to topple the Shah and his tyrannical regime. I was not sure which one of these groups Ehsan and his friends belonged to.

I could predict that something big was about to happen in Iran but never thought any of these groups were capable of starting a movement inside Iran. Not even in my wildest dreams did I imagine that the fanatics would take over.

After the meeting, we went back to Ehsan's apartment, where the discussion continued. One of the guys turned to me and asked, "What did you think about the meeting?"

"I am just learning, and I don't have any comment," I said.

Another person asked, "Having been a university student in Iran, what do you think of the situation back home?"

"The situation in Iran is unstable, and if we think rationally, we might be able to achieve democracy," I said.

"What do you think we, the Iranian students abroad can do to help?" one fellow asked.

"The best thing you guys can do is to finish your education and not be a financial burden on your parents," I said. "In the meantime, we could get together once in a while and keep current on the sociopolitical situations in Iran."

Another fellow argued, "It is selfish to think of your personal gain while our compatriots in Iran are fighting for you and me. At this point in time, what we need is a free Iran and freedom for everyone."

I argued back, "It is true that we need freedom in Iran—freedom of speech, freedom of the press, freedom to have a choice in ideology and religion—but what is freedom? Is it Communism? Is it Islam? Is it Christianity or Zoroastrianism or Judaism? In my opinion, it is none of those. Freedom is being in charge of your personal sovereignty, respecting the individual sovereignty of others, and being in control of your own destiny in the framework of morality. How dare the members of the Iranian Student Confederation in America call themselves freedom fighters while they are supporting Communism? How dare the members of the Iranian Muslim Association here call themselves freedom fighters while they are advocating the establishment of an Islamic or a communist government?" I said.

I thought everybody at the apartment was favoring Communism. However, another visitor in the apartment asked, "What is wrong with having an Islamic government?"

"I am a Muslim myself and have absolutely nothing against Islam. How can you guarantee the safety and individual sovereignty of those citizens who are not Muslims? What we are lacking in Iran is democracy. I strongly believe that a religious type government is incapable of bringing democracy and freedom for everyone."

I recall that I was being bombarded with too many questions that day until one of Ehsan's roommates by the name of Ebi interjected. Ebi was well-respected by everyone. He was well educated and I found him to be very wise. "I agree with Habib that what we need today is democracy, and that's what we hope to achieve. That is what's lacking in Iran. Once a democratic state is established in Iran, then we will worry about what type of the government is appropriate for Iran," Ebi said. He then shifted the atmosphere of the room by playing a soft traditional Persian music.

The next day, I asked Ehsan for a ride to go to the Social Security office. He said that he had a prior arrangement to go to a place near his apartment, so he offered to let me use his car. I told him that I couldn't drive. I was going to call for a cab, but Ebi told me that it was going to be very expensive. Ebi was also too busy to take me but he had a better idea; he called his sister and asked her to give me a ride. His sister, Mastaneh, showed up a few minutes later. She was a very attractive girl.

"I am so sorry for troubling you," I said.

"No trouble at all."

I was speechless for a few minutes and didn't know what to say. She started the conversation by asking, "How long have you been here?"

"A little over two months," I said. "What about you?"

"We have been here for a while," she said.

"It seems to me that most Iranian students here in America belong to the Confederation; isn't it true?" I asked.

"Almost 80 to 85 percent," she said.

If I recall correctly, I was told that there were about twenty thousand Iranian students who came to the United States within a period of four to five years, and a vast majority of them had joined the Iranian Student Confederation in the United States.

Mastaneh continued asking, "What do you think of the Shah?"

"I am not sure if the Shah is aware of everything that is going on in Iran, especially the brutality of the SAVAK on students in Iran. However, I don't think the Shah can resist all the opposition groups that he is facing internally and externally," I responded.

"What do you mean?" she asked.

"I think his government is going to collapse; it's just a matter of time," I said.

"I only hope that fanatic mullahs do not take over because they do not have any respect for women." she said.

"I don't think the mullahs will have a chance," I said.

It was not too difficult to speculate that the Shah's government would fall, but not very many people could predict that the fanatics would eventually take over. I was wrong! The mullahs led by Khomeini fooled millions of Iranians including me.

I recall that Mastaneh and I had a nice exchange of words and talked about other things as well. However, politics always dominated the conversations back in those days, and we couldn't escape from it. Just like her brother Ebi, I found Mastaneh to be very intelligent and easy to talk to. I only wished that the Social Security office was farther so I could carry on more conversations with her. I wanted to get to know her better. At the Social Security office, she patiently waited for me, and every time I had a problem with my English, she would gently come forward to help me. I started liking her too much, and just before we got back to the apartment, I asked her for a phone number, and she said, "You can get my contact information from my brother."

Usually when a Persian girl tells a guy to get her contact information from her brother, or from her father for that matter, it means that the likelihood of her being interested in him is slim to none. "Oh, well, that's the end of this love story," I muttered to myself.

I stayed at Ehsan's house for more than a week until it was time for me to head back to Dallas to get ready to go to Kingsville. It was a learning experience for me to meet Ehsan and his friends with different viewpoints. Overall I enjoyed my stay in Houston. However, I lost my passport there that got me very worried. I had heard stories about people stilling passports and misusing them. I had to go to the Iranian Consulate in Houston immediately and make a report and apply for a new passport. The next day Ehsan offered to take me back, but I insisted on catching a bus. My first ride on a bus in the United States was on Intercontinental. Travelling by bus was not as bad as I thought, the bus was comfortable and I enjoyed the sightseeing. What I didn't like about the bus ride was too many stops and layovers.

FOUR

After coming back from Houston, I started packing my belongings to get ready to go to Kingsville. Payam started a job in Dallas selling ice cream during the Christmas holidays and was not ready to pack. He told me that he might be missing the first few days of classes. Bahram, as usual, was chasing the women in town. Abdi had already packed and was ready to hit the road. He offered to give me a ride.

It was early January 1977. Abdi and I left for Kingsville. Shortly after we arrived there, we looked for a decent two-bedroom apartment close to the campus, and we found one. As soon as we settled in our apartment, classes began. I took three courses there: two math courses and a course in agricultural engineering. The same professor, Dr. David Cecil was teaching both of my math courses, statistics and advanced engineering math. He was a great teacher and a good person. He was organized, clear, and meticulous. His teaching style was unique.

My English was still very rusty and I had hard times understanding my teachers sometimes, especially in the agricultural engineering course. I was too shy to ask questions, especially in class but Dr. Cecil made me feel at ease to go to his office to ask him questions. I recall that I had to miss one of my exams in the statistics course because I had to go back to Houston to obtain my new passport in place of the one I had lost. I went to Dr. Cecil's office and asked for permission to take the exam after I came back. He said, "Yes, and I am going to give you the same test. I trust that you will not talk to anybody about the test."

"But my roommate, Abdi, is taking the same course," I told Dr. Cecil.

"I am not worried about that," he said.

I was supposed to take the exam a day after coming back from Houston. I did not have much time to study for that test, and I was worried about it. Abdi told me that Dr. Cecil had already handed back the test along with the solution. He offered to let me see the test. I adamantly refused. "Dr. Cecil trusted me enough to tell me that he was going to give me the same test, and I will not breach that trust," I said. I took the test and, incidentally, I did poorly on it, but I aced the rest of my exams.

It was surprising to me that a teacher would give me a makeup exam the same as the one he gave to the rest of my classmates a few days before. It was more surprising that, in spite of the fact that he had already passed back the tests with the solution, he had enough faith in me to give me the same test. As far as I remember, Dr. Cecil never talked to us about life; he just taught us mathematics. However, his actions, his amiable personality, his gentle mannerism, and his caring attitude taught me much beyond mathematics. I considered him as one of my best teachers and a role model.

During the weekdays, my roommate, Abdi, and I would go grocery shopping, go to the library, and do homework together. Every time we went to the library, my fellow classmates surrounded me and asked for help on the homework problems. I enjoyed doing that. I took so much joy in helping people. That really made me very popular among the Iranian and American students. Associating with many of my American classmates and studying with them made me practice my English. During the weekends in Kingsville, most often, Payam and I used to hang out together; we cooked out, watched TV, listened to music, and talked about our fondest memories of Iran.

One day while studying in the library, a couple of Iranians approached me, one of them asked, "Are you Habib?"

"Yes, I am. How do you know my name?"

They introduced themselves and said, "We have heard good things about you, and we would like to invite you to dinner tonight at our house."

"What is the occasion?" I asked.

"No particular occasion; we want to get to know you better and we want you to meet our friends," they said.

"I don't know where you guys live."

They gave me an address and left. That evening I went to their house. It was a big house, but old, and a number of students were living there. The walls were covered with pictures of revolutionary Iranian freedom fighters and anti-Shah slogans. I met a number of people there and had a good meal. After dinner, one of the gentlemen got up and asked everyone to rise for the "national anthem," their own version, and they sang some revolutionary songs. Then the leader of the group got up and, after greeting us and some other new comers, he started a speech:

"We are in the midst of a big crisis in our beloved country; our fellow citizens and our loved ones are living in misery, in fear, and in poverty for the most part. Our brothers and sisters are being arrested, tortured, and killed by the SAVAK every day for political reasons. Yet we are here in America, the most imperialistic and capitalistic country in the world, driving our BMWs, enjoying our freedom, and forgetting about where we came from. My comrades, how long are we going to suffer from the brutality of the SAVAK? How long are we going to allow a dictator to be in control of our destiny? How long are we going to live under siege by the fascist regime of the Shah? The Shah is the puppet of the United States, a friend of the bourgeoisie, and the enemy of the proletarians."

The speaker was energetic, competent, and animated. However, he sparked my curiosity by using the words "comrades," "bourgeoisie," "proletarians." Not to mention the words he quoted from Marx, Engels, Lenin, Stalin, and some other Communist leaders. I was baffled as to why these people, on one hand, were talking about freedom, and, on the other hand, were quoting from Stalin, and supporting Communism. I read between the lines that he was condemning the idea of coming to the United States to pursue advanced degrees, but promoting advancement of political awareness and hatred towards the Shah's regime. He occasionally stated, "Our primary mission should be to fight the Shah's government. Careers and everything else are secondary." I also realized that he was asking for donations to expand the organization to which he belonged.

On the way back, I was wondering what was going on. I was wondering whether those guys were for real or a bunch of hot air with no substance. Those guys wouldn't leave me alone. They called me back and invited me to their weekend meetings many times. In addition to this Communist group, there was a smaller pro-Islamist organization there and I was approached by those guys as well. However, neither of those groups impressed me, and neither could have any influence on me. In spite of my opposition to the Shah's government, I thought those people were not in touch with reality, and I could not trust any of those groups to be a more viable and trustworthy alternative to the Shah's government. I had already made up my mind that I would never join those groups and never donate a penny of my money to their organizations.

One of my fondest memories in Kingsville was meeting two brothers in the library. I had seen them in the library quite often. They were both hard working and very serious about their studies. They first approached me with some questions in math or physics and then invited me to their house for dinner. They were from a religious town near Isfahan, called Shahreza. They were religious, and my first impression was that they were probably members of the Islamist group in Kingsville.

"I would love to come to your house for dinner, but please do not ask me to join your group or anything of that nature," I said.

"No, we don't belong to any of these phony organizations," one of the brothers said.

They were very honest and decent human beings. I was very comfortable with them. We studied together, went on picnics together, and went to movies together (only the ones without sex or violence). I found those two brothers to be very gentle and peaceful. They were practicing Muslims. However, they never tried to force their ideologies on me.

I invited them to my house a few times; Abdi didn't want to have anything to do with them because he thought that they were fanatics and not worth associating with. On the contrary, they were not at all fanatical, and they strongly believed in democracy and the separation of church and state. In addition, they adamantly condemned violence. They believed in Islam as a faith, not a means for political gains.

Those two brothers taught me how to drive, they let me use their car any time I felt like, and they were very kind to me. They were nice to everybody. I had observed them helping their friends and neighbors. Their way of living, their line of thinking, and their views of Islam were very much like my father's.

Unfortunately, back in those days, not very many Muslim opposition groups shared the views of those two brothers. However, many individuals in Iran today live and think as they do. In fact, a vast majority of the Iranians are peace loving, humanitarian, hospitable, family oriented, and respectful of different religions and ethnicities. At present, the people of Iran have distanced themselves from the current regime ever since they began to know the violent and radical nature of the "Islamic Republic." It wasn't too long after the establishment of the "Islamic Republic" that the people of Iran found out how undemocratic and brutal this regime was. Not only has the current regime in Iran been isolated internationally, it has been isolated internally as well.

FIVE

The semester was coming to an end, and in spite of my poor English, I managed to do well in all of my exams. I went back to the chair of the Mechanical Engineering Department and tried to renegotiate with him to temporarily waive the TOEFL and GRE requirements and admit me conditionally. I promised him to take the TOEFL and GRE exams within one year. He was firm on his decision. Although I liked Kingsville, I liked my friends there, and I had every intention to get settled down as soon as possible, I didn't have a chance to pursue a graduate degree in the Mechanical Engineering Department and I couldn't afford wasting time. I had to move on and continue the pursuit of my dreams.

It was early summer of 1977; my good friend Payam had decided to go back home. I felt so sad saying good-bye to him. Abdi and the two brothers were happy staying in Kingsville. My other best friends, Reza and Reza T, were living far from me—one in a community college in Texas and the other one in New Mexico. They each continually asked me to pay them a visit. I wanted to, but I was running out of money. I had sent my transcripts to many graduate schools while being a student at Texas A&I, hoping to get an admission for the fall, but received no positive response from any of those universities. I had to do something; I had no admission for the fall, I had very little money left in the bank, I was not allowed to work, and time was running out. I received a call from an old friend by the name of Mustafa, who had recently travelled to the United States. He was taking some courses at a community college in a very small town in Texas. He sounded depressed and homesick over the phone. He asked me to go visit with him. "I'd love to, but I don't have enough money," I told him. He offered to help.

I paid him a visit and stayed at his place for a few days. He was thinking of going back and I tried to talk him out of it. On the last day of my visit he said to me, "Listen, Habib, I know you are struggling for money, and money is not a big

161

issue for me. I am more than willing to lend you some," he insisted. He then wrote me a check for $470. I thanked him and told him that I would pay him back. Shortly after I returned to Kingsville, Mustafa called me one day and said, "I have decided to go back home. Do not worry about paying the money back to me now. I am sure you will pay me back one day." That money helped me tremendously. It was good money back then. To this day, I can't thank him enough. He never called me to bug me about the money after he left. However, years later during one of my trips back home, I found his number through my cousin Khosro, and expressed my appreciation to him in person and returned his money. He did not ask for a penny more than $470.

After going back to Kingsville and cashing the check, I decided to make some trips to different universities and talk to the graduate admission coordinators in person. I gave a notice to Abdi that I would be leaving in about a week. I packed and left. It was particularly hard to say good-bye to the brothers, as they had been extremely nice to me.

My first choice was to stay in Texas; it was convenient and more economical for me to stay there. Unfortunately, I had received rejection letters from all the universities in Texas.

I could fit all of my belongings into a medium-size suitcase and a handbag. I decided to travel by bus from one town to another. The first university I visited was Mississippi State University in Starkville. As far as I can recall, there was no bus station in Starkville—the nearest one was located in another town. I didn't know how to get there. I was wandering around the bus station for a while feeling helpless. I asked a gentleman for the address to the university. He was waiting for his girlfriend to pick him up. He offered to take me to the campus. They were nice enough to drop me off by the university center.

It was around sunset; I went to the lobby of the University Center, and there were not very many people there. I sat on a chair to catch my breath and to rest for a while. I had my suitcase next to me, and the handbag on my shoulder. I got some snacks out of my handbag, and as I was eating, I noticed a bunch of Farsi-speaking guys entering the lobby. One of them kept staring at me. I stared back at him. He looked familiar. He came closer to me, "Mr. Eslami! Is it you?" I noticed that he was one of my former students at Bamdad High School in Iran.

"Oh, what a small world! I could have never imagined running into one of my students in the United States of America," I said.

It turned out that he was a student at a community college in a neighboring state and was visiting a friend at MSU. Those guys offered to let me stay at their house, which I refused, but we had dinner together. After dinner, they took me to a motel near the campus.

The next morning, I went to the chair of the Mechanical Engineering Department and asked him for the admissions requirements at his department. I believe they required TOEFL and GRE prior to admission. Unfortunately, things didn't work out between us. I was tired and disappointed. I went back to the University Center. I noticed a very pretty blonde girl in a cheerleading outfit sitting next to a good-looking, well-dressed Persian guy conversing together in Farsi. I went closer and said *salaam* to both. I introduced myself and they invited me to sit with them. The girl was speaking Farsi almost perfectly with virtually no accent. I asked her whether she was Persian. She said, "No, but I lived in Iran for a few years." I believe she said that her father was a petrochemical engineer or something like that in Iran.

They asked me what I was doing there. I briefed them on my story. Then I asked them if I could catch a city bus to go to the Greyhound bus station. They offered to give me a ride to the town where the bus station was located. They took me to my motel; I checked out and left for the bus station. In spite of my disappointment, I had a nice time in Starkville and was very lucky to have had a chance to meet very nice people there. I managed to spend very little money, mainly because of the help and generosity of those people driving me.

My next stop was at Baton Rouge, Louisiana. My goal was to visit Louisiana State University. The bus ride was long and tiresome. I couldn't sleep very well on the bus, and I was tired of carrying my relatively heavy suitcase, so I kept it in a locker at the bus station. It was early morning when I arrived at the campus of LSU. I had to wait for a long while for the admissions office to open. I was directed to speak with the mechanical engineering graduate program coordinator there. He was truly a gentleman and tried to help me. Incidentally he was the former PhD advisor of my professor in Iran, Dr. Aslani. However, things did not work out there either.

I immediately caught a cab and left for the bus station. My next target was Louisiana Tech University in Ruston. It was early evening when the bus arrived there. By this time, I was really exhausted and desperately needed to take a shower. I called for a cab to take me to an inexpensive hotel near the campus. The cab driver was a nice and funny person with a heavy southern accent. He was constantly talking, without a pause. I had a hard time understanding him. I was dozing off in the car and was so relieved when he dropped me off at the hotel. I immediately took a shower and went to bed.

I got up early, checked out, and left my suitcase with the hotel clerk temporarily. Then I walked toward the campus, had my breakfast at the student center, and shortly after, I went to see the chair of the Mechanical Engineering Department. I explained my situation; he admitted me conditionally—I had to take some undergraduate courses before taking any graduate course. In place of the TOEFL test, he asked me to take the university's summer English classes. His conditions were reasonable for me. I was relieved and happy. I took his words to heart and did not ask him to put his demands in writing.

Next thing for me to do was to look for a suitable and inexpensive apartment. Carrying the suitcase and the handbag on my shoulder on a hot and humid day was not fun at all. I ended up leaving it with a clerk at the kitchen who was nice enough to keep it for me for a couple of hours. I asked and looked around for a one-bedroom apartment near the campus; I did not have much luck. I felt frustrated and decided to walk around for a while. Walking around the university campuses was always very relaxing and comforting to me. I went back to the kitchen, got my suitcase, and decided to stay at the student center for as long as I could.

It was late in the evening. I wanted to go back to the hotel but I was too tired to walk back. I found a very secluded area not too far from the campus with an old tree, sat down, and leaned against the tree under the shade. I rested there for a while, and then I pulled a book out of my handbag, and started reading until it was dark. I was thinking to go back to the hotel but I felt too fatigued. I pulled my blanket out of the suitcase, laid it on the ground, used my handbag as a pillow, and slept there. Not a comfortable situation, but it could have been worse. The next day, I had mosquito bites on my hands and face. I needed to shave so badly. I took my shaving bag and a washrag with me to a bathroom in one of the buildings. It was too early in the morning and nobody was around. I brushed my teeth and shaved. Then I took my T-shirt off and started washing my body with the washrag when a security officer entered the bathroom. He looked at me curiously, probably thinking, "Who is this weirdo?"

I looked back at him and mumbled, "I am just a new student here and don't have an apartment yet but I am looking for one."

"Good luck," he chuckled, and left.

After cleaning up, I went back to the suitcase, grabbed it and the handbag, and walked towards the student center again. I sat down there waiting until they opened the dining room. I had a light breakfast there, sat on the chair for a while, and started thinking what to do next when a Persian-looking guy entered the dining center with his American friend. They got their breakfast and sat a few chairs down from mine. I waited until they finished their breakfast. Then

I approached them and sought their advice regarding housing around the campus. They introduced themselves as Charles and Saeed. I told them about my situation. They were both very gentle and helpful. They gave me some tips. Saeed asked me if I was staying anywhere. I said no. He offered to keep my luggage in his apartment until I found my own. That was a relief! The suitcase was heavy and pain to carry, and the handbag was a burden on my shoulder. Saeed drove me to his apartment and let me put my suitcase in his closet. We sat in the hall and talked for a while. A short while later, a very handsome but sleepy fellow came up to me and introduced himself as Vaheed, the younger brother of Saeed.

Saeed and I left for the campus again. I continued searching for an apartment near the campus, with no success. They were either occupied or too expensive for me. I ran into Saeed again and asked if he could take me to a hotel. He graciously offered that I stay with them that night. "I don't want to impose," I said.

"You are not imposing. We would love to have you," he said.

They had a cozy and meticulously clean two-bedroom apartment. We had a nice dinner together at the house. After dinner, I asked some questions about the university there, about the people of Ruston, the standard of living there, and so on. Everything I heard was positive. It was time to go to bed. I wanted to sleep on the couch, but they were nice enough to offer that I sleep in one of the bedrooms.

I lay awake on the couch for hours, thinking about my past, my future, my parents, my brothers and sisters, my friends, and my destiny. I was thinking and questioning, "Why should I be so far away from my loved ones and from my beloved land? Why did I have to come here to study? Why couldn't I find a job and settle in my own country? Why shouldn't we have enough universities and advanced degrees in our own country? Why do we have so much political unrest and uncertainty in our country?" I felt that I was a man with no land. It was a fretful night for me. I immediately came to my senses and reminded myself the words of wisdom from Agha Joon—always be positive and optimistic in life. Negative thoughts drain your body and soul. You want success, think success. No matter what, never forget where you came from. Those words were always comforting to me and giving me hopes for a brighter future. I finally fell asleep.

We got up, had breakfast, and left for school. I went to the bank, opened an account, and went back to school to register for the intensive English classes at Louisiana Tech. Then I started looking for an apartment again. I found one that I liked. I told the manager that I would be back to pay the deposit. It was around noontime, so I went to the university dining center again. Saeed and Vaheed showed up. They asked me if I would be interested in living with them in their apartment; sharing the rent, utilities, and other expenses.

"Sure, but it's only a two-bedroom apartment," I said.

"Don't worry, Vaheed and I will stay in one of the bedrooms and you could use the other," Saeed said. I accepted and stayed in their apartment for as long as I stayed in Ruston. The only problem was that the apartment was pretty far from the university and I did not have a car. Saeed and Vaheed gave me a ride many times but I didn't want to impose on them all the time so I commuted on foot a lot.

I had a great time with Saeed and Vaheed. We got along fine. We didn't have any problems whatsoever. They were clean, organized, and considerate. We shared the same views and values in life. I couldn't have asked for better roommates. We studied, cooked, and cleaned without disturbing one another. Saeed's friend, Charles and his roommate David paid us visit quite often in the evenings or on the weekends. We used to eat together, talk for hours, crack jokes, or we would go swimming in the community pool—they tried to teach me how to swim. Vaheed and I often played ping-pong together. Some weekends, a few of us Iranian students in the community would get together to discuss politics and the future of our beloved land without being affiliated with any student organization.

Another fond reminiscence of mine in Ruston, Louisiana involved a girl that I met while taking the English course. The English classes were very intense but enjoyable. I knew that my future depended on how well I learned the English language, so I studied hard. A group of Mexican students had come to Ruston to study English as well. Among them, there was a very good-looking girl by the name of Maria. She was perky and fun to talk to. She had such a pretty and angelic face blended with a distinctive laugh and very nice personality that made her popular with many people there. One of my friends described her laughs as "Goldie Hawn's type of laughs." We became very good friends. We had lunch and dinner together, we went to movies together, we continued seeing each other, and enjoyed each other's company. There was a great chemistry between us, but no intimacy. Maria and I became serious and somewhat romantic. I had every intention to keep her as a friend. She wanted more than a friendship—a commitment from me to go to Mexico and pursue her through her parents. I was not ready for that. She asked that we stop seeing each other. I was sad and disappointed. However, I needed to move on and focus on my career again.

It was early August; I was informed that the chair of the Mechanical Engineering Department was changed. I paid him a visit and told him about my dealings with the previous department chair. He asked for a written agreement. I did not have that, so he started all over again. He imposed much tougher admission conditions on me including the TOEFL and GRE scores prior to admission. I was disappointed.

The English classes were almost over and the fall semester was approaching. I had to do something. According to the immigration law, I had to be a full time student. I didn't want to violate any laws. I had written letters to the University of Arkansas in Fayetteville and nothing came out of exchanging letters, so I decided to go there in person. That evening I went home and told Vaheed and Saeed about my plans. David was there; he kindly offered to drive me to Fayetteville, Arkansas.

I packed my stuff, and was getting ready to leave. Sadly, I had to say good-bye to my good friends Saeed, Vaheed, and Charles. That evening, I had to see Maria so bad. I found her around the campus. We walked for a long while, then found a quiet place and talked for a long time. Maria and I had emotional moments together. We had such a hard time saying good-bye to each other. I have never forgotten the moment that Maria said, "Good-bye, my darling."

David and I left Ruston early the next day for Fayetteville, Arkansas. Riding with David was very pleasant, as he made me laugh along the way. David was a good looking guy and popular with girls. Every so often, we would stop for gas and food, and every time he saw a pretty girl, he would approach her and talk to her for a while until I would remind him that we needed to hit the road. It was early evening when we arrived in Fayetteville. Upon my request, David took me to the student center. We found the place. David left me there and decided to head back to Ruston. I offered to pay him for his travel expenses going back. The poor guy charged me very little money for gas only. I shook his hand and said, "David, I had a lot of fun, and you have been a great friend, thank you. It was very nice of you driving me down here."

"It was a joy, Habib. What is a friend for?" he said. We shook hands and said good-bye to each other.

After David left, I thought to myself, "I haven't done any favor to this guy, but he generously and unselfishly made the effort to drive me miles away from his house just to make it easier for me. I probably won't see him ever again. How can I return the favor?"

SIX

The campus of the University of Arkansas (U of A) was beautiful and peaceful. I went to the university center, as usual. I was looking and wandering around when I ran into an Iranian guy. He introduced himself as Farzan. I asked him some questions regarding the university, housing, and so on. I asked him, "What is your major?"

I expected him to say some type of engineering, physics, or computer science. He said, "Political science." It was surprising to me because not very many Iranians would come to the United States to study political science, or social sciences, for that matter.

I asked him about the reasonable hotels around the campus, and he asked if I had a car. "No, I don't," I said.

"I don't either, otherwise, I would take you. Actually there are no hotels within walking distance considering that you have to carry this heavy suitcase," he said. "I live in a very small rented room not big enough for two. If you can wait for a few minutes, there is a guy by the name of Mahdad who lives by himself in a two-bedroom apartment, perhaps you can stay at one of his bedrooms."

As he was finishing his sentence, Mahdad showed up. He had long hair and looked pretty much like a hippie! He spoke very softly and laughed for no reason. Farzan introduced us and told him about me. Mahdad graciously agreed to drive me to his apartment and let me stay there temporarily. Surprisingly, his apartment was very clean. He did not look like a person who cared about cleaning. He showed me the guest bedroom. We chatted for a few minutes and shortly after, I went to bed. In the middle of the night, I was awakened by loud noises, banging on the walls, screaming, and loud speaking. I thought that the house was being broken into and Mahdad was probably in some kind of trouble and he might need my help. I cracked the door open slightly. I noticed that Mahdad was on his hands

169

and knees and a half naked girl was sitting on his back and ordering him to go faster. The TV was also on, which contributed to the loud noises. I was relieved that nothing drastic was happening. I closed the door quietly and gently.

I woke up early in the morning. I needed to get to school early so I could talk to someone regarding a possible admission. Mahdad was nice enough to wake up early just to take me to school. After a quick shower, he drove me to the university center. I noticed that I still had my suitcase in Mahdad's car. I asked for it but he responded, "Aren't you coming back to my apartment?"

"I'd love to, but you need to have your privacy," I said.

He laughed and said, "I promise to behave tonight. She won't be there tonight anyway."

"What time are you going to be at home?" I asked.

"Probably late; however, I will call my girlfriend and tell her to leave the key under the mat in case you got there before me." I asked him for his address. He wrote it on a piece of paper and gave it to me.

I went directly to the Mechanical Engineering Department chair, Dr. Deavers, and explained my situation to him. He was kind and truly a gentleman. He admitted me conditionally. He selected only twelve credit hours of undergraduate courses to be completed with a "B" average or above before taking any graduate courses. Also, I had to take the TOEFL and GRE tests within the first year. That was quite reasonable to me. I immediately registered for those courses. Tuition was not much.

The next step was to look for an affordable apartment. I had lunch at the university dining room. Farzan was there and I met a number of other Iranian students. As usual, they were talking about the political environment in Iran. I introduced myself and hung out with those guys for a while. Then I went to check out the library and the bookstore of the university. I was always fascinated with the wealth of books that existed in the university libraries and bookstores in the United States.

I went on a tour of the campus by myself. The more I looked around the campus, the more I became enthusiastic about the University of Arkansas. I couldn't wait for classes to begin. It was around the dusk when I decided to walk to Mahdad's apartment. I had the address in my hand and didn't think that it was going to be far. His house was located in a small farmland area near Fayetteville called Farmington. I walked a very long distance. I kept on walking and walking and walking. The sidewalks were not paved, and it was not so comfortable. Unfortunately, I had underestimated the distance from the university campus to Mahdad's place. I desperately needed to find a person to ask where I was going, someone who could point me in the right direction. There were no convenience stores along the way, nor was there any person around. By this time, it was completely dark and hard to see in front of me. I noticed a small light shining from afar. I thought and hoped that I was approaching a convenience store. I walked towards that light, got closer; there was no sign of a store. Then I realized that the light was illuminating from a house. I knew for sure that the house was not Mahdad's.

I contemplated whether or not I should go knock on the door and ask for the address of the house. I decided to go ahead and walk towards the house. I heard the barking of a dog. I knocked on the door; I heard an old lady's voice. "Who is it?"

"Could you please open the door, ma'am?"

"Who are you?" she yelled.

"Please open the door, I am lost and need to ask you an address," I said.

Suddenly someone opened the door, and the next thing I noticed was a shot-gun pointed at my forehead. An old man with a rough voice who reminded me of John Wayne was holding the shotgun. The old lady was hiding behind him.

"What the heck do you want at this hour on my property?" the old man asked.

I was so frightened, and thought that he might shoot me any moment. I was shaking and started stuttering, "Sir, please don't shoot. I am so sorry to disturb you. I am not a criminal. I am not a thief; all I want is to ask you how I could find this address." I gave him the piece of paper with the address on it.

The angry old man exclaimed, "Do you know what time it is? You came at my door at this time of the night to ask me an address?!"

He handed the address to the old lady. The old lady calmed the situation and told me that I needed to go farther down. The old man said, "You need to get the heck out of my property as fast as you can or else I will shoot you."

"Please don't shoot. I am leaving now," I said.

"We are going to call the cops on you to make sure that you are not hanging around our house," the old lady warned me.

"Please do so Ma 'am. Maybe the cop will guide me to the house," I said as I was leaving.

I was relieved and embarrassed at the same time. I started walking again. After walking for another half an hour to forty-five minutes, I noticed that I was approaching a new town. The dogs in the neighborhood started barking, and some started chasing me. I thought I was going to be attacked by some dogs any moment. I knew more or less that it was the right neighborhood, but had a hard time finding the house. Then a cop pulled in front of me and asked, "What is wrong? What are you looking for?"

I was relieved. I showed him the address. He directed me right to it and followed me to the house. "Is this your house?" the officer asked.

"No, sir, it's my friend's house and I am staying with him temporarily," I said.

"Do you have the key to the house?"

"No, sir, the key should be under the mat."

I looked under the mat, and unfortunately, the key was not there. "Now what? The cop is probably going to think that I am lying to him," I muttered.

"What are you going to do now?" the cop asked.

"I guess I don't have any choice but staying here at the door until my friend shows up," I said. The cop left. I waited for a long while. I was tired and sleepy. I put my handbag down, used it as a pillow, and slept on the mat. It was not comfortable, but I was too tired and couldn't keep my eyes open. I slept for a while until finally Mahdad showed up at the door. The cop came back at the same time. I guess he was trying to make sure that I was not making up stories. Mahdad assured him of that. The next morning Mahdad took me to the campus to search for a place to live. I ended up moving into a nice and clean apartment with three bedrooms very close to the campus sharing it with two brothers Mehrzad and Jamal. These two brothers were as nice as the two brothers in Ruston, Saeed and Vaheed. That apartment was especially ideal for me because it was within the walking distance from the campus.

I finally found a good university to continue my education; I had great roommates, and enjoyed my classes. I particularly enjoyed having classes with Dr. Myklebust and Dr. Jack Cole, two of my best professors at U of A.

I was not doing so well financially. I found a job at the dining center as a busboy. One day as I was cleaning tables, Drs. Myklebust and Cole showed up for lunch. They called me to their table, and asked me to go see them in their offices. They found jobs for me grading papers and assisting them in their courses. These two professors were amazing teachers; not only were they popular teachers, they were good human beings, and cared a great deal about their students. I remember in my first semester, I was still struggling with English, Dr. Cole always made sure that I understood the subjects in class. On many occasions, he would pause and ask me, "Habib, let me know if you are puzzled and if you have any questions."

I successfully completed the courses in the first semester. I was no longer required to take the TOEFL and GRE exams, a big relief for me. Upon strong recommendations by Drs. Cole and Myklebust, I was hired by Dr. Jim Akin, the chair of the Engineering Science Department, as a graduate teaching assistant to teach the fluid mechanics lab during spring semester 1978. That was going to be my very first teaching assignment in the United States. I was determined to be a good teacher and teach my students the way I wanted to be taught. I wanted to be an organized teacher like Dr. Cecil, a kind and caring teacher like Dr. Cole, a likeable and humorous teacher like Dr. Myklebust, and a coach to my students like Lou Holtz, the coach of the University of Arkansas football team at the time.

Speaking of Lou Holtz, that semester I became a big fan of the University of Arkansas football team, the Razorbacks. I followed all of their games religiously. Lou Holtz had a very successful year with the Razorbacks team that year. He was truly a remarkable coach. One of my most pleasant memories in Fayetteville was the sweet victory of the Razorbacks versus the Oklahoma Sooners in the Orange Bowl on January 2, 1978. We were watching the game at a friend's house with a bunch of people there. We were eating popcorn, chips, and all kinds of munchies, and watching TV. The Razorbacks went into the game ranked number six in the nation, while the Oklahoma Sooners enjoyed the number two ranking. The Razorback team was an underdog by a big margin. Coach Lou Holtz had banned four of his best offensive players from playing for disciplinary reasons. In spite of all odds against Arkansas, I, being an optimist by nature, bet on Arkansas. I mean not official betting, just amongst ourselves in the house with very little money. Arkansas surprised everyone by an upset victory over the Oklahoma Sooners, 31-6. It was an amazing victory and a joyful moment for not only the people of Fayetteville, but for the whole state of Arkansas. The city of Fayetteville exploded with joy after the game.

SEVEN

The Persian community in Fayetteville was very small and consisted mostly of students of the University of Arkansas. Some weekends, a few of us would get together to discuss politics and the future of our country. We had formed our own small Iranian society with no affiliation to the Confederation of Iranian Students whatsoever. Back in those days, some of us felt that we could not be indifferent and neutral about the political climate in our motherland. We felt that it was one's moral duty to acknowledge the courage and sacrifice of those who were fighting for freedom inside the country and to sympathize with them. We felt that the least we could do was to get together occasionally in order to educate ourselves about the democracy and politics of the free world without being under pressure to follow any particular group.

Those days the news about the Shah and Iran was the hot topics of the American media and newspapers. The news about Iran was not very pleasant. My days in Ruston and in Fayetteville coincided with the debates in President Carter's administration regarding the arms sales to Iran. They were debating whether they should sell AWACS (Airborne Warning and Control System) military aircraft to Iran. Iranian student activists in the United States voiced their opinions against the proposal. Ultimately, President Carter agreed to sell five AWACS to Iran. That resulted in more demonstrations in the universities in Iran, in the United States, and elsewhere in the world. Those days also coincided with the death of Dr. Ali Shariatti, who was a religious figure and an Islamic ideologue. Shariatti was not a clergyman and did not believe in *marja-e-taghlid*. He was anti-*rouhaniat* (*anti-akhoundism, anti-mullahism*) and attracted a huge number of university students to his revolutionary speeches at his headquarters, *Housseiniyeh-e-Ershad,* in Tehran. He was considered as a big threat to the Shah's government. Dr. Shariatti fled to London during summer of 1977 and died there a few days after his arrival, apparently of a massive heart attack. The Shah was blamed for his death. There were uprisings by the students all over Iran for the death of Dr. Shariatti. Also, Khomeini's eldest son died mysteriously in Karbala, Iraq and the Shah was blamed for his death as well.

There were frequent demonstrations at the Iranian Embassy in Washington, DC. Ardeshir Zahedi, the former son-in-law of the Shah, was the Iranian ambassador to the United States at the time. He was known as a flamboyant womanizer who threw the most lavishing and expensive parties in the United States. He was known as a person who spent Iranian assets on dating and buying expensive gifts for some female movie stars and TV newscasters. He was acting as the spokesperson for the government of Iran in the United States. He traveled to different parts of the United States and made derogatory remarks against the Iranian students belonging to the Confederation, calling them traitors, treasonous, and non-Iranians. These kinds of attitudes and accusations did not help ease the tension between the angry students and the Iranian government officials in the United States.

We closely followed the news about Iran and watched interviews by Barbara Walters and Mike Wallace with the Shah. In spite of the fact that most students despised the Shah, I personally had mixed feelings about him. I did not like his arrogance, and yet I was proud of him for his candid and honest answers to some questions. For example, I did not like his statement; "Women are not as intelligent as men," which was a response to Ms. Barbara Walters' question in regards to equal rights for women.

In another interview, when Mr. Mike Wallace brought up the issue of Persian Gulf,[77] "As you know, I have been across the gulf, the gulf that you call Persian and they call Arabian..."

The shah was quick to respond by asking him, "What was the name that you read during your school days?"

Mr. Wallace's response was, "Persian Gulf."

I did not like his contradictory answers to the question that a few reporters asked him, "How many political prisoners do you have in your country?"

At one occasion, he responded, "We do not have any political prisoners."

In another occasion he said, "We have only 3,300."

In other interviews with Mike Wallace, the Shah categorized Americans as blue-eyed people who "plundered" his country over the oil. He also made remarks that the Jewish lobbyists were "pulling the strings of the presidency" and

---

77   The actual interview is detailed in the book *Between You and Me: A Memoir*, by Mike Wallace with Gary Paul Gates (New York: Hyperion, 2005).

controlling the media.[78] Those kinds of candid remarks and did not help the Shah at all and perhaps expedited his fall and the collapse of his regime.

The shah, in his speeches, repeatedly labeled the oppositions as either "the Black Reactionaries," referring to the Islamic groups, or "Red Treasonous," referring to Communist groups. Those kinds of labeling and generalization were not helpful to him either. Not all the Muslim oppositions belonged to radical Islamist organizations, and not all the non-Muslims or non-practicing Muslim freedom fighters were Communists. Most Iranians were fighting for democracy. Iranians fought for democracy long before the revolution. I tend to agree with Mr. Stephen Kinzer[79] that had it not been for the 1953 CIA-engineered coup to depose Dr. Mossadeq, Iran would probably have continued along its path toward full democracy. I also agree with my late father, who believed that if the Shah had turned some of his authorities over to the government of Dr. Mossadeq, together they could have paved the way for a full democratic state.

I thought it was unfair that some anti-Shah students in the United States labeled him as another Hitler or Ivan the Terrible or a mass murderer. He was none of those. The Shah was by no means a tyrant like Saddam Hussein of Iraq or Ferdinand Marcos of the Philippines or Anastasia Somoza of Nicaragua or Augusto Pinochet of Chile, the dictators of the time. Shah was a patriot, a pragmatic, and a visionary leader, yet an authoritarian ruler. He had many projects in his plans: to build roads, metros, a lot more universities, to start nuclear energy with the help of American companies, and more. He had a big dream for his country; he wanted to change Iran from a third world to a developed country. However, his regime was an oppressive and a totalitarian regime. The SAVAK was notoriously brutal against dissidents. Nevertheless, today when I compare the Shah with the current leaders in Iran, he was by far less brutal to his people and more credible internationally.

Around mid-November of 1977, the Shah and his wife, Empress Farah came to the United States. President and Mrs. Carter welcomed them on the lawn of the White House. A number of pro-shah Iranians also greeted the Shah and his wife.[80] A huge number of anti-Shah demonstrators occupied the streets of Washington, D.C., near the White House carrying anti-Shah placards, shouting anti-Shah slogans, and condemning the Shah's regime. Most anti-Shah students covered their faces with masks to shield their identities from SAVAK. The demonstrators tried to get closer to the White House, and a big riot erupted. In an attempt to

---

78   See the same book by Mike Wallace, pages 124 and 125.

79   Stephen Kinzer, *All the Shah's Men*, (New York: John Wiley & Sons, 2007).

80   It was believed that those people received money to attend the welcoming ceremony in Washington DC.

disperse the rioters, police hurled canisters of tear gas to the crowd, and the gas was felt by the Shah and the Empress Farah, President Carter, and the first lady. That day I watched the whole event on TV in the lobby of the University Center along with a number of Iranian and American students. There were cheers and clapping among the spectators to see the Shah shedding tears. I am sure that perhaps a number of Iranians in the crowd like me felt bad to see their king being humiliated and his pride being insulted. Despite my opposition to the Shah's absolute authoritarian ruling, I condemn the humiliation of a human being in any shape or form. The Shah and President Carter met again on New Year's Eve 1978 in Tehran, which triggered more demonstrations in Iran and America.

The student association in Fayetteville was formed and led by a popular, well-respected, and well-liked person by the name of Ali. He was an anti-Shah activist but not a radical, nor was he a hate monger. Unlike many Iranian student organization leaders back in those days, he never tried to discourage students from attending classes. He never tried to encourage us to put anti-regime activities on top of our priority list. On the contrary, he reminded us from time to time that we should not forget what we came here for, and he had high praise for studious and hardworking students. I liked that very much. Most students attended the meetings willingly and not under any pressure. The main agenda of each meeting was to be abreast of the political events in Iran and elsewhere in the world. We were not under any obligations whatsoever to be a member of the Iranian Student Confederation in the United States or to go to their general meetings, which would normally take place in big cities such as Houston, Washington, D.C., Los Angeles, or Oklahoma City. However, I voluntarily went to one of those meetings in Oklahoma City during the Christmas break, and it was not a pleasant experience. I did not find it amusing, nor was it informative to me. Different groups of anti-regime activists were at each other's throats, trying to inject their ideologies to one another. I was happy just to be a member of the Iranian Student Association of Fayetteville. I became somewhat active in that organization. We had our own radio program, two hours every Sunday. Ali and I were in charge of not only collecting news about Iran but anchoring the news on the radio as well. We also helped the radio disc jockey to pick appropriate songs for our radio program.

In addition to keeping current with the news around the world, the members of our association in Fayetteville occasionally would get together at somebody's house to have barbeque, to relax, to socialize, and to entertain each other. Word got around that I could sing. I entertained my friends by singing mostly revolutionary songs, often accompanied by Massoud playing piano. A few weeks before

Eid-e Nowruz, around the first day of spring 1978, we got together in order to strategize and to arrange entertainment programs for the big event. Ali was the producer, the writer, and the director of the programs. He was truly talented and knew exactly what he was doing. He spoke English very well and had no fear of speaking before a big crowd. The programs were to be performed before a big audience including Americans, Iranians, and some foreign nationals. I was supposed to sing a song. It was my first experience to perform before such a big crowd. Massoud and I practiced almost one hour a day for two or three weeks before the start of the program. In addition to singing, I was given a role to play in a politicized pantomime as well. The day of the program, I was extremely nervous and anxious to sing my song and get it over with. The program started with the national anthem:[81]

> *Oh Iran, oh bejeweled land,*
> *Oh, your soil is the wellspring of the arts,*
> *Far from you may the thoughts of evil be,*
> *May you remain lasting and eternal.*
> *Oh enemy, if you are of stone, I am of iron,*
> *May my life be sacrificed for my pure motherland.*
> ....
> ....

After the national anthem, a few announcements were made, followed by an electrifying speech by Ali soliciting moral support for the Iranian students struggling for democracy and against tyranny. My singing performance was scheduled in the middle. Massoud went to the stage first and started playing, and then I followed and started singing the revolutionary song[82] that we had practiced:

> *For every horrific, dark, autumn night,*
> *There is a bright spring daylight.*
> *For every mild breeze,*
> *There is a storm that will spawn a new generation.*

---

81   Ey Iran – Wikipedia, the free Encyclopedia. For the complete version of the national anthem one can refer to the website: en.wikipedia.org/wiki/Ey_Iran.

82   It is believed that the song was written by an unknown student in Iran whose fate is not known. The poem above is not the transliteration of the lyrics but the English version of the song which is done by the author.

For every foundation of slavery,
There is a movement of freedom.
For lovers of life,
Today only unity, unity.
Get up, my compatriot,
Stand on your feet and change the foundation of this land.
How long do you want to be contained under siege in this land?

For every horrific, dark, autumn night,
There is a bright, spring daylight.
For every mild breeze,
There is a storm that will spawn a new generation.

Tear these filthy clothes, destroy these rotten tents,
Let us change the rhythm of the music.
Get up, my compatriot,
Let us find our new day, and let us find our eternal triumph.

I used to be my own biggest critic but in spite of my extreme nervousness, I thought I did pretty well that evening, and my performance was well received. I got a standing ovation. About a week later, we were invited to go to Lawrence, Kansas to perform the same song at the University of Kansas. A much larger audience attended the Nowruz ceremony there. I sang the same song, and the audience was on its feet requesting that I sing another song. I sang another song at the end of the program. After my performance, I was approached by a couple of people in the audience who asked me if I wanted to record the song and perhaps an album with their company in California. I was flattered by the offer, but as a precautionary measure and out of the fear of SAVAK entrapment, I refused.

They tried to encourage me by saying things like, "This could be the stepping-stone to a successful singing career," and so on.

I told them, "I am a full-time student and singing is just a hobby for me. I have no desire to become a professional singer." One of them left a number with me and asked me to give him a call if I changed my mind. I never did.

I still sing that song, and I will keep singing it until I die or until my beloved motherland is free!

EIGHT

After the Nowruz ceremony, I realized that I was behind with my studies and I had much catching up to do. I studied my brains off, and in the meantime, I was having a great time teaching. The stipend that I was getting every month was good enough for me to get by, but not enough to pay for all of my expenses. In addition, I was planning on going back home to visit my family during the summer of 1978, so I decided to find a job off campus for extra income. I landed a job in a local restaurant. I was working in that restaurant as a dishwasher during some evenings. I had saved up enough money to purchase a plane ticket to Iran.

Spring semester 1978 ended successfully for me, in spite of my extracurricular activities. I started planning for my trip to Iran. I made my family informed of my plan. I had been told that my father was not going to be at the airport due to a cold. That got my attention; I started worrying that perhaps there was something more seriously wrong with my father than just a simple cold! Most Iranians have the habit of hiding the serious illness of a family member from the loved ones who live in a different country. My excitement about the reunion with the whole family and my angst about my father's health made me too anxious to get back home as soon as possible. I purchased a ticket a few days after the semester ended, mid-May 1978. To the best of my recollection, the flight was a direct flight via Iran Air from New York to Tehran. We finally touched down at Mehrabad Airport. After going through passport check and customs, I went to the main lobby of the airport, and I was surprised and relieved to see my father there—he was in tears and so was I. Then I saw my brothers Iraj and Ahmad, and my brother-in-law, Mr. Moemeni. I was so glad that my father seemed to be in a good health. However, later on, I was told that father had suffered a minor heart attack.

On our way home, I noticed tanks and soldiers on the streets of Tehran. Before my departure from the United States, I had read in some Persian papers that some sporadic fighting had occurred in different parts of the country, especially in Tehran, between the anti-government forces and the police. Tehran was under a semi-martial law. When we got home, I was so glad to see my mother, my teen-age sister Afsaneh, my sisters Maasoomeh and Molood, and the rest of my family members there. I noticed the absence of my brother Nasser. I asked my mother where Nasser was. She said, "Nasser is staying at a friend's house in Tehran, and he will be here tomorrow night." It was kind of odd to have everybody there except my brother Nasser, but I took my mother's words for granted. I was so glad to hear that my sister Maasoomeh and her husband, Mr. Moemeni, had rented a house in Fardis close to ours. I asked my mother about grandmother, Jaan Jaan. I was so saddened to hear that she had passed away. I loved her so dearly. She will always have a special place in my heart.

The day after my arrival, a bunch of friends and relatives came to visit, but there was still no sign of Nasser. I became more curious as to whether my family was hiding something from me. I was afraid that he might have been arrested by the SAVAK for political reasons. I went to my mother and insisted that I wanted to know the truth about Nasser. My mother said, "Nasser is doing well but he is cautiously staying away from this town for a short while."

"But why?"

"Nasser had a job as a minibus driver, driving people from one town to another (Fardis to Karadj). One day he got into a fight with two macho brothers who were loud, disruptive, and harassing a girl in his minibus. Nasser kicked them both out of the minibus. They attacked Nasser, but he managed to overpower them and beat them both. These two bullies belonged to a notoriously infamous and influential family in town. The father of the family threatened to retaliate," my mother said. "I went to see the father of the family and talked him into withdrawing his retribution intent and he reluctantly accepted. Nasser will be here tomorrow."

The next evening my brother Nasser showed up at the house, and I was extremely happy to see him. Nasser became a hero in that town for standing up to the obnoxious family. I was proud of him for that. I was also proud of my mother for standing firm against the tyrants and for resolving the dispute between the two families peacefully. My brothers and I had a great time together; we visited family and friends in the daytime and watched the 1978 World Cup taking place in Argentina during the nights. Iran qualified for the soccer World Cup for the first time from the whole continent of Asia after beating the strong Australian team. Iranians were proud of their national team.

One day I decided to pay a visit to my old university in Narmak, I had heard that Reza T was working there as a PE professor. I wanted to surprise him. When I entered the university, I noticed security officers everywhere. I went to the Athletic Department first, and I asked for Reza T. They directed me right to his office. He was surprised to see me; we gave each other a big hug, and he introduced me to his colleagues as an alumnus. He had an arrangement to play soccer with couple of his friends. He asked me if I wanted to play, and I said, "No, I will watch and cheer for you."

He insisted that I play. I thought we were going to go to the soccer field and play a serious game, but we went to the basketball court instead, to play the "salon" game or "footstall," as they call it now. To my surprise, there were only two of us against two on the opposite team. They bet on lunch money. Small, movable soccer goals were mounted on the ground, and no goalkeeper was required. The goal posts were very close to each other, which made it difficult to score goals. The team that first reached five goals would be the winner. It was a breathtaking game. After hours of running and a long struggle, we won the game. After the game, I needed a shower. I was directed to a private shower room. I opened a locker and noticed an anti-regime leaflet inside the locker. The leaflet was full of anti-Shah statements by Khomeini. In response to one of the Shah's statements that he promised to grant freedom to people, Khomeini had been quoted as saying, "Freedom is not something that you grant to people, freedom is God given— freedom is the lawful right of people. Islam has granted freedom to people. Who do you think you are, granting freedom to people? This statement by itself is a disgrace to the people." I folded the leaflet and put it in my pocket. After the shower, I went to Reza T's office. They were waiting for me to go to lunch. I showed the leaflet to those guys, and they immediately advised me to tear it up and trash it.

Reza T gave me a speech, "Habib, you are a guest in this country; do not engage in political discussions at all, as you may jeopardize your return visa to America." After lunch, Reza T took me on a tour of the university and then on a tour of the Eastern Tehran, the city of Narmak (a suburb of Tehran), and the district of Tehran Pars, where Reza T's house was located.

During the tour, I observed more tanks and soldiers on the streets of Tehran. The security in Tehran was unusually tight. I was almost certain that something big was going to happen in Iran. Reza T then insisted that I should go to his house for dinner. I was reluctant because I thought my family would get worried about me. Reza T asked me to give them a call, but unfortunately, we didn't have a phone in our house. His wife had prepared all kinds of food. She also insisted that I stay. I agreed and Reza T took me to the balcony of his house. We each had a few beers with pistachios. I told Reza T, "This could very well be the last beer in Iran that we drink together."

"Why?" Reza T asked.

"I have a feeling that the end of the Pahlavi era is coming, and if the Islamist groups take over, that would be the end of our social freedom," I said.

Reza T disagreed with me and said, "The shah and his government will be untouchable. Security and SAVAK are too strong to allow instability and a hostile takeover of the country. The Islamic groups have no chance of taking over, and Iran has no place for the leftist groups either."

After dinner, Reza T drove me from Tehran Pars, the extreme east, to the extreme west of Tehran near the Mehrabad Airport so I could catch a cab to Fardis. By the time I got home, it was around the midnight. I rang the bell and my sister Afsaneh opened the door, and she was so glad to see me, "Where were you? We were worried about you."

My father furiously said, "Don't do that to me anymore."

Unlike my father, my mother normally wouldn't go into panic; she intervened and turned to my father and said, "So what? He was late a little bit; he is young and needs to spend time with his friends sometimes." My father was worried that I might have been apprehended by the SAVAK for saying something inappropriate against the government. I apologized to my father and assured him that I would be careful. My brothers were all in the TV room watching the World Cup, and I joined them. We discussed soccer for hours before going to bed.

The next morning after breakfast, I told my father about the leaflet and its content. My father had more or less the same views as Reza T and believed strongly that the Shah's regime was too strong to be toppled. I told my father that the Shah and his regime were faced with enormous organized opposition groups and could not resist that much opposition. I predicted that the Shah would be gone before *Nowruz 1358* (March 21, 1979). Everybody in my family laughed at me. My father pleaded to me not to repeat that anywhere else. I left Iran a few days later, on August 1, 1978.

Shortly after I came back to the United States, the news about the Rex Movie Theater in Abadan[83] received media attention worldwide. The movie theater was set on fire and several hundred people[84] who were watching a critical movie, *Gavaznha*, "Deer," were trapped inside. All the doors, including the emergency doors, were locked, and, sadly, all of them died. The Shah's regime was blamed for that atrocious tragedy. The next day the people of Abadan mourned the death of their fellow citizens and held the biggest anti-government rally in the city.

---

83   Abadan is a city in the southern province of Khuzestan with the biggest oil refinery in the world.
84   Chronology of Iran (1896-1979), Vol. 2 by Bagher Agheli, *Nashr-e Goftar*, 1995, page 354. The date for the incident quoted in the book is August 18, 1978. The number of people killed is quoted as 377.

Then they started going on a rampage; they attacked the government buildings, banks, and shops, and burned buses. The people in Tehran and almost everywhere in Iran empathized with the people of Abadan. Angry and bloody demonstrations erupted all over the country. More movie theaters were attacked, windows were smashed, liquor stores were destroyed, and beer factories were set on fire. The government renounced any involvement in the Rex Cinema tragedy. Shortly after, the government of Jamshid Amoozegar[85] collapsed, and he resigned as the prime minister, after being in the post for almost one year. He also relinquished his title as the head of the *Rastakhiz* Party.

The shah appointed Jafar Sharif Emami, the speaker of the Senate, as the new prime minister. He asked the Shah to be granted full autonomy to run the government. In the boldest move, the very first thing the prime minister did was to change the imperial calendar back to the solar calendar (Shah had changed the solar calendar to Imperial calendar in 1976 which was an unpopular move; the year 1355 was changed to 2535). He closed down nightclubs, casinos, cabarets, and liquor stores. He then ordered to free most political prisoners, including the well-known ayatollahs Taleghani and Montazeri, who were greeted by tens of thousands of people. Sharif Emami's daring and reformist moves, his fiery speeches against some elements of the Shah's regime, and his calls for *ashti-e-melli*, "national reconciliation," did not work. Khomeini's messages against such reforms and reconciliation were louder.

Approximately three weeks after the Rex incident, over one million Iranian people marched towards the then *Shahyad* Square (now, the Freedom Square) in a peaceful manner. The march was organized and led by the distinguished university professors, clergies, and leaders of the National Front Party. At the Shahyad Square, a manifesto was read wherein the move to support freedom of speech, freedom of press, freedom of all political prisoners, complete sovereignty of the nation, abolishment of SAVAK, establishment of an Islamic Republic led by Khomeini, and demolishment of the Shah's regime were declared. Shahyad Square was renamed as "Freedom Square," and it has been called that ever since. Immediately after the peaceful march, a full martial law was imposed in all major cities. Despite the declaration of martial law, a huge number of people gathered in Zhaleh Squre on a Friday morning, they disobeyed the martial law rules and disregarded the order of the elite soldiers, and shouted anti-Shah slogans. The demonstration turned bloody. Several hundred people were killed and several others were wounded.[86]

---

85   Dr. Amoozegar replaced Amir Abbas Hoveida, who was the prime minister for more than thirteen years.
86   Chronology of Iran (1896-1979), Vol. 2 by Bagher Agheli, *Nashr-e Goftar*, 1995, page 360. The number killed quoted by the government officials at the time was ninety-five, and the number wounded was 250.

Zhaleh Square was named "Martyrdom Square" after that incident and that day was called "Black Friday."

The Rex and Zhaleh tragedies sparked angry and wider demonstrations by the students in Iran. We watched on TV the shooting of students by soldiers at University of Tehran. I was extremely angry and sad and felt so frustrated for not being able to be with my fellow citizens in those crucial moments. Most Iranians abroad including myself became concerned about the situations inside the country. I was particularly worried about my three young brothers back home; whom I was told participated in most demonstrations.

The incidents in Rex and Zhaleh Square expedited the fall of the Shah. However, it is now a known fact that the Shah's government had no role in the burning of the Rex Movie Theater. The main perpetrator of the crime was a person by the name of Hossein Takabalizadeh, who confessed to the premeditated crime. In his confession affidavit, he expressed no remorse whatsoever, and explained that he executed this act in response to the fatwa by Khomeini that the liquor stores, nightclubs, and movie theaters are the loci for corruption and prostitution and must be destroyed.[87] After the establishment of the Islamic Republic, the families of victims went on strike and demanded an answer. The Islamic Republic was forced to start a court session. During the fake hearing sessions, Takabalizade also confessed that he was in contact with the lead person of the Abadan Islamic Organization (AIO) at the time, and together they planned the criminal act. These two had apparently committed an arsonist act against another government building. In order to cover up the rest of the story and save the Islamic Republic from a big embarrassment, the mullah judge, Mousavi Tabrizi, ordered the execution of Takabalizadeh. However, the leader of AIO, who was one of the masterminds of the plan, was never subpoenaed to the hearing, and he later became one of the representatives of the Khuzestan province in the Parliament of the Islamic Republic.[88] This was one of the most disgraceful and deceitful cover up in the Iranian history in the name of the religion. This horrifying tragedy can only be compared with Reichstag fire on February 27, 1933 at the pivotal point of the Nazi establishment and Hitler's Ruling.

My prediction that the Shah would fall before March of 1979 came to reality. I could sense that and I could feel it. Shah did not have the support of the majority

---

However, the author of the book mentions that the numbers declared by the government are much less than the real numbers. In the book, it is also quoted from Shahpour Bakhtiar, who later became the prime minister, that 2,450 were killed while Bani Sadr, in Paris at the time, announced that three thousand were killed.

87   For more details, one can refer to *Pajouhesh* magazine, No. 99, fall 2007, pp. 8-11. In this magazine, the date was quoted as August 19, 1978, and the number killed is quoted as four hundred.

88   Ibid.

in Iran, nor did he have any support outside Iran. Not even the American government, the biggest ally of the Shah, was willing to support him any longer. I am often teased by friends and family members, "Habib, you predicted the fall of the Shah correctly; can you predict when the Islamic Republic will be gone?"

I am not a psychic and I don't have the crystal ball in my hand, my prediction of the fall of the Shah before Nowruz 1358, March 1979, was just an educated guess. However, history has shown time after time that tyrants and ruthless regimes cannot prevail against the people's democratic movements, and they will eventually be thrown into the dumpster of history. It is a matter of time that fanaticism will become a thing of the past in the Iranian history and the autocrats of the Islamic Republic will be forced out of Iran and will join their friends Saddam, Pinochet, Slobodan, Hitler, and thousands of other dictators in the dumpster of history. It is a matter of time that Iran will become Iran again, as opposed to "the Islamic Republic of Iran," and Islam will again become a religion by choice, not a religion by force.

NINE

A few weeks before the start of the fall 1978 semester, I returned to Fayette-ville from my trip to Iran. I had to move out of the apartment because, in my absence, the sister of Mehrzad and Jamal was living with them. She insisted that she was staying there temporarily. Mehrzad and Jamal wanted me to continue staying with them, but I felt that I did not want to impose, and it was to every-one's best interest that I left. I ran into a friend of mine, Jassem one day and he talked me into living in the dormitory with him. Jassem was a nice guy with a good sense of humor. Although I was not very keen on staying at the dormitory, I accepted it. The rooms were small, and two students shared each room. Jassem used to work the night shift at a restaurant and would come late to the dorm, and he would always wake me up. I decided to go to the restaurant with him and study there and come back to the dorm at the same time. A number of other students used to go there after hours to eat, drink coffee, and study. That arrangement worked to my advantage because I got a lot done during those nights.

In the meantime, I really worked hard to do well on my teaching. I had to do the labs for myself and to prepare my notes in advance in order to get ready for my classes. Preparation for my classes was time consuming but enjoyable. However, I was not so sure whether I was doing a decent job or not, whether students understood me or not, and whether or not my students and my supervisors were going to be happy with me. Above all, I was a little bit insecure because of my lack of the command of the English language, until one day, one of my students came to my little office and asked me some questions, I answered all of his questions. He then asked me, "Habib, why don't you teach more rigorous courses other than one-credit hour lab courses? You are doing a great job; keep it up."

"What do other students think?" I asked.

"Most of my classmates share my view," he said.

He made my day. I was very glad to hear that my students were happy with me.

Dr. Akin, the head of the Engineering Science Department and my boss whom I was also taking a course with—another great teacher that I had at the University of Arkansas—one day after the class asked me, "Habib, how are your classes coming along?"

"I love what I am doing, sir," I said.

"I haven't heard any negative comment on your teaching job," he said.

"Do you think next semester I could teach a more challenging course, like Statics or Mechanics of Materials?" I asked.

"I don't see why not; I will keep you in mind." He said.

I was getting tired of the dormitory life and started searching for a better alternative when Reza called me one day and asked me to pay him a visit in Stillwater, Oklahoma, where he was a student in the Mechanical Engineering Department. It was near Thanksgiving break. I purchased a round-trip Greyhound bus ticket and managed my time to stay there for almost one week.

He had a roommate who was a Zoroastrian, pro-Shah and anti-Khomeini, while Reza was a committed Muslim, anti-Shah and pro-Khomeini. These two were both opinionated and strong willed and didn't get along very well. They would sometimes get into the heated discussions and arguments about politics. Back in those days, Iranians did not dare boldly support the Shah without being labeled as an agent of SAVAK, and being a SAVAK agent was a curse. Reza's roommate was a daredevil to support the Shah bluntly. Reza was not a fanatic Muslim, as some fanatics do not even want to associate with non-Muslims. Despite his dislike of his roommate, he always defended him as being an innocent person who did not have anything to do with the SAVAK. He then introduced me to a friend of his who was a graduate student, if I am not mistaken, in agricultural engineering. We recognized each other immediately. I had met him in Kingsville before. He invited both Reza and me for breakfast the next morning at one of his friend's house in commemoration of an Islamic ceremonial occasion. To the best of my recollection, most Iranian students in Stillwater belonged to Islamic groups.

Reza and I woke up early and got ready to go to breakfast. The house was located near the campus of Oklahoma State University and was packed with people. I expected the usual Iranian breakfast, bread, cheese, butter, jelly, and tea. Surprisingly, they had *kalleh-pacheh*, lamb head, including the tongue and brain, plus the leg—all koshered. Before the start of the breakfast, we had to do the prayer for a victory of an Islamic Revolution led by Khomeini against the "evil regime of the Shah." After the breakfast, Reza, our mutual friend, and I decided to go for a walk around the campus to burn the greasy food. It was a cold and icy day. A few days before I arrived there, it snowed heavily in Stillwater. As we were walking and talking, all of a sudden we had water splashed all over our bodies and we were soaked. We then noticed a bunch of students throwing balloons full of water out of their car. The kids in the car were laughing and shouting, "Go home, camel jockeys!" We felt the water on our winter jackets turning to ice; nevertheless, we started laughing. I jokingly said, "Thanks for your hospitalities." All three of us started shivering and decided to run to keep warm. We ran back to the cars. Reza turned the heater on in the car and for the first few minutes, ice-cold air was blowing on us. By the time, the heater started blowing warm air; we had arrived at Reza's apartment.

One evening, Reza and I were invited for dinner at Mehdi's house, one of Reza's friends. The food was great. It was made by Mehdi's sister. It had been a long while since I had tasted real Persian food. There was another real nice gentleman from an African country who was a guest there as well. He was a Muslim and a doctoral student in political science at OSU. He was knowledgeable about the politics of the world and was particularly interested in the Iranian politics and Persian culture. As usual, political unrest in Iran dominated the conversation. I remember vividly while we were discussing and debating the situation in Iran, Khomeini was getting momentum and gathering support from many groups inside and outside the country, and this gentleman made a statement that I couldn't agree more, "What you need in Iran is the establishment of a democratic and secular government—not another dictatorship. Religious-type governments tilt toward dictatorship."

His statement made me think, "Is it possible that a man who keeps talking about God, Islam, freedom, humanity, and prosperity can turn into a dictator?"

We talked for hours but couldn't solve the world's problems. Reza then shifted our discussion to something else—he asked me to sing.

The next evening Reza and Mehdi took me to a local bar against my will. We met three good looking native Indian girls there. We carried on a conversation with the girls for quite a while. The girls invited us to their house. Reza and Mehdi accepted the invitation, and I had no choice but going with the flow. We followed the girls' car; it was a cold night and the road was icy. Then we noticed the girls were slowing down. They stopped the car. We parked the car right behind them. We noticed that they had a flat tire. We got out of the car to help. It was extremely cold. Reza was good with cars, and thank God, he had all the tools. We helped him changing the flat tire. But that was not the only problem with the car; the car wouldn't start. Reza found out that the battery was low, so we had to jump it. That car died on us at least a couple of times. They finally parked the car by a rundown house located in a secluded area. We got out of the car; there were not very many houses around. It was dark, cold, and scary. The girls asked us to come in. We asked the girls, "Where is this place?"

"An Indian reservation," they said. We looked at each other and didn't know what to say. We all decided to head back, but the girls insisted on going in for a cup of coffee. We reluctantly went inside the house. To our dismay, we were greeted by a huge guy in his late thirties or early forties with a rough voice. He looked like a giant.

Reza jokingly whispered, "Oh, boy, all three of us are going to be swallowed by this guy tonight." Then we noticed a young teenager, an older lady, and a bunch of little kids, all living in that little house. There were a few bedrooms there. We were directed to go to the warmest room. The source of the heat in that room was a fireplace. The girls brought us coffee and cookies and we expected them to join us, but the big guy showed up in the room. We were not at all at ease in that house.

"Where are you guys from?" The big guy asked.

"We are from Iran."

"I like the old man (Khomeini) who is standing up to the tyranny of the Shah," he said.

He began by saying that the American government must stop supporting dictators like the Shah. He talked about the politics of Iran and America. I was surprised by his knowledge about the situations in Iran. He then started talking about his ancestors, his tribe, and his Indian heritage. He talked about Christopher Columbus; called him a gold digger and a cruel person. He mentioned that Columbus imprisoned and tortured Indians who approached his boat to welcome him and his crew, and took them as hostage so they could show him gold. "We gave him and his crewmen food, corn, fruits, and gold; he took us as hostage and slaves and killed so many of us," he said.

I was shocked to hear those words, as I had always envisioned Christopher Columbus as a religious man, an adventurer, and a hero. At this time, the teenager, who was probably fourteen or fifteen, showed up in the room, and I asked him, "What grade are you in?"

"I quit going to school."

"Why?"

The big guy interjected and said, "He used to get into fights with the kids at school all the time and never enjoyed going to school. Now I am home schooling him, as I have been home schooled myself by my parents."

"You mean you have never gone to school?" I asked.

He answered, "I couldn't go to school because I don't have a birth certificate and I am not a citizen of the United States of America, yet I am the real citizen of this land."

"But you are so knowledgeable," I said.

"Because I had excellent teachers; not only did they teach me how to read and write, they taught me how to make art crafts with clay and build houses with mud. That's how I make my living now. They also taught me the native language as well. I teach the same stuff to my nephew," he said, referring to the teenager. The girls showed up at the room and showed us some interesting family pictures.

It was late and time for us to leave. We shook hands good-bye. They asked us to come back again for a visit. It was a great adventure for me, and I wished I could go back to visit them. On our way to the door, everybody came to the door, including the old lady and the little kids, to say good-bye to us.

The big guy turned out to be such a great person. He was kind, respectful, peaceful, and truly a gentleman. I guess we were afraid of him at first because we had seen so many American- Indian movies back home in which Indians were always portrayed as the bad guys. After talking to this man, I personally felt that it was not only the academics that I should focus on, I needed to be educated socially and learn more about people of different races and different ethnicities.

Overall, that Thanksgiving break was adventurous for me, and I had a great time. It was great to see Reza after almost two years. The only thing missing was the turkey! Reza and I decided that we didn't want to bother going through the hassle of cooking the big bird, so we settled with chicken.

I came back to Fayetteville shortly after final exams started. Jassem and I were busy working and studying. In our spare time, other than doing laundry, we talked mostly about politics and the future of our country. We were hearing that sporadic fighting between anti-government forces and government soldiers had intensified in Iran. The news about Iran, the demonstrations by the Iranian students in all the universities in Iran, and the off-and-on strikes by the workers in the country were hot topics of the American media. Jassem and I went to the lobby of the dormitory to watch the news every evening religiously. Khomeini was becoming a celebrity in the media by appearing on TV almost every evening. He sent anti-Shah messages to the people of Iran from his exiled headquarter in Paris on an everyday basis. The newscasters interviewed Ibrahim Yazdi and Sadegh Ghotbzadeh, Khomeini supporters in the United States frequently. Most Iranians in the United States and Europe were concerned about the fate of their country. Jassem was somewhat inclined to support Islamic groups, and to some extent, he was favoring an Islamic establishment in Iran. However, he was reluctant to support Khomeini. I, on the other hand, while admiring Khomeini at the time for fighting against the oppressive regime, never favored an Islamic regime under the mullahs.

I asked Jassem once, "What is your reason for not supporting Khomeini? You want an Islamic government in Iran, don't you?"

"Islamic government yes, but not Khomeini," he responded.

"Why not?"

"You might laugh if I tell you this story," he said.

"I promise, I won't laugh at you," I said.

"A few weeks before I left Iran for the United States, I talked to a very trusted psychic in our town and asked him about the future of Iran," Jassem said. "The psychic said that the Shah will be gone and a *seyed* (descendents of Prophet Muhammad or 12 Imams) with a turban (a mullah) will take over and will brutally rule the country, and Iran will not be the same for years."

"First of all, I am not sure if Khomeini has any intention to rule the country. Secondly, he is a devout religious person; he will not be a brutal dictator," I said.

"Don't be naïve, Habib," Jassem said.

"Do you really believe in psychics?" I asked.

"Yes, I believe in this psychic. You would have believed him if you had gotten to know him," Jassem said. I laughed. Jassem turned to me and said, "Hey, you promised not to laugh."

"You are right; I am sorry," I said.

Jassem was correct; I was naïve. I could not have imagined that we would go from one form of dictatorship to another—much worse! I guess the psychic was also correct; Iran has not been the same ever since mullahs took over. The country has gone backward for years, and the hopes for a democratic establishment in Iran have been shattered. Nobody can predict what the future will hold, but one thing is for sure, the struggle for democracy will continue in Iran.

T E N

After the Thanksgiving break 1978, I had made up my mind to leave the
dormitory and move in with one of my friends, Davar, who had a vacant
room in his apartment. For the most part, it was convenient to live in a dorm—I
had a great time there and made good friends who made me laugh quite often—
but dormitory life was not for me.

It was a relief for me to have my own room and not be disturbed in the middle
of the night, sometimes by my roommate coming back from work or often by
some drunken students banging at our room and everybody else's in the dormitory. The apartment was located in a rundown part of Fayetteville and did not have
very good acoustic or thermal insulation system. My Nigerian next-door neighbor
and his girl friend would wake me up almost every night after coming back from
work near midnight—having a loud conversation, playing loud music, and then
going to bed. My bed and theirs were separated by a thin wall. They would talk to
each other for hours, and I could hear every word they said and every sound they
made—moaning, humming, joyful screaming—and I could imagine every move
they made, and then the snoring! It was becoming unbearable for me, so one night
I decided to sleep on the couch in the living room. In the morning, Davar wondered why I slept on the couch, and I told him the story. He suggested that I talk
to the guy. This Nigerian was such a nice person and a helpful neighbor; I didn't
think it was appropriate for me to even give him a hint. I got used to sleeping on
the couch, cold and not very comfortable, but peaceful!

The news about the riots and demonstrations in Iran was getting hotter by the
hour. The Nigerian neighbor and I would often get together and talk about politics
and the situations in our countries. Everywhere we went, there were talks about
the rise of a revolution in Iran. Every morning I would wake up to listen to the
morning news on ABC's *Good Morning America* with David Hartman and Nancy

195

Dussault (Sally Hill as a frequent substitute) or NBC's *Today* show with Tom Brokaw and Jane Pauley. Then I would get ready to go to school. At school, often students and faculty members asked me about the situations in Iran. It was hard to concentrate on my studies. Every evening we would be glued to TV watching the evening news, turning the channels from Frank Reynolds, Max Robinson, and Peter Jennings of ABC to Walter Cronkite of CBS to David Brinkley and John Chancellor of NBC. Sometimes almost the whole half an hour of the evening news would be focused on the people's struggles and uprisings in Iran.

During the Christmas break, I spent most of my time reading books and newspaper articles about Iran and followed the news, interviews, and documentaries regarding the situations in Iran on TV. The uprising by the students, including high school students, spread to the streets of Tehran and other cities in Iran. Strikes, struggles, demonstrations, and sporadic fighting intensified in almost every major city in Iran.

My friends and I in Fayetteville on one hand were concerned about family and friends back home; on the other hand, we thought we were getting closer to achieving victory against the tyranny and to achieving democracy! But were we?!

Iranians heard Khomeini's messages of hatred for the Shah and hopes for a victorious Islamic revolution on mainly the BBC radio and other international newscasts. His cassette tapes were distributed to the Iranian people on daily basis. His house in Najaf, Iraq became headquarters for his anti-Shah activities and the center of attention for the media, to the extent that he was forced to leave Iraq by the Iraqi government. He left Iraq for Kuwait on October 3, 1978,[89] but Kuwaiti officials denied him asylum at the Iraqi-Kuwaiti border. He eventually departed to France and settled in *Neauphle-le-Chateau,* a suburb of Paris. Khomeini became a celebrity in Paris, and his rented house became the focal point for his political showdowns against the Shah. His house in *Neauphle-le-Chateau,* not very far from the house of the well-known French bombshell movie star Brigitte Bardot, became the house of prayer for young and old Muslims and Mecca for journalists and broadcasters coming from across the world. In France, Khomeini was given access to numerous phone lines, from which he and his assistants could talk directly to his representatives in Iran. He did not have that luxury in Najaf. He also gained access to many different news agencies and the international press.

In Paris, Khomeini, during an interview with the CBS, announced that the riots would not subside unless the Shah's regime was gone and the Shah was put on trial for his crimes. In the meantime, almost all the factory workers, government

---

89   Most of the recorded dates in this book are taken from the book *Chronology of Iran (1896-1979)*, vol. 2, Bagher Agheli, Nashr-e Goftar, 1995. Some of the dates were found through a Google search.

employees, universities, and, most notably, oil refinery workers all over the country were on strike. Prime Minister Sharif Emami could not run the country under the harsh circumstances. He resigned on November 5, 1978, after being in power for only seventy days. Soon after the resignation, he fled the country.

After the resignation of Sharif Emami, the Shah formed a military government led by General Gholamreza Azhari on November 6, 1978. Immediately after forming the new government, the Shah appeared on TV and confessed to some mistakes, ignoring the will of the people, and mishandling of the country's wealth by the past governments. He tried to implore the people for mercy and pleaded to the people of Iran to give him more time in order to overcome past mistakes. That speech, unfortunately, did not help the Shah and was interpreted by the people as a sign of weakness, an admission of guilt, and an inability to control.

The shah's so-called most loyal friends left the country one after another and sneaked several million dollars of Iranian assets out of the country. His longest-running prime minister, Amir Abbas Hoveida, stayed and was arrested by the Azhari government for inflicting corruption while being the prime minister. Several other previous government authorities were arrested on charges of corruption or abusing power or obstruction of justice. These kinds of maneuvers did not help General Azhari, and he could not resist all the pressures. He was hospitalized following a heart attack. He then was flown out of the country for heart surgery. His government lasted for only forty-eight days.

In the meantime, the populist ayatollahs Taleghani and Montazeri, who had been released from prison after several years, resumed their political activities tirelessly. Ayatollah Montazeri left for Paris to visit with Khomeini, while the influential Ayatollah Taleghani masterminded several peaceful rallies and marches against the Shah's regime. Both ayatollahs announced their loyalties to Khomeini and demanded the lifting of martial law and the resignation of the Shah. They both favored establishment of the Islamic Republic under the leadership of Khomeini.

After the fall of General Azhari's government, the Shah met and consulted with some of his longtime foes, including Dr. Gholamhossein Saddighi, an associate and a big advocate of the late Dr. Mossadeq, and Dr. Karim Sanjabi, the head of the National Front. He offered the post of prime minister to each; they both refused. He then met with Dr. Shahpur Bakhtiar, also a longtime adversary of the Shah and the head of the opposition party, the Iran Party, and offered him the position of prime minister. Dr. Bakhtiar, who was also an active member of the National Front Party, accepted the position but asked the Shah to leave the country for an indefinite period. Following the acceptance of the post by Bakhtiar, he was expelled from the National Front and Iran parties. Immediately after the formation of the new government, Cyrus Vance, the secretary of state during President Carter's administration, recognized the new government in Iran and warned against any military coup.

Prime Minister Shahpur Bakhtiar, during a press conference, expressed the highlights of his policies as follows:[90]

"It is my hope and honor to welcome Mr. Khomeini back in Iran as soon as possible. The Shah will reign (the monarchy), but the government will rule. We will break ties with Israel and South Africa and stop selling oil to those countries. The elements of corruption in the previous government will be tried. SAVAK will be abolished. My government will promote Islam and Islamic values while respecting other religions. All the political prisoners will be freed. The curfew will be gradually lifted. Individual sovereignty of the people will be respected and political freedom will be granted to people. All political parties can resume their activities."

At the end of his speech, Mr. Bakhtiar read the following poem,

"I am a bird from the storm; I have no fear of the storm.
I am a wave; not a wave that escapes from the sea."[91]

These words would have been music to the ears of the Iranian people about a year before the revolution. Bakhtiar was too optimistic that his thirty years of anti-government activities and his struggle against the corruption of the Pahlavi regime would gain him the respect and trust of the people. He gained the support of some secularists and intelligentsia. However, the people of Iran, by a vast majority, were mesmerized and hypnotized by Khomeini's charisma and his bravery and would not settle for anybody else as their leader.

Khomeini and his supporters demanded the resignation of Shahpour Bakhtiar. Iranian people poured into the streets and chanted, *"Bakhtiar, nokar-e bee-ekhtiar,"* "Bakhtiar, a puppet with no power." On the other side, Bakhtiar's supporters, very few that he had, chanted, *"Bakhtiar, Bakhtiar Sangaretto Negahdar,"* "Bakhtiar, Bakhtiar, hold on to your trench."

Ayatollah Taleghani, who had become Khomeini's main associate in Iran, rejected Bakhtiar's government and announced that the only acceptable government is the one that is formed and led by Khomeini.

---

90   Translated from *Chronology of Iran (1896-1979)*, vol. 2, Bagher Agheli, Nashr-e Goftar Publishing, 1995, page 387.
91   Ibid, page 388.

During an interview by one of the French news agencies, Khomeini was quoted as saying, "Any interference by the Soviet Union will cause a global chaos, and Iran will not accept the Russian red flag."[92] In another interview, this time with the French newspaper, *Le Monde,* he expressed, "I will not accept the position as the president, nor will I ever accept any other governmental positions. I will only be a religious leader and continue to guide people as I have done in the past."[93]

In response to Khomeini's speech regarding the Soviet Union, *Pravda,* a leading Soviet newspaper, announced that Moscow did not intend to interfere with the internal political affairs in Iran. However, it warned Iran of a military coup d'état. There was some truth to this claim by the Russian newspaper, as rumor had it that four-star General Gholamali Oveisi tried to convince President Carter that the only solution to the crisis in Iran was to establish a military government. These rumors seemed more realistic when General Feraydoon Jam refused to be a member of Bakhtiar's cabinet, and when Khomeini alerted the people, of a military conspiracy. In addition, the rumors seemed more realistic when General Khosrodad made a threat to Bakhtiar that he would dig his own grave if he insisted on the Shah leaving the country. In the meantime, George Brown, the former foreign minister of the British government and the so-called mastermind of the military coup in Egypt,[94] arrived in Iran, which was another reason to believe that a military coup was about to occur.

The situation in Iran was out of control and somewhat explosive; all the schools, colleges, and universities were closed, and strikes and political unrest continued in almost all the cities and every corner of the country. Oil exporting, the most vital resource of the Iranian economy, was stopped, and the oil and gas distributions were not sufficient for internal consumption. Furthermore, a huge number of soldiers escaped from their military bases, smuggled guns and military ammunitions out, and distributed them to ordinary people. Most newspapers and media employees were on strike to protest censorship. Most government employees were also on strike. Almost all the internal and international flights to and out of Iran were stopped, because most of the pilots and airport employees were on strike as well. The future of our country was uncertain.

The tension between the United States and the Soviet Union over Iran was reaching a boiling point, and the two countries were accusing each other of trying

---

92 Translated from *Chronology of Iran (1896-1979),* vol. 2, Bagher Agheli, Nashr-e Goftar Publishing, 1995, page 388.

93 Translated from *Chronology of Iran (1896-1979),* vol. 2, Bagher Agheli, Nashr-e Goftar Publishing, 1995, page 389.

94. It is believed that it was George Brown who helped Jamal Abdul Nasser topple King Farouk through a military coup.

to take advantage of the turmoil and the unrest in Iran to their benefits. I was extremely worried that perhaps my motherland was going to be a battleground for the superpowers and was going to be tormented into pieces by the Russian, British, and American governments. I am certain that most other Iranians shared the same views as mine. We were fearful of a bloody takeover by the Communist groups as happened in Afghanistan by the People's Democratic Party of Afghanistan, PDPA, led by Nur Mohammad Taraki in 1978, and later by Babrak Karmal.

The crisis in Iran, Afghanistan, and South Africa, prompted a call for a conference by the leaders of the most powerful Western nations: President Carter of the United States, Valéry Giscard d'Estaing of France, Helmut Schmidt of Germany, and James Callahan of England. The conference was held in the first week of January 1979 in Guadalupe Island in France. The focus of the conference, however, was mainly Iran. In that conference, the participants decided that the Shah was no longer capable of sustaining power or his reign. They also decided that Khomeini, with the help of the National Front[95] and the Liberation Movement,[96] would be able to secure the interests of the West once the Shah was gone.

Khomeini fooled everyone, including the Western leaders of the time. He cut ties with the United States and intended to limit trades with some European countries until the war started between Iran and Iraq. The Western countries got what they wanted during the Iran-Iraq war: cheap oil and profits from selling weapons to both sides at inflated prices. Israel also benefited a great deal by selling weapons to Iran directly and indirectly.

General Gharabaghi, the chief commander of the army, air force, and navy at the time, during a press conference announced, "There will not be any military coup in Iran after the Shah leaves the country." He also mentioned that there would not be any military intervention in the formation of a new government. The general, in a way, was sending a signal to Khomeini that he was paving the way for his safe return to Iran.

---

95   The National Front was founded by Dr. Mossadeq in late 1940. The National Front was an official party in Iran and held power in the Parliament until the 1953 coup d'etat. It became an opposition force against the Shah's regime after the coup.

96   The Liberation Movement (the Freedom Movement) of Iran is a political organization founded in 1961 by Mehdi Bazargan, Mahmoud Taleghani, Ibrahim Yazdi, and Sadegh Ghotbzadeh. The main difference between the National Front and the Liberation Movement was that the National Front was a secularist party and the Freedom Movement was religious. During the revolution, the National Front and the Liberation Movement formed a coalition movement to fight against the tyranny. In 1981, after the Parliament passed the *qias,* or "eye for an eye," the National Front called for a national demonstration against the law. Khomeini outlawed the National Front Party, labeled it as apostate, and ordered the execution of the leaders of the party and anybody who was associated with the party. He demanded that the Freedom Movement disassociate itself from the National Front.

It was around one o'clock January 15, 1979, that the Shah and Empress Farah left the Mehrabad Airport for Cairo. At the airport, Prime Minister Bakhtiar and his bodyguards, General Gharabaghi, and some other high-ranking military officers were present. Moments before the Shah's departure, an army colonel of the elite Imperial Guard bent down, kissed the Shah's shoes, then his hand, and pleaded to him to come back. It was a moment of agony, sadness, affliction, and disbelief for many Iranians, while a vast majority celebrated the moment. The headlines of the *Kayhan* and *Ettellaat*, the prominent newspapers in Iran, boldly stated, *"Shah Raft!"*—"**The shah is Gone!**"

The next day people poured into the streets of Tehran and everywhere in the country, carrying the papers and celebrating the departure of the Shah.

I was alone at home watching the people's joyous moments of the departure of the "dictator" on TV. I was sad for not being with my fellow citizens to celebrate those historic moments. Despite the fact that we predicted and anticipated the fall of the Shah to happen any day, I felt heartbroken, and somewhat shocked that it actually happened and that I was not dreaming.

About an hour later, the doorbell rang; I was hoping that it wouldn't be my roommate to see my sad face. I didn't want him to think that I actually had feelings for the Shah. It was our next-door neighbor, the Nigerian guy. "Man, I am so happy for you and the people of Iran. He is finally gone," he said. "You don't seem to be happy; what is wrong?"

"I don't know what is wrong with me. I have a bad feeling that things are going to get worse. I don't think Shah's departure was going to be the end of the dictatorship in Iran." I said those pessimistic words, in contrary to my optimistic nature.

Yes, the Shah left, and took with him the peacock throne, two thousand five hundred years of kingship, and some of the past pride of Iranians.

ELEVEN

The next evening after my classes, I went to the student union and met a bunch of friends there. The Iranian students were happy for the Shah's departure, or maybe pretended to be happy. They were shaking hands and extending congratulations to each other. Mahdad showed up with his famous big smile, and we were all happy to see him after a long time. He then so calmly and gently asked, "Is it true that Prime Minister Hoveida is gone?" We all started laughing, and he was laughing with us. He then paused for a moment and repeated his question: "Is it really true?"

One of the kids turned to him and said, "You've got to be kidding."

Another fellow said, "You don't live in this world, do you?"

Another guy asked, "Mahdad, are you stoned?"

Another explained, "After Hoveida, we had several other prime ministers who are also gone. Not only are all the butlers gone, the big devil is gone, too. Don't you know that?"

"What do you mean by that?" Mahdad asked.

"The shah is gone," we all said.

"Is he really gone? Is he gone for good?" he asked.

He was shocked and couldn't believe it. His big smile all of a sudden turned sour, and I could see agonizing facial expressions in him. The group dispersed, and I went to him to thank him again for letting me stay in his house. I asked him, "Are you all right?"

He turned to me and said, "I am not sure how I feel, but I am afraid that we are headed for more disastrous moments in our history."

In Iran, Mehrabad Airport was seized by the tanks and soldiers, and all the international airliners were warned against travelling to Iran. During a French radio interview, Bakhtiar announced, "It is too soon for the ayatollah's return. He must give me a chance to make arrangements for his safe return." He added, "We are in contact with the ayatollah in this regard."

Khomeini, in response to a rumor that he was secretly coming to terms with Bakhtiar, denied such secret dealings and asked for his resignation. Bakhtiar responded: "Mr. Khomeini is free to come back, but I will not resign under any circumstances." Khomeini then sent harsh and uncompromising messages to Iran asking the people to revolt against the treasonous Bakhtiar. He also demanded that the Shah must return the assets of the Iranian people back to people. He also demanded that the Shah must be returned to Iran to be put on trial.

Karim Sanjabi and Mehdi Bazargan, whose names were mentioned in the media as possible prime ministers of the provisional government, separately criticized Bakhtiar for closing the airports and urged him to lift the seizure of all airports in order to avoid civil war. In the meantime, the streets of Tehran were seized by the students; they were fighting the army—first with rocks, Molotov cocktails, and small grenades, and later, as soldiers gradually joined the people and disobeyed their superiors, ordinary people carried guns and other heavy artilleries. Tehran was becoming a city of war; sandbags were everywhere, many ordinary people, and young and old, were carrying machine guns—they were determined to fight to their last drop of blood.

Sadegh Ghotbzadeh, who became the interpreter, spokesperson, and aide to Khomeini in Paris, quoted Khomeini as saying, "Newspapers must be at the liberty of writing whatever they want, the movie theatres will not be closed, and all the political parties, including Marxist organizations, will be free to continue their functionalities." In addition, Khomeini, in his very last interview before his departure from Paris, mentioned, "We will establish a government based on the will and desire of the people. The people have already spoken; they did not want the Shah and his appointees to rule any longer. We are not against civil liberty, nor are we against modernization of the country; we are against the Shah's version of modernization and his conduct. Under his ruling, the movie theatres were being misused to promote prostitution and corruption. He increased the prostitution centers, and he provided the means of drug addiction for the youth." In another interview, Khomeini mentioned, "In an Islamic government, there won't be a place for dictatorship. Freedom will be granted to people and the economy will be repaired under the Islamic regime."

Finally, under tremendous pressure and after days of street fights between people and the army, Bakhtiar's government had no choice but to open the airports. With the opening of the airports, almost 40,000 Americans who still lived in Iran and did not feel safe any longer left Iran. It was decided that on

January 31, Khomeini would leave France for Tehran. A huge number of Iranians planned to travel to Tehran from every corner of the country to welcome their religious leader. Tehran became overly crowded. People were all united, sharing foods, drinks, blankets, and so on. It was a cold day on February 1, 1979, when millions of Iranians impatiently waited for the arrival of the Air France 747 at Mehrabad Airport. Peter Jennings was reporting live from Tehran. Most Iranians in Fayetteville boycotted classes that day. We were all worried that some lunatic air force officers loyal to the Shah might blow up the airplane bearing the seventy-eight-year-old leader into pieces. It was a moment of joy, excitement, anxiety, and somewhat fear for many Iranians. The streets of Tehran were jampacked with people. People were chanting, *"Allah-u-akbar, Khomeini rahbar,"* "God is great, Khomeini is the leader." It was estimated that the line of people waiting for Khomeini's arrival was almost twenty miles long. The Air France jet finally touched down around 9:30 in the morning. Khomeini returned to Iran after fifteen years in exile. No incident occurred. It was a historic moment for all Iranians who thought their long struggle for democracy was over!

I had no idea where my brothers were, whether they had survived the street fighting or not. I only knew that my brothers Nasser and Ahmad were away from home for a few days and nobody knew where they were. I was extremely worried about them. After many unsuccessful attempts to call back home, I managed to get through one day. I called a neighbor and requested to talk to my mother. My parents both came to the phone. I was assured that both Nasser and Ahmad were okay and they finally came home. My father sounded very happy and excited about the future of Iran. He enthusiastically talked about the revolution and said, "Son, your wish and your prediction came true; the tyrant regime is gone. Under Khomeini's leadership, we will never go wrong."

"I hope so," I replied. I was surprised to notice a big shift in my father's line of thinking. Later on, during one of my visits back home, I asked my father, "What made you change your mind about the Shah?"

"Son, I have not changed my mind about the Shah; he was a good man and a real patriot. He surrounded himself by corrupt people, his regime was corrupt, and he was not aware of all the un-Islamic conducts of his government."

Khomeini's arrival in Iran on February 1, 1979, was broadcast live by the national Iranian TV, and worldwide, while the national Iranian radio refused to do so. However, Iranian national TV broadcast the event for only twenty minutes and suddenly stopped. That angered many Iranians to the extent that many of them broke their TVs. After a short speech in Mehrabad Airport, Khomeini was escorted to the well-known Behesht-e-Zahra Cemetery, where he delivered a fiery speech against the Shah and the government of Shahpur Bakhtiar. An interesting thing that happened inside the airplane before reaching the Iranian territory was Khomeini's response to one of the foreign correspondents, who asked him, "How do you feel about going back home after almost fifteen years in exile?"

"*Hitchi*, nothing!" Khomeini responded. Ghotbzadeh was sitting next to him and translating. He repeated the question to Khomeini in Farsi and his response was the same, "*Hitchi*, nothing!"

Finally, Ghotbzadeh turned to the reporter and said, "He does not want to make any comments." To this day, it is puzzling to many Iranians including his biggest advocates, as to why he made such an abrupt statement. I expected him to say, "I have feelings of joy, pride, anxiousness, mirth, the love for my country, the love for my people, sorrow for the loss of lives, I can't wait, and things of this nature." At the least, I expected him to say it was an indescribable feeling.

I had heard comments like "Oh, he was being cautious," or "Khomeini was not a sentimental person," or "Maybe he was shying away from the camera," which to me is not at all acceptable because Khomeini by no means was a shy person.

Some people interpret his "*Hitchi*" response as his true feeling—a lack of any feelings for the people of Iran, resentment, revenge against the nation, or just settling a score against the Shah, and nothing else.

In Behesht-e-Zahra Cemetery, Khomeini made a long speech, some of which is worth mentioning: "The Pahlavi regime was illegal from the first day it was established. Those who are in my age group have observed that the parliament originally was instituted by force of javelins, not by the vote of the people. The representatives of the parliament were forced to vote for monarchy and Reza Khan as the king—the first king of the Pahlavi Dynasty. Hence, the monarchy was illegal from the beginning, and the monarchy regime was injudicious and in violation of human rights. Let us suppose that people voted for a person to be the king fifty years ago; what rights did those people have to decide about the destiny of the future generations by voting the king's descendants to be the future kings? What rights and qualifications did Mohammad Reza have (to be the king)? People of the past generation had no rights to determine the destiny of the people of this time. The people now want to be in control of their own destiny and they voted no to monarchy." He continued, "I will slap across the face of this government. And with the support of the Iranian people, I will appoint a government."[97]

---

97   Translated from *Chronology of Iran (1896-1979)*, vol. 2, page 354, Bagher Agheli, Nashr-e Goftar Publishing, 1995, page 469. It was hard to translate Khomeini's speech, as he did not speak Farsi with proper grammar.

A few days after that speech, Khomeini appointed his provisional revolutionary government with Mehdi Bazargan as its first prime minister. A power struggle started between the two governments—one official, the other de facto—which eventually resulted in surrendering of the Shah's military to Khomeini's provisional revolutionary government.

Khomeini denounced the monarchy as illegal but his *"velayat-e-faghih"* was declared as legal! Where is Khomeini today to see that his doctrine of *velayat-e-faghih* has drawn many youths including teenagers under the age of eighteen to drugs and prostitution, a higher percentage than ever before in Iranian history? Where is Khomeini today to see that the civil liberty is virtually nonexistent in Iran? Where is Khomeini today to see that his current *vali-e-faghih,* supreme leader is the most brutal dictator on the face of the earth? Where is Khomeini today to see that his *velayat-e-faghih* is far from Islamic values and has done the most damage to Islam and Iran? Where is Khomeini today to see that the economy is a sham and, for over three decades, nothing has been done about it other than making the rich richer, destroying the middle class, and expanding poverty and starvation? Where is Khomeini today to see that his Basij army, under the direct order of his *valy-e-faghih*, "supreme leader," is brutally murdering our young brothers and sisters for rallying peaceful demonstrations? Where is Khomeini today to see that currently in Iran, air pollution and contaminated water are the worst in the world and killing people of Iran more than any time in the history.

Shahpur Bakhtiar's government collapsed and he went into hiding. A few days later, he fled to Paris.[98] Bakhtiar was the last prime minister of the Shah, and his government lasted for about six weeks. Yes he was a wave all right, as he claimed when he first became the prime minister, but he had no choice but to escape the sea.

---

98   Mackey, *The Iranians: Persia, Islam, and the Soul of a Nation,* page 285.

TWELVE

In the spring semester 1979, I got my wish when Dr. Akin was so kind as to assign an important engineering course, Statics, for me to teach. I was determined to do a good job and leave a good impression. Unfortunately, the news about Iran, the threats of confrontation between the United States and the Soviet Union over Persian Gulf domination, and possible annihilation of Iran was distracting. It was hard for most Iranian students to ignore the news and focus on their studies. In that particular semester, I was taking two courses, teaching a difficult course, and working on my thesis.

The provisional government of Prime Minister Bazargan was practically inefficient. He was a religious man and a peaceful person. He was not a shrewd politician. He lacked charisma and decisiveness. He could not make any decision of his own. Khomeini was the ultimate decision maker. He overruled most of Bazargan's decisions.

Khomeini in exile on many occasions had announced that he had no aspiration to be the ruler and had advised the rest of the mullahs to avoid high-ranking government positions. However, he did not keep his promises and was indeed the man in charge from day one after the establishment of the provisional government.

He ruled from the very first days. For example, about a month after his arrival, he literally waged a war against women.[99] He fired all the female judges and announced that women were not allowed to become judges any longer. Women were forced to wear a head-to-toe covering, the so-called *hejab*.[100] He segregated boys and girls in the elementary, middle, and high schools.[101] He ordered segregation of men and women in public, for instance, men and women were not allowed

99   Azar Nafisi, *"Reading Lolita in Tehran,"* Random House, 2004, Page 111.
100   The hejab was mandatory before Reza Shah became the king. Reza Shah removed the hejab and encouraged women to be productive members of the society.
101   It wasn't too long ago that Mohammad Reza Shah had integrated all the school systems.

to sit next to each other on the buses,[102] not even husbands and wives. As stupid as it sounds, husbands did not side with their wives, nor did brothers with their sisters, when women voiced their opposition against Khomeini's chauvinistic ruling through demonstrations. He crushed the demonstrations of the women, not only by using force against them but also by polarizing men and women on the issue. Men, mainly fanatics and members of Khomeini's *Komiteh*,[103] demonstrated against the women in support of Khomeini's order. The Komiteh members poured into the streets of Tehran, chanting, *"ya roosari, ya toosari,"* "either head scarf or bop on the head." I had heard so many stories about Khomeini supporters pouring acid on the faces of women who violated his orders on hejab.

Khomeini banned the nightclubs, alcoholic beverages, and casinos. He closed every newspaper that opposed his harsh ruling. He declared music as being one of the causes of corruption and banned all kinds of music on radio and TV. For a long time, radio and TV were playing only classical music. Rumor has it that one day a foreign reporter asked Khomeini, "If music brings corruption, why do you allow classical music by Beethoven, Mozart, Bach, Tchaikovsky, and so on?"

Khomeini turned to his interpreter and asked, "Who the heck are those people?"

"Those people were classical musicians," the interpreter replied. He ordered to ban those kinds of music as well.

Khomeini and his disciples formed the Revolutionary Council and Revolutionary Guards. Then the bloodbath by the Khomeini regime started. The Revolutionary Council issued the execution orders, and the Revolutionary Guards executed people. Many of the Shah's cabinet members, military generals, and his friends were executed without trials.

To this day, the bravery of two of the Shah's generals is talked about by everyone: General Mehdi Rahimi and General Nader Jahanbani. They both died heroically for what they believed in without bowing to the Islamic Republic.

While many military personnel and generals recanted during harsh interrogations and torture by some criminal elements of the provisional government, General Rahimi chose not to dishonor himself. The infamous Khalkhali, "the hanging judge," was the chief interrogator and the head of the "Revolutionary

---

102 Years after the revolution, the Islamic Republic designed buses made of two doors; men enter through one of the doors, and women through another.

103 *Komiteh* means "committee." During the revolution, Khomeini's disciples organized committees of mostly young people, blue-collar workers, and volunteers to be on the front lines of all the anti-Shah demonstrations. Immediately after the revolution, these committees were turned into rival authorities to the police. The intelligent members of these committees soon separated themselves from the rest. The remaining were mostly illiterate and from lower-class parts of Tehran and other rural parts of Iran, and they imposed Khomeini's orders through violence and force. These committee members later on turned to basijies.

Court." One of the interrogators of General Rahimi was Dr. Ibrahim Yazdi. He asked the general, "Who do you recognize as your commander–in-chief now?" he firmly replied, "His Majesty the Shah is my commander-in-chief." He continued, "I am an elite Imperial Guard. I have sworn allegiance to the Shah and the constitution, and I will never back down on it." Moments before his execution on February 15, 1979, General Rahimi shouted, *"Javid Shah,* Long Live the Shah." Even Khomeini is quoted as admiring Rahimi's bravery.

General Jahanbani, one of the most prominent air force generals—I knew one of his nephews as a classmate in high school—was another heroic figure after the Shah left. He was known in the air force as the blue-eyed general. He was well known as a very honorable air force general. I recall from high school years that General's very funny and humorous nephew described him as a patriotic, composed, decisive, athletic, serious, and very conscientious person. In fact, a few months before the revolution, he had become the head of sports and physical education. During his fake trial, General Jahanbani was charged as being a CIA spy and an element of Zionism.[104] Their rationale was that he lived in the United States for a few years. The court also accused General's father of being a Russian spy. Furthermore, he was accused of being the commander of the operation against the pro-Islamic Republic groups.[105]

In response to Khalkhali's question asking the General whether he wanted to defend himself or not, General Jahanbani firmly responded, "The charges are ridiculous, stupid, and baseless. They are not worth defending." He continued, saying, "However, it is obvious from your lies that a verdict has already been rendered against me. You people are not true believers of Islam; you are a bunch of traitors, anti-religious, and mercenaries. You are a bunch of despicable people who have been ordered by your masters to destroy the true army of this country and to destroy my beloved land." He went on further to say, "My father was not a Russian spy; he was an Iranian army officer who studied in Russia. I was not an element of any foreign national either, but an air force officer who was being trained in America and was chosen as one of the best pilots while you despicable and treasonous mullahs were going door to door and from one mosque to another, repeating stories about Imam Hussein's head for a slice of bread. How dare you accuse me of treason? These past few months I have been training the body and soul of the youth in this country by providing and purchasing sports facilities. I have had no role in suppressing people. You ought to be ashamed of yourselves for making false accusations. Who do you think you all are? You are all a bunch

---

104 *Pajouhesh* magazine, No. 105, Spring 2009, page 39.
105 Ibid.

of hostile occupiers, bloodthirsty and anti-human, who are destined to destroy this nation and all Iranians. I have nothing further to say in my defense. Go ahead and don't delay any further; obey the orders of your masters. But rest assured that Iranian people will one day wake up from their deep sleep; they will come to know your true colors much sooner than you think and will annihilate your oppressive and inhumane regime."

Many other generals, military officers, and government affiliates were murdered by Khomeini's regime. Former Prime Minister Hoveida was also murdered, not via execution, but by a mullah who pulled a pistol from under his cloak and shot the former prime minister twice in his neck during a court recess. This inhumane act of the mullah who murdered the former prime minister was never condemned by the regime. For years, the regime covered up for that mullah, and people were under the assumption that the prime minister was executed. That mullah was not tried for his crime and he is still walking freely on the streets of Tehran. Khomeini then started cracking down on non-Islamic government associates. He ordered all non-Muslim forces to be removed from the military, judiciary, and educational system. Following that order the government executed many non-Muslim leaders and non-Muslim entrepreneurs, and confiscated their wealth. The wave of executions in Iran angered many Iranians and international communities. Khomeini dismissed all the internal and international demonstrations for human rights violations by declaring: "criminals must be executed without trials." The provisional Prime Minister, Mr. Mehdi Bazargan, was not at all happy with the situation and pleaded to Khomeini and other influential clerics to end the bloodshed. The executions continued. Khalkhali, the man who was known as a person who took joy to strangle cats in his youth, took so much joy in executing people without trial.

On March 30, 1979, Khomeini called for a referendum to say either "Yes" or "No" to the establishment of the "Islamic Republic" without educating people or describing what Islamic Republic was all about. What was it that the people were voting for? The answer was unknown. "Islamic Republic" was undefined. Prime Minister Bazargan, many of the intelligentsia, and some moderate mullahs argued that the referendum should be based on two choices, either "Religious" or "Secular." Khomeini adamantly refused. That added to Mr. Bazargan's dismay and disappointment with Khomeini's abrupt decisions. People went to the polls and voted yes to the Islamic Republic. They voted yes to the undefined Islamic Republic before the constitution was written. They thought they were voting for Islam. They had no idea that they were voting for a different form of dictatorship.

Ayatollah Taleghani was not very happy with Khomeini's decision either. He was upset with the vicious executions of people without trial. He made a speech in April 1979 and warned that Iran was going back to the dictatorship. Soon after Taleghani's speech, the Revolutionary Guards arrested his Marxist son, and Ayatollah Taleghani went into hiding. That angered many Taleghani supporters, who went to the streets of Tehran and chanted, "Taleghani, you are the soul of the revolution," and "Down with the reactionaries."[106] Later on, Khomeini summoned Ayatollah Taleghani to his headquarter in Qom and expressed his displeasure on Ayatollah Taleghani's actions. Immediately after, Khomeini, in a press release, disrespectfully referred to Ayatollah Taleghani as Mr. Taleghani. He declared that Mr. Taleghani was with him.

Personally, I don't think that Ayatollah Taleghani came to a compromise with Khomeini. It was early into the revolution, and Ayatollah Taleghani did not want to cause any clashes between his supporters and those of Khomeini's. He, therefore, kept his calm and acted as a peacemaker between Khomeini and the Kurds and between the left and right wings until he suddenly died on September 9, 1979. His death ended the hopes of the people to have a more humanistic and a more civilized government.

It didn't take too long for the Iranian people to realize that they were fooled by Khomeini. Prior to and during the 1979 revolution in Iran, a vast majority of Iranians embraced Islam as a way of fighting the Shah's regime. They embraced the mullahs as their spokespersons. Clerics were well respected by intellectuals, different opposition groups, and most people in Iran. They all had one common goal: to get rid of the tyranny and replace it with democracy. Unfortunately, Khomeini and his circle of disciples hijacked the democratic movement and the people's revolution and replaced it with one of the darkest and the most brutal dictatorship in the modern era. Not only did they hijack the revolution, they hijacked the peaceful, divine, soothing, and uplifting religion of the people by replacing it with fanaticism, radicalism, extremism, and terrorism. Yes, they hijacked Islam in Iran as well. General Jahanbani was correct when he referred to mullahs as not being true believers of Islam. True spiritual and religious leaders don't kill under the name of religion!

I want to emphasize here that it is the "mullah-ism" that I oppose, not all the "mullahs." By the word "mullah-ism," I mean reactionaries; those who belong to organized profiting religious groups and organizations, those who claim that only mullahs are the moral authorities, and those who claim that only their religion is the true religion and the rest should be wiped out. I also mean those who claim

---

106 Sandra Mackey, *The Iranians: Persia, Islam and the Soul of a Nation* ((New York: Dutton, 1996), page 291.

religion and government are inseparable. To me there is no difference between these groups of people and the Nazis. Both groups are hate mongers and racists.

I look at mullahs as individuals. Today in Iran, there are many mullahs who work hard like the vast majority of Iranians to bring food to the table. Many of them suffer the current circumstances in Iran. Many of them oppose the brutal ruling of the current regime. Some of them have joined the people in their quest for freedom and justice. Ayatolloh Taleghani realized from day one that the whole establishment of the Islamic Republic was headed for dictatorship and corruption. Unfortunately, his short-lived life after the revolution was a misfortune for the Iranian people but a blessing for stakeholders of the Islamic Republic. In my opinion, had he been alive, he would have continued fighting for democracy. He would not have been a follower of Khomeini; he would have followed his dreams of ultimate justice and freedom for Iranian people. Ayatollah Montazeri was one of those very few mullahs who separated himself from the Islamic Republic the moment he realized that the regime had become totalitarian. He realized from early on that the path that Khomeini and his disciples were spearheading was not what he was teaching and preaching for years. He stood firm to Khomeini and opposed his authoritarian ruling in spite of the fact that he was chosen as the heir to Khomeini. He fought the previous regime for injustice and went to prison for years, and he opted to continue fighting for his principles rather than becoming the next *velayat-e-faghih* for an un-Islamic "Islamic Republic." He chose to be under house arrest for the rest of his life rather than bowing to Khomeini's ferocious ruling. He chose to distance himself from the corrupt leaders of the Islamic Republic rather than becoming filthy rich like the current supreme leader and his butlers.

Islam in Arabic has multiple meanings, such as peace, purity, submission to God, salvation, and reconciliation. A true Muslim leader, in my opinion, is the one who conveys the messages that imply the true meanings of Islam. A true religious, spiritual, or government leader is the one who believes in pluralism; the one who believes in creating a peaceful society encompassing all three monotheistic faiths as well as all other divine faiths, in which the sovereignty and beliefs of every member of that society would be respected. When Shiism became the official religion in Iran during the Safavid Dynasty (1502-1722), it was marked by pluralism and diversity.[107] The Islamic Republic is not following any of these principles.

All three monotheistic religions—Jews, Christians, and Muslims—trace their beliefs back to Ibrahim (Abraham) and worship the same God—the God of Ibrahim. They believe in the same God but they don't tolerate each other's points

107   Ray Takeyh, *Guardians of the Revolution* (New York: Oxford University Press USA, 2009), page 17.

of view! They believe in the same God but they are not at the liberty of switching from one Ibrahamite religion to another! People of Iran don't have the right to change religion. They will be labeled as "apostates" and according to the rules of the Islamic Republic; anybody who apostatizes will be sentenced to death.

Today many Christians, Jews, Zoroastrians, and Baha'is live in Iran and love their country. Many of them opted to stay in Iran and live under the discriminatory and harsh ruling of the mullahs while a huge number of them fled the country. Many Iranian Jews who fled to Israel after the revolution and became citizens of Israel still consider themselves as Iranians and are proud of their heritage and their ancestors. Of all the minorities, Baha'is have been scrutinized and terrorized the most by the thugs of the Islamic Republic, especially under Ahmadinejad. Many of these non-Muslim people are more patriotic than the leaders of the Islamic Republic, and yet they are not allowed to serve their own country. Under the Islamic Republic, only Muslims (believers of Islamic Republic, not true Islam) have the right to become president, vice president, ministers, parliamentarians, CEOs, military and police officers, and so on. The Islamic Republic in Iran is not based on the true meaning of Islam, but based on bigotry and violence.

In addition to bigotry against minorities, today the war against women which started by Ayatollah Khomeini continues. Women are subject to more violence, more sexual discrimination, and more discriminatory Penal Codes. In an article by Ms. Zohreh Arshadi, a former practicing lawyer in Iran who is now exiled in France, she states:[108]

> "The theoretical foundation of the Islamic Penal Codes is a social model based on sexual apartheid. The chief elements of this model are first: a belief that women are deficient in their natural and "innate" potentials and abilities, including their psychological-makeup and intellectual capacity. Second, a belief in a social and family order where men must be guardians over women, and women must submit. Third, a belief in an unequal system of rights and consequently, wherever the question of the reproduction of such an order is concerned, of a system of punishment that is also unequal."

In another part of the article she writes:

> "These are laws which in their entirety are more in keeping with a society still in the age of barbarism. At a time when most countries

---

108 Islamic Republic of Iran and Penal codes – Restructuring society on the basis of violence and sexual apartheid, by Zohreh Arshadi. This article is found in the following web page: www.Iran-bulletin.org/political_islam/punishment.html.

are banning the death penalty to have punishments such as cutting of
hands, and feet, stoning to death, cutting off of tongues and gouging
out eyes on the statutes is totally unacceptable."

Such discriminatory laws and violence against women especially stoning women to death increased under Khamenei-Ahmadinejad duo ruling. That
reminds me of the story of the woman, caught in an act of adultery, during the
time of Jesus; she was sentenced to death by stoning. Following a confrontation
between Jesus and a crowd of Pharisees and Scribes[109] over the fate of the woman,
Jesus stated, "Whichever one of you who committed no sin may throw the first
stone at her." This statement by Jesus put everyone in the crowd to shame, and
resulted in the aversion of the execution.

I don't think the statement by Jesus who condemned stoning people to death
almost 2000 years ago put the sinners like Khamenei, Ahmadinejad, and the rest
of the criminals of the Islamic Republic to shame in this modern era, but it might
have contributed to the aversion of the execution by stoning of an Iranian woman
convicted of adultery and murder, at least temporarily. Her case received a world-
wide attention, and leaders of the free world demanded to halt stoning her to
death. Perhaps the statement by Jesus awakened the whole world of the criminal
and barbarianism acts of the current Iranian regime in the 21st Century.

---

109 Definition given by Britanica online: "In the 1st century, scribes and Pharisees were two largely distinct
groups, though presumably some scribes were Pharisees. Scribes had knowledge of the law and could draft legal
documents (contracts for marriage, divorce, loans, inheritance, mortgages, the sale of land, and the like). Every
village had at least one scribe. Pharisees were members of a party that believed in resurrection and in following
legal traditions that were ascribed not to the Bible but to 'the traditions of the fathers.'"

THIRTEEN

After the revolution, many Iranian students living in the United States were struggling for money. Many of them depended on money coming from back home. They were not receiving a penny from home, or they had to wait for a long time to receive some, because of the new restrictions and regulations of the provisional government.

Most other Iranian people in the United States felt humiliated for the unnecessary anti-American government demonstrations orchestrated by the Iranian government on the streets of Tehran and other major cities in Iran. The demonstrators, often would burn the American flag in front of the cameras, and shout, "Death to America." The American media broadcast those kinds of government orchestrated demonstrations almost every day, while most Iranians inside and outside Iran were opposed to flag burning and death to America slogans.

I lived in a small apartment very close to our school. I was teaching an early-morning class and walked to school every morning. There was an older fellow in the neighborhood who used to go for a walk around the same time I did. He would often stop me along the way and would speak about different subjects and especially about politics. The political news about Iran was hot those days. He would mostly talk about Iran and complain against the "savagery" of the Iranian people who were burning American flags in Tehran. He believed that Iranians who lived in the United States should all be kicked out. I would just listen and wouldn't make any comments for the most part. One day on my way to class, he asked me where I was from, and I said Iran. He paused for a moment and then said, "Why don't you go back to your damned country?"

"Sir, I have a class to teach in a few minutes; I will think about it after my class," I said. I told that story to my students that morning, and they all laughed. The old fellow stopped talking to me after that. I liked the man. He was fun to talk to. I saw him in the mornings occasionally and would wave at him, but he wouldn't wave back at me.

During the summers, I was on my own. I only had a teaching assistantship during regular semesters. I had no choice but to work during summers. The summer of 1979 was very adventurous for me.

I found a job as a cook and in a newly built Mexican restaurant, which was within a walking distance from my house. Two people, Harry and Jerry, co-owned the restaurant. Harry was too serious; he was difficult to deal with and hard to please, but Jerry and his wife and their two cute daughters were very pleasant. They were nice to the workers. I was working four or five days a week in that restaurant while taking a graduate course and working on my master's thesis. The food in that restaurant was excellent, and it quickly became very popular in town. Weekends were extremely busy, and Harry would most frequently come to the kitchen and would yell at everyone. I found a good friend there, by the name of Gene, who was hard working and very honest. Gene and I got along very well and became fast friends. Harry put us both in charge of cleaning after dinner and in charge of closing the restaurant. Late one evening, after everybody was gone, Gene and I were very busy washing dishes, sweeping, and mopping the floors when someone knocked on the kitchen door. I thought it was one of the boys or girls who had come to keep us company. I opened the door halfway; I notice a huge guy who tried to force himself into the restaurant. I tried to close the door on him, but I couldn't. I called Gene for help. We both pushed the door, but we could not overpower him. Gene quickly grabbed a frying pan and whispered to me to let go of the door. I did, and the guy came in. Gene hit him hard on his head with the frying pan. He got dizzy and started tottering. He was stinky as if he had not bathed for days, and we could smell the alcohol coming from him. We then each grabbed one of his hands and took him back to the heavy kitchen door, held the door, and pushed him out the door. We were both scared that he might have had a gun. He started yelling, and a few minutes later, he appeared at the front door. Luckily, the door was locked. Gene went to the phone and called the police. He could see us through the window. I told him that the cops would be there any moment. He was drunk and out of control. By the time the cops arrived, he was gone.

That incident secured a strong bond between Gene and me at work. We both worked hard and took our jobs very seriously. We gained the respect of everyone at work, which included all the workers and Jerry and his family. Harry, on the other hand, had a very rough personality and hardly ever smiled. He never appreciated our hard work. One evening during a weeknight, everyone in the kitchen was sweating and working nonstop. Harry came to the kitchen and started yelling and cussing at everybody. He had done that a few times before. I ignored him and turned my back to him every time he came to the kitchen in a rotten mood, but I ran out of patience that evening. I got very upset. I took my apron off, threw it down, and turned to Gene and said, "I can't take this anymore. I am not going to work for this mad bully anymore." I started walking out.

Gene said, "If Habib is not working here, I am not going to work here either." As we walked a few feet away from the restaurant, Jerry, his wife, and his daughters ran to us begging us to come back to work. Gene and I imposed a condition that we would come back to work if Harry promised not to come back to the kitchen. Jerry and his family assured us of that. Had it not been for my respect for Jerry and his family, I would not have gone back. When we went back to the kitchen, every worker there clapped for us. We were told that every one of them was getting ready to walk out.

Harry never showed up at the kitchen for as long as I was working in that restaurant. Jerry and his family showed up in the kitchen occasionally and gave us each a pat on the back. Not only were they good to us, they were great with customers as well. Gene and I made the kitchen very organized and made sure that everyone worked hard and had fun in the kitchen. Harry and Jerry had different styles in management, and I found Jerry's style much more humanistic and effective. I vowed to myself that if I ever became a manager, I would follow Jerry's style.

That summer I bought my very first car, a used Toyota Corolla for about $600. It was not the best-looking car, but it was decent and ran well. I was tired of living in rundown apartments, and since I had a car, I looked for a better apartment. I heard that two Persian guys were looking for a third roommate in a two-bedroom apartment to share the expenses. The apartment was located in a better part of the town. I paid them a visit and I liked their apartment. They offered me the smaller bedroom while they shared the bigger one. A few weeks later, I met the Hendricks family, who had recently moved to Fayetteville. They had temporarily rented a three-bedroom apartment next to ours with four children. Their oldest child was Lisa. One evening on my day off, Lisa stopped by our apartment and one of my roommates introduced us. She cooked for us that evening. The food was good, but having her as company was much better. Lisa was a good-looking girl, extremely charming, and friendly. We ate dinner, we played cards, and then she asked me to go for a walk. The very first question she asked me was, "You are hardly ever at home; do you have a girlfriend?"

"No, I don't have a girlfriend, I just get up early to go to school, work in the evenings, and come home late. I don't have time for social life," I said.

Lisa and I developed friendly relationship. She came to our apartment very often. We cooked together, washed dishes together, and played card games. One day, Lisa told me, "I am engaged, you know, but if I feel that there is a future between you and me, I will leave him," she said.

"What kind of future are you talking about?" I asked.

"I mean marriage," she said.

I was surprised that she made sort of a marriage proposal within the first few weeks of our acquaintance. I asked her, "How old are you?"

"I am seventeen," she said.

"I am twenty-seven," I said. "You are not even of legal age yet."

I found Lisa to be blunt, honest, strong-minded, and straightforward. She would never hide her feelings. One day she asked me for a dinner date. I accepted. We set a date for an evening. That evening I asked her where she wanted to go. "I just want to be with you. I don't care where we go," she said. "Let's go to McDonald's."

"I can afford taking you to a more expensive place," I said.

She insisted on McDonald's, and that was okay with me. After dinner, I suggested that we go see a movie or have an ice cream. She said, "I don't want you to spend your money on me. I just want you to keep me company."

I was impressed. She gave me the impression that she was not a gold digger, and I thought that she behaved more maturely than others did of her age groups. However, I didn't want to get intimate with her for two main reasons: first, because she was underage, and second, because she was still engaged.

Later on I heard from a mutual friend that Lisa broke her engagement and made a statement to our mutual friend that "I will one day marry that guy (referring to me)." When I heard that statement, I laughed and said, "I have no intention to get married any time soon."

Lisa and I became very good friends. In fact, I felt privileged to have become a friend of the family. Lisa's mother, Linda, was a kind person and a good cook who would often invite me to their house for lunch or dinner. Lisa's father, Ramon, was also a kind person with a great sense of humor. He was a great handyman. He knew so much about cars and could fix everything around the house. I remember that my Toyota had a broken window on the driver's side and I was too busy to fix it. One early morning on a weekend, Ramon knocked on my apartment and asked me for my car key. I gave it to him and went back to sleep. He gave my car key back to me a few hours later. When I went back to my car, I noticed that my window was fixed. I was surprised. I saw Ramon the next day. I was speechless and didn't know how to start thanking him. I offered to pay him for his time and efforts plus the parts. He refused to charge me. I insisted, and he said, "You could only pay me for the parts, if you insist." He did not charge me more than a couple of dollars.

I went to church with Lisa and her family a few times upon their invitation. Through Lisa and her parents, I met another great family at church: Dan and Laurie Sain and their two young children, Jason and Alison. Dan and Laurie invited me to their house numerous times. They were hospitable, easygoing, and extremely nice to me. I felt so much at ease with them. It was in late August 1979 that my roommates were about to graduate and leave, and I was not able to find roommates to share the apartment. I could not afford the rent by myself. Time was running short, and I was supposed to notify the apartment manager whether or not I was going to continue staying in that apartment for the fall. I was too busy with school and work to look for an apartment. Dan and Laurie knew that I was looking for a place to live. I invited them once to the Mexican restaurant that I was working at. I was off that day and was having dinner with them. That evening Dan and Laurie made an offer to me to go live with them. They had an extra fully furnished bedroom that they wanted me to use.

"Well, that is a great offer, but how much do I have to pay for rent?" I asked.

"Nothing," they said. "We want you to be part of the family. The room and food will be on us."

"I can't accept living there for free and not pay for my food," I said.

We settled on a very small rent payment that included room, utilities, and food. Not only was I relieved that I didn't have to search for another place to live, I was happy to have found such nice people to stay with. I had a great time staying at the Sains' house. Dan and Laurie were not much older than I was, maybe just a few years, so we had some common interests to talk about. Laurie was an excellent cook. They had two very well behaved kids. It was a great experience for me to stay at their house. They were very kind to me.

FOURTEEN

Fall semester 1979 started. I was working on my master's thesis and was taking a couple of courses. I was taking a course called Elastic Stability. Dr. Steiyer taught the course. I had taken a course with him before. He was a great teacher with fatherly attitude. He would often ask me to stop by his office for a chat. In his office, we would talk a little about engineering and more about politics, and especially about the events in Iran. He believed, like many Iranian people, that Khomeini was an old man and his clerical regime was not going to stay in power for long. He was concerned that the Soviet Union might invade Iran and forcibly convert the country to a Communist nation, in which case the United States would not stay silent. There was some validity to his concerns, as the tension between the two superpowers was growing over Iran. For example, Radio Moscow was being loud in warning Iran of a CIA plot for a military coup, or *Pravda* was quoting Brezhnev as saying, "The Soviet Union will not tolerate an American invasion of Iran."[110] The media would interpret such statements by the Soviet leader as a threat of war with America and perhaps the start of World War III.

Dr. Steiyer and I developed a good relationship. In addition to politics, we often discussed different approaches to tackle an engineering problem that dealt with stability of structures. However, that particular semester, I could tell that he was not feeling well and was not as enthusiastic about teaching as before. He asked me a few times to take over his classes, and I gladly did. I really liked Dr. Steiyer. Sadly, he died in the middle of that semester of heart attack. His death was hard on me and the rest of the class. We all liked him. Teaching was his passion, and he was really a dedicated teacher. He made me interested in the field of structural analysis and I ended up doing my PhD in structures.

---

110 Translated from the *Rouz Shomar-e-tarikh-e-Iran az mashrouteh ta enghelab-e-eslami, Jeld-e Dovom,* Chronology of Iran (1896-1979), Vol. 2 by Bagher Agheli, *Nashr-e Goftar,* 1995, page 376.

From mid-January until late October of 1979, the homeless Shah who had been suffering from cancer, traveled from Egypt to Morocco, then to the Bahamas, and then to Mexico. In Mexico, the Shah's illness got worse. His twin sister, Ashraf, and his wife decided to move him from Mexico to New York for surgery. President Carter's administration met and decided to admit the Shah to New York, in contrast to their original refusal decision. Despite the fact that President Carter had expressed his concern over the hostile seizure of the American Embassy[111] by the Iranian government, the Shah was admitted to a New York City hospital on October 23, 1979. President Carter's nightmare came to fruition on November 4, 1979.[112]

It was an evening time. I had just come home from school. Laurie was fixing dinner, the kids were playing in their room, and Dan was watching the evening news on TV. I asked Dan whether there was anything new on the news, and he said, "Yes, your fellow countrymen have seized the American Embassy in Iran and held Americans hostage." At the beginning, I didn't think that the crisis was serious. I thought that the hostages would be released soon. Most of my friends were under the same impression—that the hostages would be freed in a matter of a week or so, but we were wrong. The militant Islamist students loyal to Khomeini were the masterminds of the attack on the embassy. They took sixty-six Americans hostage and called the American Embassy the "nest of spies." When Khomeini was first informed of the situation, he was opposed to the militants' action and asked for mediation between the government officials and the militants to end the crisis, but the students wouldn't negotiate with any Iranian officials. They would only listen to Khomeini. Surprisingly, after talking to some militant students, Khomeini announced that he would support the students. Prime Minister Bazargan, who was already frustrated with Khomeini's radical and unruly decisions, resigned soon after Khomeini's announcement. The militants, who enjoyed the support of their spiritual leader, demanded the extradition of the Shah. Khomeini and his followers interpreted the Shah's admission to New York Hospital as perhaps the intention of the Carter's administration to plan a similar coup d'état as in 1953. Many Iranian people back then were upset with President Carter for allowing the Shah to be admitted in the US, many Iranian people now are upset with President Carter for allowing the Shah to be "ousted" and they blame him for allowing the 1979 revolution to occur. I personally think that the Shah's departure from Iran was inevitable and President Carter had no choice but to respect the will of the people.

---

111 Translated from *Pajouhesh* magazine, No. 104, Winter 2008-9, page 7.
112 Ibid.

Anyhow, the decision by Khomeini to side with the militants was not pleasant news to President Carter and his administration. The administration adamantly refused to negotiate with the militants over the Shah's extradition. President Carter ordered to freeze all the Iranian assets in American banks. However, there was a break in the case when the militants announced the release of thirteen hostages on November 19, 1979—among them, women, and African American men. Many of us Iranians in the US were glad to hear the good news, and we were hopeful that the rest of the hostages would be released soon. That did not happen.

The situation worsened every day. There was an order by Carter's administration to the then Immigration and Naturalization Department to search all the Iranian people to see if they were living in the United States legally. Soon after the president's order, we were lined up in the university union center, holding our passports to be checked for the proper visa or lack thereof. It was a long line; we had to wait for a long time, and it was somewhat humiliating because we were treated by some immigration officers like criminals. Among Iranian students in the United States, a rumor quickly spread that we were probably going to be placed in the internment camps, similar to Japanese descent that lived in the United States after the Pearl Harbor attack during World War II. We were under the impression that perhaps the hostage crisis was a good excuse for the American government to start a war with Iran before Iran fell into the hands of the Soviets. However, President Carter was wiser and smarter than that. Any military action against Iran would have possibly resulted in not only a death sentence to all the hostages, but a war between "Islam and infidels" as well. At that time, Khomeini's popularity had grown beyond Iranian borders. His anti-American rhetoric had resonated with many people in the Muslim world. In addition, the Soviet Union, under the leadership of Leonid Brezhnev, would not have stayed silent, if there had been any military attack by Americans against Iran. The whole region would have been a mess.

One evening at home we were hosting some of Dan's friends. They brought up the hostage crisis and political uncertainty in Iran. We had a heated discussion about the situation in Iran. One of the guests believed that the United States should send troops to Iran. Obviously, I disagreed with him.

"Let's think and talk logically here; by sending troops to Iran, other than killing innocent people, including the hostages, and stirring the pot in the whole Middle East, what else would the American government gain?" I said.

At this point someone said, "We should go and nuke Iran!" I got very upset and couldn't keep my cool.

I told him, "You are an irrational person; you are an advocate of mass killing, and thus you are anti-people." I later on realized that I was wrong and I should not have lost my temper. I could have said the same thing with a better tone. Dan and Laurie, as gentle as they always were, calmed the situation down, and changed the subject. We then started talking about football. Incidentally, the person who got me upset over nuking Iran used to be a football player himself. He was tall, well built, and very strong. Before he left, he turned to me and said, "Habib, if anybody bothers you or harasses you because you are an Iranian, come and tell me. He is going to have to deal with me before he causes any harm to you." I then apologized for losing my temper. After they left, it dawned on me that during our political discussion, I was the only one who lost my temper. I was the one who used the word irrational, and the rest of them were calm. I was the one who indeed was irrational. I don't think that person was serious about nuking the whole country and killing innocent people, but I was the one who took it too seriously.

During the televised debates, American people and politicians express their opinions and attack each other's views, but at the end the day, they would smile and shake each other's hands. Americans, for the most part, have a higher tolerance for different points of view. Relatively speaking, the American people are trained to respect different religions, races, nationalities, cultures, accents, and ethnicities. Diversity is one of America's greatest strengths. This has been recognized by many American scholars and politicians. I admire that so much about the people in this country. This is one good reason that many people from all over the world are attracted to this country. Merchants, investors, scholars, and people from all walks of life immigrate to the United States because they feel more secure to advance and excel in this country than their own. In my humble opinion, Americans owe these noble characteristics, for the most part, to the work of their founding fathers, who wrote one of the most democratic and humanistic constitutions ever.

During the 2008 presidential campaign in America, the honorable general and former secretary of state, General Colin Powell, in an interview with Mr. Tom Brokaw on "Meet the Press," in response to the rumors that President Obama was a Muslim, stated:

> "Well, the correct answer is, he is not a Muslim, he's a Christian. He's always been a Christian. But the really right answer is what if he is? Is there something wrong with being a Muslim in this country? The answer's no, that's not America. Is there something wrong with some seven-year-old Muslim-American kid believing that he or she could be president? Yet, I have heard senior members of my own party drop the

suggestion, 'He's a Muslim and he might be associated with terrorists.'
This is not the way we should be doing it in America."[113]

Now, my question for the current "Supreme Leader" in Iran or President
Ahmadinejad is: "Is there something wrong with a seven-year-old Baha'i or
Christian or Jewish or Zoroastrian kid in Iran who loves his or her country to
dream or to believe that he or she could be president, or a judge, or an army officer,
or a minister of some sort?"

Persian culture is comprised of many different ethnic backgrounds: Farsi
speaking people, Turks (Azeris, Turkmen), Lures, Kurds, Gillakis, Ghashghaees,
Bakhtiaris, Balouchies, Iranian-Arabs, -Armenians, -Assyrians, -Georgians; with
different religious backgrounds: Shia'ats, Sunnis, Jews, Zoroastrians, Christians,
and Baha'is; they all consider themselves as *Parsis,* Persians, and they are all proud
of their heritage and their founding father: King Cyrus the Great. Cyrus believed
in respecting all religions, all beliefs, the sovereignty of all neighboring countries,
and he believed in equal rights for all citizens. He was against slavery, oppression,
suppression, and against despotism. These principles were the basis of Cyrus's ruling 2500 years ago. Those who do not believe in Cyrus and his principles, do not
represent Persian culture, and do not deserve to rule Iran.

The ruling of the Islamic Republic is not the Persian way; they are only representing a very small minority in Iran; the reactionary mullahs (not all mullahs)
and those who think like them. Iran was a haven for different religious beliefs,
and bigotry, racism, and hate mongering don't have any place in the Persian
culture.

---

113 www.msnbc.msn.com/id/27265369/ns/meet_the_press/

FIFTEEN

The tension between Iran and the United States escalated. Anti-Iranian sentiments by some angry American people started to boil. Many Iranians were attacked or beaten all over the United States. In Fayetteville, we didn't dare show up in public. Dan and Laurie expressed concern over my safety on many occasions.

I remember one day, one of my Turkish friends asked me for a ride to a nearby mechanic shop to pick up his car. I had parked my car off campus, so we had to walk a long distance to get to my car. While we were walking, a kid from the passenger side of a car rolled his window down and threw a banana peel at us that hit my friend and shouted, "Go home, you camel jockeys." My friend shouted back and said, "I am not an Iranian, I am from Turkey, you dummy."

I chuckled and jokingly turned to my Turkish friend and said, "You should be thankful that it was just a banana peel."

"You shut up, you are the Iranian one, and I have to receive the banana peel," he said. "I am going to stick my passport to my chest from tomorrow on."

Just before the start of spring semester 1980, I received a call from my boss, Dr. Akin. He asked me to stop by his office. I was really concerned and worried that he was going to fire me because of the situations between Iran and the United States. I depended on the financial support and enjoyed teaching. When I went to his office, I was nervous; he closed the door and asked me, "How many classes are you going to be taking?"

"I have taken more courses than required for my MS degree. I am just going to be working on my thesis," I responded.

"I wanted you to stop by for two reasons: first off, I might give you more courses to teach for more money, and secondly, I want you to go see Professor Cook, the course monitor of Statics (the course I was teaching)," Dr. Akin said.

I was relieved and jokingly said, "You mean you are not going to fire me even though the tension is high between Iran and America?"

Dr. Akin very kindly and gently said, "Why should I fire you? You are doing a fine job, students are happy with you, and so am I. Politics is not my forte, and I am going to leave politics with politicians."

I was happy because not only did he not fire me, he offered to give me more money, and he appreciated my hard work. Then I thought to myself, "Some of my countrymen are holding Americans hostage; they chant death to America, they burn American flags on the streets, and they disrespectfully step on the picture of the American president. Yet I am being supported financially in this country, living with a family who are extremely nice to me and charge me virtually nothing, continuing my education free of tuition (because of my teaching assistantship), and following my dreams."

My fellow countrymen even held rallies in the middle of the hostage crisis in different cities in America in support of the militants in Iran and demanded the return of the Shah. Yet they were being protected under the law of this land without being harmed. Although there have been some isolated cases in which Iranians were attacked by angry Americans, we felt safe for the most part. The Iranians who lived in America could express their anti-Carter feelings in America without being prosecuted, but the people of Iran wouldn't dare express anti-Khomeini feelings.

Upon Dr. Akin's request, I went to Professor Cook's office. He gave me the new syllabus for statics and asked me to give my students a so-called, "Mechanics Readiness Test" at the beginning of the course. They had just decided to do this. The purpose of the test was to evaluate students' math and physics background and their readiness for the very first core and important engineering mechanics course—Statics. Questions were of multiple-choice types, true or false, filling blank and very short-response types. I did exactly as I was told. Students were not thrilled to take an exam the very first day of the classes. One of the students in my class had very funny answers to many of the questions. For example, in response to one of the questions on the first page he wrote, "The answer is given on the back of the page." I turned to the back of the page, he had written, "The answer is on the back of the next page." He had written the same message on that page and finally on the last page he had this message for me, "Hey Mister, what are you looking for? If I knew the answer to the question, I would write it on the first page!"

When Khomeini was in exile in France, some of his disciples referred to him as "Imam." After the revolution, Khomeini was officially given the title of Imam—he officially became "Imam Khomeini." In Arabic, the word "imam" means "the leader." Sunnis use the term "imam" to refer to the lead prayer in the mosque. To the Shiites, the word "imam" refers to someone infallible, a saint, and a divinely appointed successor to Prophet Muhammad. There are twelve imams in the Shiite faith; Imam Ali was the first, plus his eleven descendents. The Shiites believe that the twelfth imam, "the promised Mahdi," who was believed to be granted the imamate at the age of five, is hidden (by God) and will emerge with Jesus Christ together to bring peace, prosperity, and justice to the world. This is one of the main differences between Sunnis and Shiites. In Iran, our religious leaders and theocracy teachers always told us that there were only twelve imams—the twelfth one was supposed to be the last. We were told that it was a sin to refer to anybody else as imam. The Shiite faith has always been referred to in Arabic as *Shia Asna-Ashar*, and in Persian as *Shia Davazdah Emami*, both of which mean believing in twelve imams, the "twelvers." How did the mullahs in Iran come up with the justification of naming Khomeini as the thirteenth imam!? That is beyond me and I have absolutely no idea.

In the heat of the revolution, Khomeini's cadre spread the rumor that they had seen Khomeini's reflection on the moon.[114] Khomeini's naive believers interpreted that as proof that he was a saint. His disciples went even further and named Khomeini *Naeb-e Imam Zaman*, "deputy of the twelfth imam." His title became even more divine when a parliamentary member asked him whether he was Mahdi. Khomeini refused to answer that question.[115]

On January 25, 1979, a presidential election was held in Iran. Abolhassan Banisadr was elected as the first president of Iran after the revolution, receiving almost 79 percent of the votes. He was the foreign minister and the finance minister of the provisional government under Prime Minister Bazargan. Banisadr was one of the most important allies of Khomeini. These two first met in 1972 in Iraq, when Banisadr went to Iraq for the funeral of his father, Seyed Nasrollah Banisadr, who was a clergyman and revered by Khomeini as Ayatollah. Khomeini and Banisadr had kept in close contact ever since until they were reunited again in Paris in 1978. In fact, Abolhassan Banisadr was the temporary host of Khomeini when he sought political asylum in Paris and remained under Banisadr's protégé for as long as he stayed in Paris. Khomeini, on some occasions, referred to Abolhassan Banisadr as his son. He made Banisadr the commander-in-chief of the army in February 1980. That decision by Khomeini was not well received by the clerics.

In the late April 1980, a rescue operation by the U.S. military (Operation Eagle Claw or Operation Evening Light) in an attempt to rescue fifty-three hostages

---

114 Vali Nasr, *The Shia Revival* (New York: Norton, 2007), page 131.
115 Ibid.

failed. Subsequently the Iranian authorities scattered the hostages in different parts of Iran. In July 1980, another hostage, Richard Queens, was released due to a serious illness.

Shah died on July 27, 1980, in Cairo, Egypt. I was personally saddened to hear the news, but also relieved. I was relieved because I did not want the Shah to be sent back to Iran. By that time, the brutal nature of the Khomeini regime was proven to most Iranians including myself. I was afraid that the government would use all kinds of humiliation tactics to show its hatred toward the Shah.

After the death of the Shah, negotiations over the release of hostages continued. In the meantime, the triad of clerics—Mohammad Beheshti, Akbar Hashemi Rafsanjani, and Ali Khamenei—became the biggest adversary elements against Banisadr. The first two were the founders of the Islamic Republican Party (IRP). Banisadr, on the other hand, was the founder of the newspaper *Jomhoori-e Eslami*, Islamic Republic. He used his newspaper to criticize the IRP. Banisadr was against the cleric domination and hostage-holding of Americans. Rafsanjani and Beheshti, the key members of the IRP, used their influence to gain a sweep victory in the parliamentary elections. They appointed their favorite candidate, Mohammad Ali Rajaee, another opponent of Banisadr, as the prime minister. The tension between the IRP and Banisadr intensified when an attempted military coup was neutralized in July of 1980. The masterminds of the coup held key positions in the army. They were all executed, and Banisadr was severely criticized.

The war broke out between Iran and Iraq in September of 1980. Saddam Hussein's forces took advantage of the internal power struggle and the weakened armed forces in Iran and invaded the Iranian territory on September 22, 1980. This war was not a war between two nations. It was a war between the leaders of the two nations. It was not a war between Shiites and Sunnis, nor was it a war between Iranians and Arabs, as many reporters and commentators interpreted. In other words, it was not a religious war, nor was it an ethnic war. Shiites, Sunnis, and Arabs in Iran, and Iranians who lived in Iraq were in peace long before the Iranian revolution. During the Shah's reign, Iran and Iraq had a border dispute over the waterway of Arvand Rood (Shat-Al-Arab), but it was resolved peacefully in 1975. Khomeini and Saddam didn't like each other. Khomeini didn't like to be forced out of Iraq and he insisted to export his revolution beyond the borders. Saddam, on the other hand, aspired to become the most powerful man in the region.

At the beginning of the war, the Iraqis had the upper hand. They advanced into the province of Khuzestan and captured some border villages and the key city of Khorramshahr. They savagely killed many of our young soldiers, as well as many innocent civilians. They destroyed the biggest oil refinery in the world at the time in the city of Abadan and inflicted so much casualties on Iranians. Banisadr spent most of his time near the war zone and away from Tehran, and he wanted a quick resolution to the hostage crisis. The mullahs, led by Beheshti and Rafsanjani, used this opportunity to lash out at President Banisadr. They blamed him for all the casualties of the war. They accused him of not being competent in handling the war. He was accused of attempting to work out a secret deal with the United States for the release of the hostages. Furthermore, Banisadr was criticized for ignoring the Revolutionary Guards and favoring the armed forces still loyal to the Shah. He was also criticized for seeking the support of the opposition group, Mujahedin-e Khalgh (MEK) and the Communist Toudeh Party. All the criticisms and accusations against Banisadr had taken a big toll on his presidency.

The mullahs managed to convince Khomeini that Banisadr was not competent to remain as the commander-in-chief of the army, and that he was not capable of running the country as the president. Khomeini stripped Banisadr of both of his positions on June 10, 1981 and ordered impeachment of President Banisadr. Banisadr went into hiding. In his hideout, he called on all Iranians to "unite against fundamentalists and the unprecedented dictatorship they are imposing on the country."[116] A few days later, Banisadr fled to Paris with the help of the Mujahedin and some military and junior noncombatant air force officers. One of those junior noncombatant air force officers was a friend of mine whom I used to play soccer with, by the name of Yaqub (same as Jacob). Yaqub was a good person, a good-looking guy, and a very athletic young man. He was extremely popular with all of his friends and the people in our neighborhood. He was always ready to give a hand to anybody who needed help. He possessed a calm, gentle, and very pleasant demeanor. He was accused of helping Banisadr to flee Iran. He was executed without trial. He was in his mid twenties when he was murdered by Khomeini's murderous squad. I learned of his execution during one of my trips back home. I was disturbed and sad to hear the bad news; I cried for hours.

The notorious Mullah Mohammad Gilani was the chief of Tehran's "Revolutionary Court," who ordered Yaqub's execution along with many other young and innocent people. He sentenced twelve young girls to death just for supporting Banisadr. The oldest was eighteen years old. When Gilani asked them to identify themselves, they each replied, "Mujahed" ("Crusader"). He asked them to identify their parents, they each replied, "The people of Iran." Gilani photographed all the girls and then consigned them to the firing squad. As the guards began to blindfold them, the girls started chanting, "Death to facism!

116 http://www.time.com/time/magazine/article/0,9171,922597-2,00.html#ixzz0bdXmmbOK.

Death to Khomeini!"[117] Three days later, one of the clergy-controlled newspapers, *Ettelaa't*, printed the girls' pictures with a curt message to their parents to call for the bodies. Under the cruel rules of the Islamic Republic, not only are the parents responsible for the bodies, but they have to pay a ridiculous amount of money for the bullets used to kill them.

At a press conference, Gilani defended the trials and execution of the minor girls. "By the Islamic canon," he said, "A nine-year-old girl is mature. So there is no difference for us between a nine-year-old girl and a forty-year-old man."[118] This heartless, cold-blooded murderer executed two of his own children for standing up to the brutality of the regime and the senseless and inhumane execution orders of their own father! This so-called ayatollah still lives in Iran, but I can't imagine how he could live with his conscience and how he could sleep at night!

---

117 Ibid.
118 Ibid.

SIXTEEN

In the summer of 1980, Dan and Laurie left Arkansas for their birth state of Tennessee, and I moved to a one-bedroom apartment near the campus. I was working on my thesis full time and living off my savings. In the meantime, I was searching for a suitable university to start a PhD. Reza and I had been in contact with each other. He had already transferred to Old Dominion University (ODU) in Norfolk, Virginia. He was happy at ODU and insisted that I move there. I decided to apply for the PhD program at the Department of Engineering Mechanics at ODU. I also applied for financial support there. Luckily, I was admitted to the PhD program with financial support. I was notified of the admission in early July 1980. The next step for me was to defend my master's thesis and leave Fayetteville, Arkansas, for Norfolk, Virginia.

I defended my thesis successfully in mid-August to the full satisfaction of my advisor, Dr. Myklebust. I sold my car and some small furniture items and bought a one-way bus ticket to Tennessee to visit the Sain family and from there to Norfolk. It was great to see Dan, Laurie, and the kids in their newly built countryside home in Bradyville, Tennessee, and I met most of their relatives. What a nice group of people. They treated me as one of their own. I really enjoyed their Southern hospitality and the Southern food there. After a relaxing and joyful reunion with the Sain family, I continued my journey to Norfolk.

It was a long and tiresome ride. There were too many bus stops, but I met so many interesting people on the bus. At one point along the way, on a dark night, I found myself riding with only two people in the bus: the driver and a man sitting behind the driver's seat wearing boots and a cowboy hat. I was sitting on the other side of the cowboy, to his right. The driver brought up the hostage issues. "Here we go again!" I muttered. He was cursing Iranians. He complained that his daughter, to the best of my recollection, a student at the University of

235

Kentucky, had applied for two different campus jobs and both jobs were taken by Iranian students.

"We educate them here, they go back to their country and protest against us," he said. "We should kick these bastard terrorists out of this country."

The cowboy added, "We should go there and bomb the crap out of them."

Then the driver turned to me and said, "You are so silent and not making any comments." It was late at night. I was really tired and sleepy but I could not sleep because those two people were too loud.

"I am just listening. I have no comments," I said.

The driver noticed my accent and asked, "Where are you from?" I felt that I was cornered. I was fearful that if I revealed my real nationality, they would harm me or kick me out of the bus in the middle of the night, so I decided to disguise my nationality—I declared that I was Lebanese. That was the first time I had hidden my real nationality. Those guys continued using nasty and hateful language against Iran and the Iranians. I felt so bad and like a coward for lying about my origin. By early morning, the cowboy was already gone and we had a few more passengers sitting in the back of the bus. I changed my seat and sat right behind the bus driver.

I moved forward, leaned my hands and chest against the bar behind the driver's seat, and whispered to the driver, "Sir, I have a confession to make."

"What is that?" he asked.

"I lied to you about my nationality. I am from Iran," I said. "Are you going to kick me out of the bus now?"

"No, I am not going to kick you out," he said. "What is going on in your country? Why are the people of Iran holding so many grudges against us? Do these people have anything else to do other than burning our flags? Why are they taking Americans hostage?"

"I believe you are watching too much TV, and, unfortunately, the American media show exactly what the Iranian-controlled media want the Americans to see. They do not go to the people's houses to ask them what they really think about the hostage crisis and the current regime in Iran. The vast majorities of Iranians are not supporting the regime and are against the hostage taking. Iranians are very hospitable people, and it is against their nature and their customs to mistreat their guests," I said.

"Iran used to be one of the biggest allies of the United States, and the people of Iran have always paid respect to our past presidents when they visited Iran," he said.

"The people of Iran are still the same. It is the leaders of the new government that are promoting hate against not only the United States, but anyone who doesn't see the world or doesn't think the way they do," I said. "I felt insulted and uncomfortable when you made wrong allegations and racial slurs against the Iranians."

"Your leader, the ayatollah (Khomeini), calls us 'the Great Satan,' " he said. "What do you say about that?"

"He is wrong. He does not speak for me nor does he speak for the whole nation. I am ashamed that the leader of my country calls this great nation 'the Great Satan.' Iran is also a great nation and I am proud of my nationality and my heritage. I do not appreciate the use of the words 'bastards' or 'terrorists' against my country and my fellow citizens. We are neither, sir," I said. The driver was nice enough to apologize, and I apologized for lying to him about my origin. We finished our conversation with a handshake and wished success for the people of both nations.

When I look back at those days, more than thirty-one years ago, I often think that we have advanced in science and technology, we have made many discoveries, we have learned to coexist with people of different origins, and we have made progress in removing racial barriers. However, in my humble opinion, we have not made much progress in the world of politics. In third world countries, the politicians, for the most part, blame the West for their impoverishment and promote hate and terrorism against Western nations. In some Western countries, the politicians see violence as the only means to fight terrorism instead of trying to find the roots of all the troubles. Internally, in the nondemocratic world, powerful politicians rig the elections and commit all kinds of crimes, including assassinations of people for political gains, and, in some democratic nations, politicians, more than before, instead of focusing more on real issues, use all kinds of bashing techniques and character assassination against their opponents, for that matter.

Over thirty-one years ago, the people of Iran revolted against dictatorship, injustice, censorship, and against oppression. They revolted because they wanted freedom and they wanted to move forward socially, economically, politically, and technologically. What was the outcome of their revolution? The byproduct of the Islamic Republic was worse dictatorship, more injustice, more censorship, and more oppression. The people of Iran now face much less freedom, and the country has gone backward socially, economically, and politically.

The Iranian people wanted stability and peace internally and a peaceful relationship with the outside world, especially with their neighboring countries, based on mutual respect of their sovereignties. In particular, they wanted fair and mutually beneficial economic trades with the American government, and all the Western countries, for that matter. The Islamic Republic brought them instability, a reign of terror internally, war and hostility with their neighbors, and tension with the West.

In the heat of the hostage crisis, Khomeini used the term "the Great Satan" to refer to the United States. That upset Americans, including the bus driver. Many people in the United States demonstrated against the use of such words by the Iranian leader, and many of them called for the deportation of all Iranians. Unfortunately, the clerics in Iran including the sitting supreme leader, Ali Khamenei, still use similar derogatory words against the United States and other western countries. I am baffled as to why a person who claims to be a religious leader uses hateful rhetoric against other nations.

It is unfair and morally wrong to name a country that has been home to many oppressed people who escaped the brutal ruling of dictators and totalitarian regimes, "The Great Satan." I appreciate living in a country in which their laws protect and respect people. The laws in this country prohibit torturing their dissidents to death; they prohibit hanging their people in public or executing their oppositions for political reasons. There are no discriminatory laws against minorities and women in this country. The government in this country does not instigate their people to go on the streets to burn Iranian Flag, nor do they instigate them to shout "Death to Iran." They do not train thugs and mercenaries to crush people's peaceful rallies violently nor do they imprison or kill innocent young people for just voicing their opposition against their government. This country is tolerant of all kinds of ideologies and religions and its constitution would not allow the return of the dark ages—the ruling of the cleric regimes and dictators who commit the most horrendous crimes against humanity in the name of religion.

I believe rhetoric and name-calling such as "Great Satan," "Terrorist Nation," or "Axis of Evil," etc. are in contrast to human ethics and should not be used by politicians especially the heads of states. I appreciated President George W. Bush for always separating Iranian people from the Islamic Republic in his state of union speeches; nevertheless using such terminologies against other nations are inappropriate and distasteful.

Promoting hate, using nasty remarks against western nations, and blaming them for all the world problems, lying to and cheating on people have been the tactics of most of the leaders in Iran since the establishment of the Islamic Republic. Such tactics worked for a while but not any longer. Today many people in Iran, especially the younger generation, feel that they have been betrayed by their religious leaders. They don't trust the leadership of the Islamic Republic.

They think that if these corrupt clergies are the voices of Islam, they don't want to be Muslim. They are drifting away from Islam and looking for something else. That was not the case during the reign of the Shah. Islam was a soothing religion and was much more respected and accepted by the people of Iran. However, as mentioned before, people in Iran under the current regime do not have the right to change their religion publicly. "Apostatizing" is not allowed in Iran; it means death sentence. These so-called religious leaders, for the past three decades, have been trying to sow the seeds of hatred in Iran while making themselves very rich.

During the recent uprising in Iran, some of the high-ranking mullahs of the Islamic Republic have made statements that were outrageous and worse than barbaric. For instance, Mullah Ahmad Jannati, the chairman of the Guardian Council during the Friday prayer sermon on January 29, 2010 expressed pleasure and praised the judicial authorities for the executions of two political dissidents. He urged the officials to continue execution of the dissidents until the protests by the opposition was subsided. The notorious Mullah Mesbah Yazdi, during an interview on August 11, 2009, justified and religiously legitimized sodomy, emotional and physical pressure, drugging with addictive substances, raping, and torturing by any means against dissidents.[119] Such disgraceful, inhuman, and sinful statements are far from Islamic values, and such atrocious actions and crimes are, by no means, legal in Islam.

These hate mongers, however, while being rejected by most of the Iranian people, especially the youth, managed to recruit, brainwash, and arm a considerable number of young people from mostly uneducated, poor, and rural areas to work for them as thugs, mercenaries, and basijies (the term mullahs use for "army of Islam" mercenaries). The basijies have been brainwashed to be loyal to the Islamic Republic. The minds of the basijies have been corrupted. Instead of training them to be productive and responsible citizens, to protect lives, to be the crime patrollers, and to be volunteers as guardian angels and security forces, they have been trained to use violence against people, to invade people's houses, to harass young people on the streets, to beat mercilessly on university students and freedom fighters, and to kill. They get direct orders from the "Supreme Leader." What is so scary about these basijies is that a huge number of them appear in ordinary clothes but carry guns and knives, which is in violations of the constitution. It is believed that many of the "basijies," especially those who brutally attacked women and children during the demonstrations after the election, were foreign nationals who did not speak Farsi. I am not certain as to the authenticity of such claims, but I personally had a hard time seeing and believing the criminal acts of some of the

---

119 http://raheazadi.com/1388/06/11/ayatollah-mesbah-yazdi-sodomy-and-rape-of-protesters-is-ok/

bassijies and the police forces against their own fellow citizens on TV. However, many other basijies have a conscience and refuse to use violence against ordinary people. During the recent crackdown, people have witnessed some basijies trying to distance themselves from the rest. My message to all the young basijies is the following poem by Feraydoon Moshiri:[120]

Put your gun down,
For I hate to see this crooked bloody object.
A gun in your hand speaks the language of fire and steel,
But I, in the presence of this evil, destructive object,
Have nothing but language of the heart,
The heart of affection for you; oh, you enemy of peace,
The language of fire and steel is the language of bloodshed and anger,
The language of mad Genghis Khan,
Come, sit, talk, and listen—perhaps
The light of humanity will find a way in your heart.
Brother,[121] as you call me, sit and act like a brother.
Put your gun down,
Put your gun down, for this physical body of yours,
The human killer demon comes out.
What do you know about humanity?
If life is God given,
Why should you destroy it?
Why should you, in a moment of madness, splash your brother in blood and soil?
You may be right and just, but, my dear brother,
You must not use this flaming, despicable weapon to seek justice.
If your slumbering conscience awakened this time,
Put your gun down.

---

120   Fereydoon Moshiri (1926 – 2000) was a contemporary poet. This poem is translated by the author. The master Iranian singer Mohammad Reza Shajarian sang a song in Farsi based on this poem.
121   At the beginning of 1979, these basijies called everyone "brother."

SEVENTEEN

I arrived in Norfolk just before the fall semester 1980. Reza picked me up from the bus station. Reza and Mehdi both transferred to ODU, and they lived together in a small two-bedroom apartment near campus. They were both so courteous to let me stay with them for a while. I enthusiastically started my PhD classes and worked as a research assistant. About a month into the semester, I decided to look for a new apartment. Reza and Mehdi both insisted that I stay with them for the entire semester. I felt like a burden in that small apartment, as they would not accept any rent or utility money from me. I started searching for a suitable, inexpensive, and preferably a furnished apartment. I could not find any reasonable apartment near campus. I found one, half-furnished, a few miles away from the campus. It was a long walking distance to the campus. I did not have a car yet. Often I walked to school, but most often, I would catch the city bus. Commuting became a burden.

I soon realized that I was living in an unsafe neighborhood. In addition, a young couple lived next door to me who were too loud and argued frequently, especially during the nighttime. They were too annoying, so I started looking again for a better apartment. I saw an ad at school that said, "Looking for a roommate to share the rent and utilities." I immediately called the person and paid him a visit. His apartment was located right across from the campus and within a five-minute walk to my classes. The apartment was neat and clean, but it had just one bedroom. My first impression of the guy was that he could be into drinking, marijuana, and loud music, but he said that he was going to stay until May and then I could have the whole apartment to myself. I figured that I was going to spend most of my time at school anyway; I could tolerate him for one-and-a-half semesters. In the bedroom, he had a bunk bed, but he gave me the option of either using the bunk bed or he could make it into two separate beds. I chose the two

separate beds. Luckily, I did not have any long-term lease with the previous apartment manager, so I moved in to the new apartment immediately. My roommate,
Scott, was a typical cool *American Gigolo* who was into rock and roll and pretty
girls, but I found him very clean and organized. Unlike my first impression, he
was not into alcohol, nor was he into any kinds of drugs. He loved women and
was infatuated with Charlene Tilton of *Dallas* episodes, and one of his hobbies
was to read *Playboy* magazine! I remember one day Scott was lying down on his
bed and was "reading the articles" of the latest *Playboy* issue. The doorbell rang, I
opened the door, and it was Scott's mother. I told her to wait for just one second.
She gently said, "Sure."

I went to Scott and said, "Scott, it's your mother."

"Come in, Mom," he shouted.

"But Scott, you have the *Playboy* magazine in your hand," I said.

"She already knows. I don't hide anything from my mother," he said.

"Ma'am, I apologize for keeping you waiting," I said. "Come in, please."

Once she found out what was going on, she laughed and said, "He has boxes
of *Playboy* magazines at home." Scott's mother was living locally, and she used to
bring us food, fruits, and cookies often.

Another time, Scott and I were watching an episode of one of our favorite sit-
coms, *Three's Company*. There was a pause, and a special bulletin came on the news
regarding the hostage negotiations. Khomeini was still defiant about the release
of hostages. After the news bulletin, I turned to Scott and said, "Scott, you know
I am Iranian."

"Of course, I know you are an Iranian," he said.

"But you never asked me where I was from."

"Oh, come on, a name like 'Habib' couldn't be French," he said. "Don't be
silly, Habib. I don't care what nationality you are; I care about who you are."

Scott was a few years younger than I was but was more mature for his age. He
was extremely considerate—he was not at all a distraction to my studies. What
distracted me the most was the Iran-Iraq war, the hostage crisis, and the internal
power struggle back home. The news about the casualties and loss of innocent lives
in the senseless war was disturbing. I was constantly worried that they might draft
my brothers for the war, even though they all had served their military duties.

My parents were influenced by the media in Iran that Iranians were being
humiliated, apprehended, attacked, and killed by Americans over the hostage crisis. They were worried that my life was in danger and suggested that maybe I
should return to Iran. I had a hard time convincing them that what they heard on
Iranian TV was blown out of proportion and I am in no way, shape, and form in

a danger; most of the news were either somewhat isolated, or distorted facts and far from the truth.

During the presidential campaign between Ronald Reagan and Jimmy Carter, many of my friends in the United States were under the impression that if Reagan won the election and the hostages were not released, America would attack Iran militarily and Iran would become another Vietnam. However, in the last stages of the presidential race, the media in America speculated that some secret negotiations were taking place in Europe between Reagan's aides and Iranian officials regarding the hostages. On the other hand, Khomeini, during his speeches, sent messages and signals to Americans that "Carter must go"—the same slogan he used against the Shah. He even sent messages to the American people not to vote for Carter. On November 4, 1980, Khomeini got his wish: Carter lost reelection. Ronald Reagan won in a landslide. Many political analysts and commentators concluded that Carter's failure to gain the release of the hostages was the main cause for his loss in the presidential race. Others suggested that the poor economy was the primary cause and the hostage crisis was secondary. In Iran, Khomeini's followers interpreted Carter's second-term loss as "the will of the imam" and a "victory for the Iranian people."

Khomeini used the same slogan against Saddam in the heat of the war between Iran and Iraq—"Saddam must go." As a part of his plan to export his "Islamic revolution" to the Muslim world, he insisted that the war would continue until Saddam was gone. The loss of lives, and especially young and innocent lives, the loss of oil revenues, the disastrous consequences of the war, and economic pressure on the people did not matter to him. His ego and his desire to expand his "*Velayat-e-Faghih*" version of Islam, and to escape from the internal pressure, were indeed his ulterior motives to continue the war at any cost. In some of his speeches, he made statements such as, "This war is a blessing" or "a gift from God," or "War is good for people's spirit."

The Iran-Iraq war was not a blessing for the Iranian people, but it sure was a blessing for the Islamic Republic. Just before the war started, the vast majority of Iranians were disappointed, disenchanted, and unhappy with the government. There were criticisms of the inept nature of the Islamic Republic to face national and international crises and to resolve them peacefully. There were warnings by the intellectuals about the restoration of dictatorship and an even darker despotic regime. There were uprisings in different parts of the country. The Iran-Iraq war helped a great deal to deter the attention of the people from the immediate internal social, economical, and judicial battlefront to the battle at the border. Khomeini, who in exile repeatedly talked about freedom and promised to grant freedom of speech and freedom of press, used the war to polarize the people and to crack down on the opposition. Anybody who opposed the Islamic Republic was labeled as "infidel," imprisoned, or sentenced to death.

Khomeini's regime negotiated directly and indirectly with the very same regimes that they called "satanic and evil," namely, the United States and Israel. There is no argument that negotiation over the release of the hostages was necessary, and in fact, it should have taken place at the early stages of the hostage crisis. There is no argument that Iranian government negotiated arms deal with the Israelis and purchased weapons from them—the country was at war, and they needed weapons. The argument is the hypocritical and deceitful nature of the Islamic Republic that kept the negotiations away from the people of Iran.

The fact of the matter is that taking the Americans hostage was a mistake in the first place, and it should not have happened. It absolutely served no purpose other than the Iranian assets being frozen by the U.S. government, and causing frictions with the West and further isolation of the country. The war with Iraq was a more detrimental and costlier mistake. It is true that Iranians did not start the war, and in fact, throughout Persian history, rarely have Iranians ever started any war. It is true that the war was imposed upon Iranians, but it could have been prevented had it not been for Saddam's ego or Khomeini's idea of exportation of his revolution and his attempt to exact vengeance against Saddam. It could have been stopped after the city of Khorramshahr[122] was liberated.

In 1982, most Iraqi forces were pushed back to their own territory. The regional countries led by Saudi Arabia came up with a plan to end the war; they offered close to $90 billion to pay Iranians as reparation for the war damages. In addition, the Iraqis agreed to evacuate Iranian territory completely. That was a huge amount of money back then. It still is. The Iraqis accepted all the terms. The Iranians would have received compensation for the war and would have come out as the winner of the war. Unfortunately, the Iranian government, led by Khomeini as the supreme leader, Khamenei as the president, and Rafsanjani, the then speaker of the parliament, refused the plan and insisted that Saddam must go.

I had heard the story about a twelve-year-old Persian kid throwing himself in front of the enemy tank. I read stories about young, middle-aged, and old men voluntarily running on the minefields to clear the way for the Iranian soldiers, or stories about girls in Khorramshahr carrying guns to defend themselves from being raped, and mothers heroically protecting their children. Hearing such sto-

---

122   Khorramshahr is a port city in the Province of Khuzestan in the southwest of Iran. It is located approximately ten kilometers (6.2 miles) from the important oil city of Abadan. This city extends to the right of Arvand Rood, also known as Shatt-al-Arab, near its confluence with the Karun River.

ries and reading articles about people's sacrifice to defend their territory, and their patriotism and love for their country would make me feel cowardly for not being able to be a part of it. In the meantime, such stories would make me proud to be an Iranian. It is beyond the scope of this book to write about the inhumane acts of Saddam's army against the defenseless citizens of Khorramshahr and his use of chemical weapons against Iranian soldiers. Conversely, books can be written about the heroism of the Iranian people ranging from the age of eleven to sixty five to recapture Khorramshahr, some even with bare hands.

Yes, Khomeini was right, the war was a blessing. It was a blessing for Khomeini to impose his "*Velayat-e-Faghih*" doctrine on the people of Iran. It was a blessing for some mullahs and elements of the regime to make themselves rich over arms deals. Furthermore, this war was a blessing for the West and many other nations who bought oil as low as $8 a barrel, while one barrel of oil sold for $36 just before the Shah left. It was also a blessing for American arms dealers, Brazilians, Chinese, French, Israelis, North Koreans, and Russians who sold weapons to both sides.[123] Saddam used chemical and biological weapons furnished by the Centers for Disease Control and the Virginia-based company[124] against Iranians, and killed many Iranian soldiers. He killed so many of Iraqi Kurds using his chemical weapons. In an article in Counterpunch[125] dated October 10, 2002, Elson E. Boles writes:

"A PBS Frontline episode, 'The Arming of Iraq' (1990) detailed much of the conventional and so-called 'dual-use' weapons sold to Iraq. The public learned from other sources that at least since mid-1980s the US was selling chemical and biological material for weapons to Iraq and orchestrating private sales. These sales began soon after current Secretary of State, Donald Rumsfeld, traveled to Baghdad in 1985 and met with Saddam Hussein as a private businessman on behalf of the Reagan administration. In the last major battle of the Iran-Iraq war, some 65,000 Iranians were killed, many by gas."

It is mind boggling as to why the whole world stood silent and didn't stop Saddam back then for his crimes against humanity. Approximately 1.5 million people lost their lives or their loved ones on both sides in this senseless war. Many other people lost their homes or their limbs. Unfortunately, no concerted efforts made by the United Nations to stop the flow of arms.[126] Moreover, no serious efforts were initiated by any country, or the United Nations, for that matter, to stop the bloody war.

123 Michael Brzoska, "Profiteering on the Iran-Iraq war," *Bulletin of the Atomic Scientists*, vol. 43, no. 5, pages 42-45. Found through a Google search.
124 Reza Aslan, *No god but God* (New York: Random House Publishing, 2006), page 253.
125 http://www.counterpunch.org/boles1010.html
126 Ibid.

EIGHTEEN

I was about to get comfortable having Scott as a roommate when he decided to leave early, not in May as he mentioned before, but in mid-December, right after the final exams. We were not acquainted for very long, but I was sad to see him leave so soon. After Scott left, I enjoyed my privacy in the apartment for a while, but I had two problems—first, the apartment complex did not have laundry facilities. The closest coin laundry was located a few miles from my apartment. When Scott was there, he was nice enough to give me a ride back and forth to the laundry. Secondly, the rent in that apartment was too expensive for me.

I had some savings and decided to search for a car. I found an inexpensive 1970 Mustang that ran well but was not in a very good shape. It needed some repair done to it, and I did not have enough money to fix all the problems in the car. It was, however, good enough to get me around the close proximity of the school to do laundry and shop for groceries without asking my friend Reza anymore, even though Reza always helped me willingly. Although the rent was a bit too much for me, I was tired of moving around and decided to keep the apartment.

I was not making a whole lot of progress on my research due to harsh circumstances and my lack of interest in the project, even though my advisor was a great person. Shortly before the Christmas break, when I was just about to get situated in my apartment, I found out that my research assistantship was not going to be continued. My advisor had accepted employment elsewhere. However, Dr. Goglia, the chairman of the Mechanical Engineering Department asked me to see him in a few days to decide what he could do for me. I started panicking and thinking, "What if he doesn't come up with any kind of financial support for me? What if he finds me something that pays less than what I was getting paid?"

A few days later, I stopped by his office as he said. Before I opened my mouth, he said, "Habib, don't you worry. I already have a plan for you. You will be teaching

'Statics.' I know you taught that course before. Your tuition will be paid and we'll pay you a stipend."

I was speechless and did not know how to express my gratitude. I only said, "Dr. Goglia, you won't regret this."

Dr. Goglia was a great person, a likable man, and one of the finest human beings I have met in my life. He was admired and loved by many students. He was known as "Father Goglia" in the Mechanical Engineering Department. He was pro-academic advancements, pro-faculty, and pro-student. We were lucky to have him as the chairperson.

Spring semester 1981 was off to a good start for me. I was all set with my courses, I had an assistantship that paid my bills, including my tuition, I was settled in a nice apartment, and I had a car. Moreover, the hostages were released after 444 days in captivity in Iran, and that made me happy. The release of the hostages coincided with President Reagan's inauguration day on January 20, 1981. In fact, one of the leaders who contributed to Reagan's election was Khomeini, whether intentionally or not. I was overly optimistic that Iran and the United States would start a new chapter in their diplomatic relationship and was hoping that President Reagan would end the war between Iran and Iraq. Unfortunately, the war did not end until late 1988, and the diplomatic relationship between Iran and the United States has yet to resume.

Reza had just finished his Bachelor of Science degree in December of 1980. A few days after the graduation ceremony, he came to me and told me that he had decided to leave the United States for Iran for good. During the course of my first semester at ODU, Reza was a good companion to me and helped me a great deal. He was the one who encouraged me to attend ODU. For that, I will always be indebted to him. Attending ODU was a turning point in my life. It is a great university, and I learned so much from my professors there. I tried to talk Reza into pursuing a Master's degree at ODU, but he had already made up his mind. His intention, as he put it, was to go back home and help his fellow citizens. It was very sad to see him leave. Reza and Reza T were the first people I met in the United States. I have had great memories of both of those nice gentlemen. As I mentioned earlier, Reza T had already left for Iran and was working in the Athletic Department at my former university. Reza, after leaving the United States, worked for some engineering firms for a few years and then started his own business. I have kept in touch with both of them all these years. I always enjoyed hanging out with them every time I visited Iran. I visited Reza T many times at my former university. He was an athlete, a vibrant person, a family man, and a true gentleman. He had a great deal of respect for his students and used to refer to them as his kids. Sadly, he died of cancer in 2005. I was informed of his death through one of my telephone conversations with Reza one early morning. The news came to me as a shock. I was sad and depressed the entire day. He was too good and too young to die so soon.

One of my fondest memories during spring of 1981 was to meet George. I was doing laundry one day, and after I was done, I put my clothes in the car. The car would not start. I tried a few times with no luck. I was approached by a guy who was also doing laundry. It was a cold and icy day. He came to me and gently said, "Is there anything I could do for you?"

"I think my car needs a jump," I said. "Do you happen to have a jumper cable?"

"I came in my girlfriend's car," he said. "Let me ask her."

"I don't have a jumper cable, but I could get it from my dad," the girlfriend said.

"Thank you, don't bother, please. I will call my friend," I said.

"No bother at all. Her dad lives nearby," George said.

She left, and while she was gone, we talked for a while. I learned that he was a student in the Computer Science Department and that he lived right across from my apartment in an old two-story building. He then introduced himself as George Rojas. George's girlfriend came back shortly. They helped me jump the car. We exchanged telephone numbers and left. George and I became good friends and got together often at his house. We cooked many times, watched TV, ate out occasionally, went to movies, and studied together. We talked about politics and the hostage crisis in Iran sometimes, but not very often. George was not much into politics, he was more into sports. He was a good volleyball player, an excellent tennis player, and a reasonably good chess player. We played chess together occasionally, we were pretty much equal but I think overall he beat more than I did. I remember one day when George and I were discussing people of different background, he said, "I had a different image of most Iranians. All I knew about Iranians was what I learned from TV. After attending college and meeting people of different nationalities, I learned not to rush to judgment." He continued saying, "Good human beings, as far as I am concerned."

Speaking of good human beings, George was a great person himself. During the summer of 1981, on one hand, I was deeply concerned about the future of my country and especially the safety of my family members back home. The government crackdown on people expanded. People, especially the youth were being arrested arbitrarily, jailed, and many executed. The war between Iran and Iraq was turning uglier and deadlier every day. On the other hand, the rent money and other expenses were too much for me to handle. I thought about finding a room-mate, someone to talk to and share the expenses with. George made me an offer to move into the vacant room next to his in that old house. At first, I thought that we might ruin our friendship if we became roommates. Then I decided, why not? George was a good friend and a reliable person. The rent was of course much more reasonable, so I moved in. That was a good decision, George and I got along better than I thought. I found him to be unselfish, humble, generous, and chivalrous. Every time he cooked, he tried to cook for both of us whether I was home or not.

During the course of my friendship with George at ODU, he helped me on many occasions emotionally as well as financially. I remember I was having emotional problem with a girl that I dated for a while, and I became depressed when she decided to leave. I had a hard time concentrating on my studies. George sympathized with me as he went through the same experience with his ex-girlfriend. He constantly reminded me that life must go on and I should not let this to cause any distraction to achieving my goals. Another time, during a summer in the middle of my PhD studies, I was not getting any financial support from school and had a hard time keeping up with the expenses. I seriously contemplated quitting the PhD and looking for a job. George realized that I was going through financial hardship, and not only did he pay for the rent and other expenses, but, without my knowledge, he borrowed money from some source and lent it to me. He said, "I am lending you this money because I don't want you to interrupt your PhD," he said. I was speechless and flabbergasted. To this day, I feel I am indebted to him.

In the meantime, the power struggle in Iran climaxed. My best sources of news were TV, American newspapers and magazines in the university library, and the *Iran Times* (Persian News Paper published in the United States). Often we would follow the news about Iran via shortwave radio; we would listen to BBC news, and a number of other radio stations belonging to opposition groups. As mentioned before, President Banisadr was ousted and fled the country along with Massoud Rajavi, the leader of the MEK. Five days after they left, Ali Khamenei, the current supreme leader, who was a key member of the Islamic Republican Party (IRP) and one of Khomeini's closest disciples, lost the use of his right hand when a small bomb exploded during his speech in the Friday sermon. The bomb was planted in a tape recorder at the podium. The following night, during a routine meeting of the IRP members at their headquarter in Tehran, a sixty-pound bomb which was planted in a trash can next to the podium exploded and killed seventy-four people. The government of Iran blamed the MEK for the terrorist act and placed the death toll at seventy-two to correspond to *"haftad-o-dow tan (shahid),*" "seventy-two bodies (martyrs)," with Imam Hussein at Karbala.[127] Among the dead were Ayatollah Mohammad Beheshti, the most powerful man after Khomeini, and many government officials. Beheshti was known as the mastermind and the strategist of the Islamic Republic. Not only was he the leader of the IRP, he was also known to have been the founder of Hezbollah in Iran. Hezbollah (the Party of God) virtually does not exist in Iran any longer. The main headquarters of Hezbollah is now located in Lebanon.

Iranian people opposing Islamic Republic in the United States and many European countries in a way celebrated the death of Beheshti. In spite of the fact that Beheshti was notoriously unpopular among the opposition groups, but what happened was a terrorist act; I wonder why sometimes we celebrate the loss of a human life?! I often think and question myself, "Why do some of us humans in the golden ages of scientific and technological advancement behave the way we do? Why do some of us humans still act like a bunch of primitives who cannot resolve our problems civilly and peacefully? Why do some of us humans still act like a bunch of savages who cannot tolerate other viewpoints and must kill each other to satisfy our egos? Why do some governments still act like a bunch of bloodthirsty barbarians against their own people?"

On July 24, 1981, almost eighteen months after the very first president (President Banisadr) was inaugurated in Iran, another president was elected. Mr. Ali Rajaee, the IRP's favorite candidate, became the second president of Iran. Almost a month later, on August 30, at a conference in Tehran that Mr. Rajaee and his prime minister, Mr. Bahonar, were attending, a bomb went off and killed both of them along with ten other government officials. Millions of cleric supporters poured into the streets of Tehran and chanted, "Revenge, revenge, revenge."[128]

This was another human tragedy, retaliation by the opposition against many unjustified killings and executions of the cleric regime. Unfortunately, the assassination of Mr. Rajaee and Prime Minister Bahonar made some people happy and made others seek revenge! What was sad about all this was that the cleric regime of the Islamic Republic waged war against any organization and anyone who opposed the government in any shape or form, and has done so ever since that incident. They started imprisoning and killing many people of other religions. They imposed censorship on the newspapers and the media. They cracked down on the university professors and students. They imprisoned and executed many intellectuals without trials. The revenge of the Islamic Republic continued. They were killing people either by labeling them as *"mofsed-ol-felarz,"* "infidels on earth," or

---

127 Sandra Mackey, *The Iranians: Persia, Islam and the Soul of a Nation*, page 304.
128 Ibid., page 305.

"*monafeghin*," the "traitors," or by sending young people to the war zone. In the meantime, they were spreading hate, and terrorizing people in Iran in the name of religion. They encouraged parents to turn in their children if they belonged to anti-government organizations, "Those who turn in 'the infidels' or 'enemies of God' will go to heaven." Government officials used this statement in their media. Unfortunately, some parents fell for such deceitful words and were foolish enough to turn in their loved ones. They encouraged neighbors to spy on neighbors and turned relatives against relatives. I heard stories that some of those parents, who sent their children to the execution squad, after getting to know the brutal nature of the regime, could not carry the burden of guilt, and committed suicide.

NINETEEN

On October 2, 1981, not even two years after the revolution, in the midst of the reign of terror inside Iran and the war with Iraq at the border, the third presidential election took place. Despite Beheshti's and Khomeini's declaration that clergymen should not run for president, *Hojjat-ol-eslam* (a religious title, one step below Ayatollah) Ali Khamenei, who had lost the use of his right hand a few months earlier, was elected as the third president.

The newly elected president chose Mr. Ali Akbar Velayati, the foreign minister under Rajaee, as his prime minister. The Iranian Parliament rejected Velayati by a majority vote, and Mir Hossein Mousavi, one of Khomeini's favorites, became the prime minister. President Ali Khamenei's focus was limited to the war and external affairs, while Prime Minister Mousavi was in charge of internal affairs and executive decisions.

Prime Minister Mousavi became more popular among Iranians as a capable man who handled the economy very well during the Iran-Iraq war. His pseudo socialist and food-rationing policies at the time allowed basic supplies to be distributed to the public—rich and poor equally.[129]

Prime Minister Mousavi and President Khamenei did not get along very well for the most part. Although they were both members of the same party, the Islamic Republican Party (IRP), the prime minister joined the left wing of the party while the president remained in the conservative right wing.[130] However, other than the new economic platform presented by the prime minister, the new president and his administration did not present any new pattern of government conduct, nor did they make any changes in the ongoing war strategies. Street fighting, most, if not all, involving Mujahedin forces and the Revolutionary Guards, had

---

129 *Payvand's Iran News*, February 26, 2009, by Arash Farid (original source: Farsi pages of *Mianeh*). Arash Farid is a pseudonym used by a journalist in Tehran. Payvand's Iran News and Mianeh are internet newspapers.
130 Ibid.

intensified. Small and big bombs exploded occasionally in different parts of the country, especially in Tehran. The government executed and killed more than eighteen hundred people between the months of June and November of 1981. In most cases, the arrests and executions were arbitrary. It sufficed for any innocent bystander to be caught in the middle of a fight.

The government continued using human waves of young people, including minors as minesweepers in the war zone by putting "keys to paradise" around their neck. Saddam Hussein called the war another *Qadisiyyah Battle*,[131] and Khomeini called it a revenge for the murder of Imam Hussein at Karbala.

One of the biggest surprises of the Iran-Iraq war was the complete destruction of the Iraqis' Osirak nuclear reactor by the Israeli forces (Operation Opera or Operation Babylon). On June 7, 1981, a flight of Israeli Air Force F-16A fighter aircraft with an escort of a number of F-15A bombed the Osirak reactor.[132] Israeli military intelligence believed that the Iraqis had purchased an "Osiris class" nuclear reactor from France to produce plutonium in order to further an Iraqi nuclear weapons program.[133]

Saddam killed more than forty-two thousand Iranian soldiers through chemical weapons only.[134] One of his biggest aspirations was to produce nuclear weapons. He would have used them against Iran had he achieved his goals of becoming atomic. This action of the Israelis made so many Iranians happy. Ordinary people demonstrated their happiness on the streets the day after Osirak's destruction.

On April 1982, the government announced the neutralization of a coup by the elements of the inner circle. One of Khomeini's top aids, Sadeq Ghotbzadeh, who stayed with Khomeini during his exile in France appeared on national TV and confessed to his role in plotting to assassinate Khomeini and topple the government. He also confessed that Ayatollah Shariatmadari, the influential spiritual leader and the *Marjaa-e Taghlid* during the Shah, was aware of the assassination plot. The radical mullahs led by Khomeini immediately stripped Shariatmadari

---

131 The Battle of al-Qādisiyyah in 636 was the decisive engagement between the Arab army and the army of the Sassanid Dynasty of Persia during the first period of Muslim expansion. It is regarded as the decisive battle in the Islamic conquest of Persia. This battle ended the Sassanid rule of Iran. Arabs invaded Iran after defeating the Persian army, which resulted in killing the Sassanid king, Yazdegerd III. In the battle of *Qadisiyyah* Persians were defeated by Arabs and were occupied by the Arabs for over two hundred years. After the Arab invasion, Iranian territory has been invaded by Mongolians, and then occupied by Ottomans, British, and Russians. However, the defeat of Iranians by Arabs has been very costly and we are still paying for the bad consequences of that defeat. One of the bad consequences of that defeat was the creation of the Islamic Republic. Books can be written on this very subject.

132 Wikipedia, the free encyclopedia.

133 Ibid.

134 Farhang Rajaee, *The Iran-Iraq War: The Politics of Aggression* (Gainesville, FL: University Press of Florida, 1993), page 34.

of his position as spiritual leader and sentenced Ghotbzadeh to death. In the eyes of the mullahs, Shariatmadari was as guilty as Ghotbzadeh, but he had the overwhelming support of many Azari (or Azeri) people and many people in the country. Executing Shariatmadari was not going to be an easy task, but Ghotbzadeh was an easier target.

Shariatmadari was a moderate and a kind person. He was opposed to the dictatorship of the Shah's regime and wanted the Shah to limit his authorities and adopt the constitutional monarchy established in 1906. Unlike Khomeini, he encouraged peaceful demonstrations and adamantly condemned violence. Ayatollah Shariatmadari and his predecessor, Ayatollah Boroujerdi, were both opposed to Khomeini's doctrine of the *Velayat-e Faghih* and believed that the major role and the responsibility of Muslim clerics in the modern world was to preserve the spiritual character of the Islamic state, not to rule it directly.[135] After the confession by Ghotbzadeh, Mullah Mohammad Reyshahri,[136] known as "Scary Mullah," forced himself and his agents into Shariatmadari's house and interrogated him regarding Ghotbzadeh's confession. Shariatmadari denounced his knowledge and participation in the coup. Reyshahri slapped the seventy-year-old ayatollah across his face and forced him to read a confession letter and apologize to Ayatollah Khomeini.

Ayatollah Shariatmadari was a respectable, peaceful, and honest man. He would not have allowed the assassination of Khomeini. The radical mullahs did not like the moderate and nonviolent nature of Shariatmadari. This was a plot to set him up and to defrock him. It was a plan to pave the way for the establishment of a totalitarian regime. Ghotbzadeh, the former foreign minister, who was a frequent guest of Mr. Ted Koppel's "Nightline" television news program, underwent severe torture and was forced to say what the mullahs wanted him to say. Later on, Ghotbzadeh denied the assassination accusations but confirmed the plan for a government change.

Rumor has it that Ghotbzadeh attempted to speak with Ayatollah Khomeini numerous times without any success. In addition, Ghotbzadeh's mother pleaded to Khomeini to pardon her only son. I was not a fan of Ghotbzadeh personally but felt so sorry for him, and I was hopeful that Khomeini, who once called Ghotbzadeh

---

135 Reza Aslan, *No god but God* (New York: Random House Publishing, 2006), page 192.
136 Mohammad Mohammadi-Nik (born in 1946) was given the name Reyshahri (or Ray-Shahri meaning from the city of Ray near Tehran) by his father-in-law, Ayatollah Ali Meshkini. Reyshahri married Meshkini's nine-year-old daughter at the age of twenty-two. Immediately after the revolution, he was given the post of chief judge of the military revolutionary tribunal. He then became the first Iranian minister of intelligence under Prime Minister Mir-Hossein Mousavi. He has been in charge of several other government positions in the Islamic Republic. During the early revolution, he discovered two failed coups d'état: the Nozheh Coup, masterminded by Bakhtiar's supporters and then the Ghotbzadeh coup. Among Iranian dissidents, Reyshahri is known as the Islamic Republic's most senior criminal/politician.

"my son," would order a lighter sentencing for him. I thought Khomeini was going to do what Pope John Paul II did to his would-be twenty-three-year-old assassin, Mehmet Ali Agca, pardoning him from his hospital bed five days after the assassination attempt. The difference was that Khomeini was not even touched, the coup d'état did not succeed, and the veracity of Ghotbzadeh's involvement in the coup was unknown, while the pope was actually shot and wounded in his abdomen on May 13, 1981.

People do or say strangest things under torture. In recent crackdowns and arrests in Iran after the tenth presidential election, many prisoners, including young teenagers, confessed to the wrongdoings that were obvious to TV spectators as lies, deceptions, forced confessions, and ridiculous showdowns of the governmental propagandas. In some cases, the prisoners could not even read the forced confession letters. The following confession story is said to have happened during the reign of a dictator in the previous century:

The story has it that a delegate of several representatives met the despotic ruler of their country in his headquarter to discuss politics with him. After the meeting, the dictator noticed that his pipe was missing. He called his security chief to the office and asked him to find out if any member of the delegate had taken his pipe. However, the dictator found his pipe a few hours later inside a drawer of his desk. He called his security chief back to his office and told him to release the members of the delegate. The security chief said, "Sorry, your Excellency, almost half of the delegates confessed that they had taken the pipe, and the rest died during the interrogation and torture."

TWENTY

George and I had to evacuate the apartment because the property owner had sold the rundown old house to another person, who demolished the place and eventually made new apartments. We rented rooms in a house owned by an old lady a few miles away from the campus. We stayed there for about a semester or two until George finished his degree and found a job in town. Neither of us had a good experience with the grouchy old lady, so we had to move again. George moved in with his new girlfriend, whom he eventually married, and I moved back to the previous apartment complex on the second floor. Those apartment complexes were convenient mainly because they were only a few minutes' walk from the campus, but they were mostly occupied by freshman and sophomore students who were loud and played loud music. My next-door neighbor was a Turkish guy by the name of Jevat who was also a PhD student in the Mechanical Engineering Department. He was living there with his wife and his toddler daughter. They were extremely nice to me. They cooked for me on many occasions. Jevat's wife was an excellent cook, and I always enjoyed the food at their place.

Jevat and his wife often complained about the young students living in a different apartment complex right behind their apartment. They complained that the students were rowdy and played loud music. Luckily, those apartments were situated in such a way that had little noise impact on my apartment. One late evening as Jevat was studying and his wife was trying to put their baby to sleep, a few of those guys were playing football. Jevat opened the window and started yelling at the guys to be quiet. They wouldn't pay any attention to Jevat. He went downstairs and started swinging at one of them. The guy swung back at Jevat with a punch to his face and another one to his ribs, and he knocked Jevat down. Jevat's wife, who was observing the fight from upstairs, came knocking at my door continually. I was asleep. I woke up hastily, went to the door, and opened it quickly. She was crying and yelling repeatedly with her broken English, "Habib, they killed Jevat."

"Who killed Jevat?" I asked. "Where is Jevat?"

"He is downstairs."

I was still in my pajamas. I immediately changed my clothes and went downstairs. I noticed Jevat on the ground, almost knocked unconscious. Those guys were standing and watching. I turned to them and asked what was going on. One of them said, "I hit him in self-defense." I picked Jevat up. He was half-conscious. I could barely carry him to his car, and as I was trying to put him in the car, the guy said, "Take him back to Iran; take him to Khomeini."

I put him in the car, got the car key from his wife, and went to the guy and said, "If you hit this person because you thought he was from Iran, you are wrong; he is not from Iran. If you have anything against Iranians, you should hit me."

"No, sir, I am not a bigot, and I have nothing against you. He swung at me first. I only defended myself," he said.

At this time, the police arrived at the scene and asked me questions. I only told the police, "I am just a neighbor, the man is hurting, and I need to take him to the hospital."

I noticed that Jevat's wife pointed out to the police the young man who hit her husband. I took Jevat to Norfolk General. They treated him for minor injuries and released him. It was early morning. I took him back to his house. His wife was happy to see him safe and sound. Jevat consulted with me about whether or not he should press charges against the guy.

"This is entirely between you and your wife," I said.

"What would you do if you were me?" Jevat asked.

"I would just let it go if I were you," I said.

"Habib, you are right; this might be a lengthy process. I should focus on my studies. I will forgive him," he said.

I then quoted the Persian proverb to Jevat that says, "There is a joy in forgiveness that you can't find in vengeance."

A few days later, as I was walking to school, I saw the person who hit Jevat. He came up to me and said, "Hey, man, listen, I didn't mean to be disrespectful to your country and to your leader."

"That country is mine and I am proud of it, but the person who you are referring to as my leader is definitely not my leader," I said.

The tumultuous situation in Iran, the war between Iran and Iraq, and my concerns about the safety of my family and particularly my younger brothers back home were distractions to my studies. I was worried about my PhD qualifying exam and was behind with my PhD research. Two weeks before the qualifying exam, I went to our graduate program coordinator, Dr. Suren Tiwari, and asked to be withdrawn from the exam. He asked me, "Why?" I told him that I was not ready for it and wanted to postpone the exam to the following year. Dr. Tiwari was one of those professors who always guided the graduate students in the right direction. He was level headed, soft spoken, and a good person. I never had the pleasure of having him as a professor, but I had heard great things about him. He told me, "Listen, you have two weeks left; you could do a whole lot for the next two weeks."

My response was, "My friends who have registered for the exam have been studying for it for the past six months or more. We have only two chances for this notorious exam, and I don't want to lose my chance."

"You have fourteen days, eight or ten subjects, more than a day for each subject. Forget about your other problems and just focus on your studies for the next two weeks, and keep telling yourself that you can do it. Think about the joy of passing the exam," he said.

"What if I don't?"

"You will have another chance," he said. "You will get familiar with the format and typical qualifying-exam questions and you will pass it the next time, but do not think failure."

He sounded like my father. I could not talk him into letting me withdraw from the exam. I decided to do exactly what he told me. I studied hard. I saw him a couple of days later. He asked me, "Are you focusing?"

"Yes sir, I am," I said.

I kept reminding myself that I could do it. After taking the whole-day exam, I felt good. I was confident that I probably passed the competitive exam. Two weeks later, I heard from a good friend of mine and a former roommate, Rahi that Dr. Tiwari was looking for me. I went to his office nervous and anxious. "How do you think you did?" he asked.

"I think I did pretty well," I said.

"You did excellent," he said. "Not only did you pass, you made the highest score of all the participants."

"I owe it to you, Dr. Tiwari. I did exactly what you told me."

God bless his soul. Recently, I heard from a friend that he passed away not too long ago. He was a good man and an inspiring person.

After successfully passing the qualifying exam, the Iran-Iraq war escalated and Iraqis started air attacks on civilians in Tehran. My worries and anxieties about my family started again. I was desperately missing my family and friends back home.

Every time I planned to go visit, I was discouraged by my own family warning me about the uncertainty of the situations in Iran. On the other hand, in the United States, I was hearing stories about Iranian students who went back home for a visit and were not able to return as their student visas were not renewed.

However, I had a nice visit from my brother Iraj, who came to the United States on a tourist visa during summer of 1984. He stayed with me for a period of almost two-and-a-half months. I really enjoyed having him around while I was teaching a summer course. I wanted him to renew his visa and stay with me longer. He was worried about his wife and his one-year-old daughter, so he left. I felt extremely lonely and depressed after he left. I felt even more desperate to go back home. I tried to get myself busy with my PhD research, but, unfortunately, I was not making much progress on that. At times, I even thought of quitting and leaving the United States for good. I started dating a girl for a while, hoping that having a female companion would make me happy. That relationship didn't go anywhere.

I was living a boring and lonely life; going to school and working on my dissertation and then going to my apartment. In order to have a little bit of livelihood around the house, I decided to buy a parakeet with a cage. Every time I came back from school, I would get him out of the cage, feed him, and talk to him. He would jump on my shoulder while I was reading newspapers or watching TV. I had kept the parakeet for about six months or so. I had to get prepared to go to Virginia Tech to present a paper at a conference there. I cleaned the cage, put plenty of food and water in the cage containers, put the bird in the cage, and left. I came back after about forty-eight hours. I noticed a drastic change in the bird's attitude. He was not as friendly as before. He bit me a few times and wouldn't sit on my shoulders any longer. I was wondering what was happening to the bird, and then it dawned on me that he was probably angry at me for leaving him in the cage for such a long time. Although I liked the little bird and was getting used to having him around, I felt that he wanted to be free, so I let the bird go. For a while, my PhD life had become so routine and boring that I felt I was caged myself between my apartment and school. I wanted to be free. For me, the only way to escape from the cage was to finish my dissertation.

Today in Iran, the youth are angry because they feel that they are being caged. They do not have the freedom to express themselves. They are not at the liberty to have long hair, to have any contact with the opposite sex, to have parties or gatherings in their own houses under their parents' supervision, to dress any which way they like, and so on. For a long while after the revolution, people were not allowed to play music in their own cars. The police forces were stopping cars to search for tapes. They would storm houses to stop parties; anybody who resisted, would be arrested or occasionally would be thrown from the balconies, which, on many occasions, resulted in the deaths of many young people. Most often, the authorities would storm houses to search for satellite dishes or videotapes and things of that nature.

It is noteworthy to acknowledge a few names that helped me during the intense period of my life that I was working on my dissertation: my friends George, Rahi, and Nader and Maryam. George visited me quite often; we went to dinner, played chess, or watched movies together. Rahi, another PhD student at ODU, was one of my most disciplined and hardest-working friends. Rahi and I had a lot in common. We were both from the same country, we both loved the same kinds of food, we listened to the same kinds of music, we played card games, and we exercised together, but he had a better study habit than I did. My friend Nader and his wife, Maryam, invited me to their house numerous times for lunch and dinner. I always had the best foods at their house. Maryam was a fantastic cook. Not only was she a good cook, she was a great mother, a computer expert, and a good manager of a reputable company in Virginia. Her house was always spotless. Our friends used to call her a superwoman. She was like a sister to me. Nader also was like a brother and my biggest patron; no matter what I did, he supported me. Rahi finished his PhD, worked in Sweden for two years, and went back to Iran. I was in touch with him for a while and visited him a few times in Iran but lost touch. George and I still keep in touch. I also kept in touch with Nader and Maryam ever since I left Norfolk. Sadly, Maryam had a devastating near-fatal car accident in the late nineties. It was a miracle and the will of her husband that she came alive after being on life support for weeks. Words cannot describe Nader's devotion and self-sacrificial efforts that kept his wife alive.

TWENTY-ONE

The war continued well into the cities, and Saddam started air attacks on the civilians. Iranians retaliated. The targets were random—schools, hospitals, shopping centers, houses, etc. The victims of the air attacks were mostly innocent and defenseless people on both sides. The two governments violated every international law. The then United Nations Secretary General Javier Perez de Cuellar made numerous attempts to put an end to the war of cities, but the Iraqi regime continued the air and missile attacks. The Iranian regime retaliated. Saddam was desperate to put pressure on Iranians to end the war. He hit several cities during the Persian New Year.

I was constantly worried about the safety of my family members in Iran. Right after spring semester 1985, I decided to take a trip back home before finishing my PhD. The last time I had visited Iran was during the summer of 1978. The main purpose for my travel back home was to visit the family, but I also wanted to explore the possibility of finding employment after finishing my education. In spite of all the odds against this decision, I was very determined to travel to Iran, and nothing was going to stop me. Most of my friends thought that I was not going to be able to come back. I went to Dr. Ash, the then newly appointed chair of the ME department at ODU, and Dr. Kandil, my thesis advisor, and one of my best professors, and asked each for a letter of recommendation.

Most of the international flights, if not all, stopped traveling to Iran due to the war of the cities. The only way I could travel to Iran was to fly to Turkey and from there, travel to Tehran by bus. First, I had to make sure that I would be able to obtain a student visa in order to come back to the United States. There was no diplomatic relationship between Iran and the United States; therefore, I had to go to a third country to apply for the proper return visa. I was told that it was almost impossible to get the visa from Turkey, as the line of applicants trying to get visas to the United States was too long. Moreover, the American Embassy and Consulates in Turkey were too restrictive against Iranians. I decided to travel to Amsterdam first and apply for my student visa there. I went to the Netherlands Embassy in Washington, D.C., and applied for a tourist visa. The embassy gave me a tourist visa for one week. I bought my air ticket to, packed, and departed for Amsterdam on May 29, 1985.

I arrived at Schiphol Airport on May 30th. I was tired, lost, and needed to take a shower. I decided to catch a cab to take me to a reasonable hotel near the American Consulate. I thought the cab driver was going to charge me an arm and a leg but it wasn't too bad. The dollar was very strong back then in comparison with the Dutch currency; each dollar was worth over three guilders.

The cab driver took me to a reasonable hotel all right, but the hotel was not what I would call a five-star hotel! It was cold in Amsterdam for the last day of May, and I was too tired to look for a more decent hotel. What I needed was a quiet room with a decent, hot shower. The room had two small beds, apart from each other. I went to the bath, turned on the hot water, and waited for a long while for the hot water to come on. There was no sign of water getting hot. I had no choice but to take a cold shower. There were two tiny beds there. After the cold shower, I slept on one of the beds. When I woke up, it was late in the afternoon. I decided to go for a walk around the hotel. I walked for a while. I was hungry and started looking for a place to eat. I found myself in an alley full of sandwich shops; McDonald's was one of them, and the place was packed. I was looking for something different. I smelled some sort of Middle Eastern food. I was checking the place out, and this Middle Eastern-looking guy asked me to come in. "What do I smell?" I asked.

"The best doner kabob sandwich (gyro sandwich) in town, that's what you smell my friend," he said.

I did not know what doner kabob was. I asked him to make me one. He asked me whether I was an Arab.

"No, I am from Iran," I said.

"Oh, you're *Irani* (Iranian)," he said. "I am Syrian."

"Nice to meet you," I said.

"What do you think of Khomeini?" he asked.

"I am really too hungry to think of Khomeini," I said.

He prepared the sandwich and French fries with melted cheese on top and a soda for me. It was not bad at all. Then he asked, "What are you doing in Amsterdam?"

"I came here to get a visa to the United States of America," I said.

"Are you crazy?" he said. "You came all the way from Iran to get a visa here! You should have gone to Turkey. They don't give visas to Middle Eastern people here."

"No, I live in the United States, and I am going to Iran to visit."

"You are crazy! You live in the United States and you want to go back to Iran at this time!" he exclaimed. "There is madness going on in Iran right now with the war, inflation, street fighting, arrests of people, etc."

"How do you know all this?" I asked.

"I know so many Iranians who escaped the country and sought political asylum in Holland. They told me stories about Iran. In addition, I read papers." He said.

I paid him, thanked him for the food, and, as I was leaving, he sarcastically said, "When you get your visa back to America, come and take me with you."

After hearing those words, I regretted coming to Holland for obtaining the return visa. I walked back to my hotel and decided to go to my room and watch TV. Surprisingly, there was no TV there. For all those hours that I stayed in that room, I was too tired to notice the lack of a TV there. I went back to the tiny hotel lobby and asked the clerk to move me to a room with TV. He said that there was no TV in any of the rooms in the hotel. I complained that there was no hot water in the bathroom. The clerk said, "If you don't like it, you can leave."

"Okay, give me my money back and I will leave," I said.

"No, you have already stayed for half a day," he said.

"All right, give me half of the money and I will leave." I said.

The answer was no. I figured that there was no point arguing with the hotel clerk. It was cold and late in the evening, so I decided to stay overnight and leave first thing in the morning. I looked at some English newspapers in the lobby and went to my room. The room was very cold and the heater was not working properly. I went to bed and covered myself with two blankets from both beds. I said to myself, "Nothing works in this room, but at least I have my privacy." I went to bed and slept for a while. A loud noise woke me up. Suddenly, I heard a bang on the door. I thought that perhaps it was someone trying to get into the room next door. Next thing I noticed was that someone was trying to get into my room. I got up frantically and pushed at the door to keep him from coming in. The person unlocked the door and entered my room.

He was big and smelled like alcohol. I was scared. He threw some Dutch words at me. I told him that I did not speak Dutch. I asked him who he was, and with broken English he said, "I rented this room."

"No, I rented this room!" I exclaimed.

"There are two beds here, one for you, and one for me," he said.

He then took one of the blankets off me and went to bed. He fell asleep as soon as he went to bed and started snoring immediately. "Here goes my privacy," I muttered. In addition to his loud snoring, I could not trust him and was very much concerned that he might rob me. I had some cash in my pants' and in my jacket's pockets. I slowly got up from the squeaky bed, slowly went to the closet, and quickly removed all of my paper money and put it under my pillow. I also put my small handbag carrying my passport, small souvenirs, and my other personal belongings next to me on the bed. For all the noise I made, luckily, he did not wake up, but I could not sleep. I felt bad that I misjudged him; he turned out to be a harmless person. I stayed in bed and could not wait to get up in the morning and leave.

The next morning, I checked out and left the hotel as fast as I could. I was carrying my bag in one hand and my heavy suitcase in the other hand. I could not go far. I found another hotel in the same alley nearby. I asked the hotel clerk whether I was going to have full privacy, hot water, and TV. The rent was a bit more expensive, but the hotel clerk assured me that I was going to have full privacy and hot water but no TV. I could live without the TV. The first thing I did was to take a hot bath. Then I went back to the clerk and asked where the American Consulate was. He said, "It is far from here; you need to go to the Central Station and take a train to American Consulate." I realized that the cab driver did not bring me to the right place.

I managed to get to the American Consulate via train. By the time I got there, it was somewhat late, and I was advised to get there early in the morning the next day. I went back to the hotel, stayed there overnight, and left for the American Consulate again early morning the next day. There were about a dozen of us waiting patiently to be called for an interview. The person sitting next to me, to the best of my recollection, was from Morocco. He asked me where I was from. "I am from Iran," I said.

"This is the third time I am coming here," he said. "They hardly issue visas to non-Europeans here. They are particularly tough on Iranians and Arabs."

I did not need those discouraging words at those early hours. They called my name, and I was very nervous. I believe the counselor who interviewed me was the chief counselor there. He asked me a few questions about my status and my study stages in the United States and then asked, "What is the purpose of your trip to Iran?"

"Visiting my family," I said.

"How are you traveling to Iran with all the air fares ceasing to fly to Iran?"

"I am flying to Istanbul, Turkey, and then I will catch a bus to go to Iran from there," I said.

"What are you going to do after you finish your PhD?"

"I don't know, sir," I responded.

"Are you going to go back to Iran to work or you will work in the United States?"

I did not know what to say. If I had said that I would go back to Iran, I would be lying to him. If I had said that I would work in the United States, he could have stamped a reject sign on my passport. I had to come up with an answer instantaneously. I responded, "If there is a stable government in place in Iran by the time I finish my studies, I will go back because I would like to serve my people in Iran. If not, I will stay in America only if they want me." That was my honest response.

The counselor looked at me and said, "Our policy is to wait for four weeks to grant a student visa. We need to do more investigation about you. If you have a clean record, you will receive a visa. Come back in four weeks."

"I don't have a visa to come back to Amsterdam, and it is almost impossible to get a return visa back to Holland from Iran," I said.

"This is our policy," he said.

I was discouraged, but thanked him and left. Just as I was stepping out the door, he called me by my first name and asked me to come back. I thought maybe he reconsidered his decision and was going to approve my visa. Not quite so! However, he said, "If you want, I could Telex your case to the U.S. General Consulate in Istanbul."

"That would be great, sir," I said.

I left the consulate and went back to my hotel. I stayed one more night in Amsterdam and left the next day for Istanbul. My experience in Turkey was like déjà vu. I asked the taxi driver to take me to a decent hotel near the American Consulate General. He took me to a shabby hotel with a very tiny bathroom, again with no hot water. Luckily, Istanbul was not cold and I did not mind a cold shower. Surprisingly, there was a TV in the room, but I did not notice any English channels. After the shower, I watched TV; I could tell most news revolved around the Iran-Iraq war. The newscast showed Khomeini's picture several times. I wished I could speak or understand Turkish as most Iranians do. In the evening, I went for a walk around the hotel. I noticed commonalities in the infrastructures between Tehran and Istanbul to some extent. That made me more anxious to go back home after seven years. I went to a Turkish café and ordered Turkish coffee and pastry and went back to my hotel. I sat in the lobby of the hotel for a while. I noticed a lady sitting right across from me in a hot miniskirt, smiling and blinking at me.

I looked around me and noticed nobody but me. I had seen the lady earlier, while I was registering. She came up to me and said, "I have been noticing you. Are you going to invite me for a drink?" Her English was not bad at all.

"I am too tired to drink," I said. "I need to go to bed early, but thank you."

I went to my room, watched some more TV, and read the book by Dale Carnegie that I was carrying with me: *How to Stop Worrying and Start Living*. I started yawning and felt sleepy. As I was fixing to go to bed, someone started knocking at my door, "Oh, God, not again," I muttered. I thought I was going to have to share the room with someone again as I noticed two beds in the room, like in the hotel in Amsterdam.

I cautiously opened the door; it was the same lady who I met in the lobby earlier. "Do you want to have company?" She asked. It was tempting, but I said no, because I couldn't trust her. I don't waste my money for instant pleasure; I'd rather give away my money to a needy person for a rewarding and a more satisfying pleasure. I learned that from my father.

I woke up early in the morning and left for the American Consulate. I noticed a huge line behind the consulate; almost all of them were Iranians who were trying to escape the war and the Islamic Republic for the United States. I went to the guard and asked him to check if they had received a Telex on my behalf from Amsterdam. The guard was very polite; he wrote my name on a piece of paper, went inside, and came back shortly. He notified me that they had not yet received any Telex on my behalf. I was very disappointed. I was not quite sure whether I had to take a number or stay in a big line, but I figured that it was going to take a few days for them to call my name for an interview. I did not have much time to waste; I was too anxious to see my family. I decided to leave the next day. In the meantime, I decided to go sightseeing and explore the city of Istanbul on foot. I found Istanbul to be a pretty city with friendly people, especially if you spoke English with them.

I walked a very long distance and bought some small Turkish souvenirs and some Turkish delights. I remember while shopping in one of the souvenir shops, I got into a bargaining negotiation with the shop owner. He gave me a figure for one of the items that was almost twice as much as the item was worth. I knew that because it was priced less expensively in another shop. I put everything down and told him, "I think you are trying to take advantage of the fact that I am a tourist and don't speak your language. These are all overpriced and I am going to buy them from another store." As I was leaving the shop, he told me to come back, he would give me a better deal. I went back and he gave me a much better deal.

He then asked me, "Where are you from?"

"I am from Iran," I said.

"When Homeini [Khomeini] tells you something, you wouldn't get into an argument with him, would you?" He said. "If you do, he will cut your head off." He continued saying, "The Iranian people were fooled by Homeini. However, he taught the Turkish people a lesson not to fall into the trap of some of their religious power mongers."

I then jokingly said, "Yes, we were fooled by Khomeini, but I wouldn't be fooled by you." We both laughed and shook hands.

I went to the Istanbul International Bus Station the next day and bought my ticket for only $20. The bus was packed with Iranian travelers, except the driver and his partner, who were Turkish. The driver was a young and funny person who would change seats with his partner in the middle of his driving without stopping the bus. He played Persian and Turkish music, mostly dance music, and would invite people to get up and dance in the walkway between the two seat rows. Other than making very dangerous and scary passes, he made it fun.

On the bus, I was surrounded by a group of Iranian relatives. They had brought so much food, fruits, Persian and Turkish sweets, and they were eating constantly. They offered me all kinds of food and hot Persian tea out of the thermo flask; I would not dare say no to them. I ate so much food that I didn't spend a penny for food throughout the travel period which took more than forty-eight hours. The person sitting next to me was one of the relatives. He was a tall and strong-looking guy named Zia. Every time the bus stopped at restaurants for food, Zia and I would go sightseeing and would take pictures. These people were so hospitable and so much fun to travel with that I did not feel the travel time and the fatigue. They were extremely nice to me, especially Mr. Ghaffari and his wife, who were sitting one seat in front of us.

The fun time was over when we arrived at the Iran-Turkey border, the so-called infamous Bazargan border. The stoppage time for passport check and custom check was long, boring, and not fun at all. The custom officers of the Islamic Republic were harsh and unfriendly. That was my very first experience in dealing with the Iranian officials after the revolution.

From Bazargan we headed to Tehran, and I was becoming more anxious to see my family. The driver kept on playing loud music even in the Iranian territory. We were stopped by the Revolutionary Guards in Iranian Azarbaijan around midnight when everybody was sound sleep. Two young Revolutionary Guards came inside the bus. They were looking at everyone as if each person in the bus was a criminal. Then they asked everyone to get out of the bus. People started leaving the bus one by one without saying a word. I whispered to Zia, "What do they want?"

"They are looking for things like alcoholic beverages, videos, and cassettes," he said.

"What right do they have to treat people like this?" I said.

"They are a bunch of bullies and they have guns. They are given autonomy to do whatever they like to scare people," he said.

There was a lady in the bus with a young child sleeping on her lap and her husband next to her couple of seats behind us. The husband begged the guard to let his wife and his child stay on the bus. The guard said sternly to the lady and her husband, "No, everybody must leave the bus, now."

I became so agitated and could not continue staying silent; I turned to the guard and said, "Don't you have any manners? Why are you being so rude and disrespectful? It is cold out and the child is asleep, why don't you let the lady and the child stay?!"

"Who do you think you are talking to me like this?" The guard said.

"Who do you think you are, talking to people like dirt?" I said.

At this point Zia kept elbowing me and whispering to me to be quiet. The guard turned to me and said, "I am going to deal with you later." However, he let the lady and the child stay. Zia rushed me out of the bus. Outside the bus, the guards were removing the suitcases from the luggage compartment and searching them on random basis. It was dark out there and unseasonably cold.

Zia grabbed my hand, forcibly rushed me away from the guards to the back of the bus, and said to me, "What are you doing? Are you out of your mind? These people can kill you right now. You don't know these people; they are ruthless, uneducated, and irrational. They are getting paid to terrorize people, and they have no mercy."

"What are they going to do with my suitcase?" I asked.

"Forget about your suitcase; just stay here, and don't show your face to them," Zia said. We waited until they let everyone get into the bus again. Zia and I cautiously got onto the bus. We sat and waited until everyone came in.

The bus driver started counting people while his partner got behind the wheel. He came up to me and, in broken Farsi, said, "No, no! Don't get into an argument with them."

When we completely settled and the bus started running, Mr. Ghaffari, his wife, and Zia spoke to me about the brutality of the regime. They all said to me that I was lucky they let me live. Zia said, "You are lucky the guy got sidetracked and probably forgot about you. He could have shot you on the spot." Then they started telling me horror stories about young boys and girls who were shot just for talking back to the Revolutionary Guards. They told me sad stories about so many young Iranians who left Iran and were living under the harshest conditions in Turkey just to escape the brutality of the regime. Zia told me about many young runaway girls who sold their bodies in Turkey to make a living. These stories brought tears to my eyes.

"I understand why they searched for alcoholic beverages and perhaps obscene videos, but why cassette tapes?" I asked Zia.

"The Islamic Republic banned almost all kinds of music belonging to the Shah's era—Classical music, Pop music, Jazz music, Western music, and all kinds of music sung by female singers," Zia said.

"How come they did not interrogate the driver? He has so many cassettes," I said.

"They normally don't harass the drivers, especially the Turkish drivers," he said. "The drivers usually bribe them with money."

"What is so un-Islamic about music?" I asked. "Music is banned, but bribery is allowed!"

"The Islamic Republic is a government of blood and terror that promotes sadness, crying, and horror. They don't want to see happiness and laughter on the faces of people. As for the Revolutionary Guards and the so-called bassijies, they can violate many Islamic laws: bribery, harassing people, killing innocent people, raping women, whatever they please, and get away with it," he said.

We finally arrived in Tehran after a long trip, in the middle of the day. We got off the bus. We each picked up our suitcase. It was time to say good-bye to everyone. Zia and I gave each other a big hug. I thanked him for his kindness, and for perhaps saving my life. The family that I defended and got myself into trouble for, came up to me and thanked me for sticking up for them, but advised me not to do that again. I went to Mr. and Mrs. Ghaffari to say good-bye but they both kindly offered me to go with them to their house to freshen up before going to my family. They were very sincere about their offer and I accepted. I felt stinky and needed a shower so bad. Luckily, their house was within a couple blocks from ours in Tehran. They were so kind as to let me take a shower and then a nap in their guest bedroom. After I woke up, Mr. Ghaffari offered to take me home; I knew whereabouts my family lived, but not the exact location. My parents had recently moved to Tehran from Fardis and purchased a house very close to the one we had before moving to Fardis. I called my parents and told my mother where I was. My father and the rest of the family were still at work. My mother showed up with one of the next-door neighbors in about fifteen minutes. I was so happy to see my mother. We were both in tears. At home, my teenage sister Afsaneh was waiting for me, and I was so happy to see her again. Later on my father showed up from work. I noticed that he had aged so much. We both cried. Then my youngest brother, Ahmad, showed up, and, later on, my brothers Iraj, Nasser, and their wives and children, and my sister Molood, her husband, and her children came to visit. I enjoyed the family reunion so much, and in spite of being tired, I stayed awake well after midnight talking to everyone.

Within the first week or so, I met so many of my friends and relatives. I noticed most of my friends and relatives had aged beyond their actual age. The war, the economic disasters, and harsh circumstances, all created by the Islamic Republic, had taken a big toll on the lives of ordinary citizens in Iran.

TWENTY-TWO

One interesting note about my journey in Istanbul was that wherever I went, I noticed the pictures of Kemal Ataturk, the founder of modern Turkey, on the walls in the shops, restaurants, government offices, airports, etc. I personally oppose idolatry and worshiping of political characters, but I sensed that the people of Turkey mostly respected Kemal Ataturk and admired him for his many reforms and for his sense of allegiance and love for his country. Unfortunately, the Islamic Republic could not even tolerate having Reza Shah's dead body in a graveyard in Iran. His body was removed from the grave and moved to Egypt by his son, Mohammad Reza Shah, to protect his tomb from being destroyed. Reza Shah was indeed the founder of modern Iran. Reza Shah and Kemal Ataturk had a lot in common: they both were born in the late 1800 (Reza Shah in 1878, Ataturk in 1881), they were both from poor families, and both were army officers and military geniuses. They were both secularists, and they both ended two disastrous dynasties (Reza Shah ended the Qajar Dynasty and Ataturk, the Ottoman Empire). They both rose to power in 1921 (Reza Shah became the king and Kemal Ataturk became the president). They were both visionaries. They both industrialized and rebuilt the whole infrastructures of their countries from scratch. They both reorganized their armed forces into army, navy, and air force for the first time in their respective countries. They both gave more freedom and a boost of self-determination and self-esteem to women. They both made many vital reforms for their people. They both revamped their educational systems completely and built many elementary schools, high schools, universities, hospitals, railroads, and more. They both performed these tremendous feats within fifteen years. Reza Shah achieved all of these remarkable accomplishments despite the fact that the Qajar regime was quite corrupt and left Iran in dire economic straits.

Reza Shah was indeed as subservient to Iran as Kemal Ataturk was to Turkey and George Washington was to America. Kemal Ataturk and George Washington are credited by their people as the founding fathers for their nations, but it is shameful that Reza Shah's dead body had to be removed from his very own grave in his homeland. The main reason, in my opinion, is that George Washington successfully, and Kemal Ataturk to some extent managed to separate church and state but Reza Shah did not succeed to fulfill that important mission. In addition, Reza Shah did not allow freedom of press and freedom of speech. However, the historians and the true patriots in Iran have acknowledged him as one of the greatest leaders in the Iranian history.

The current leaders in Iran have no sense of allegiance and patriotism to the country. They have more passion and devotion to their own version of Islam (not true Islam) than their motherland. They have condemned the great leaders who truly served the people of Iran such as King Cyrus, King Darius, Babak Khorramdin,[137] Reza Shah, and Mossadeq. They labeled Reza Shah as an element of the British government because he came to power through a British-supported military coup. It is true that Reza Shah came to power with the help of the British government, but he did not have any choice. The British controlled half of Iran and Russians controlled the other half during Qajar dynasty. However, when Reza Shah became the ruler of Iran, he succeeded in cutting the influence of both foreign occupiers.

The mullahs in Iran despised Reza Shah and labeled him as Reza *Gholdor* (bully). They considered him a brutal dictator. He certainly was an iron-handed dictator and I am not sure if he could have run the country any other way at that time. Reza Shah's dictatorship was of benevolent type. Nevertheless, he was not nearly as brutal as the current leader in Iran. He was an authoritarian leader who utilized his political authorities to build the country for the benefit of all Iranians. On the contrary, the founder and current rulers of the Islamic Republic have exercised their religious influence and political power for self-interest and for

---

137   Babak Khorramdin was born in the eighth century in Balal Abad region of Azarbaijan (currently part of Azerbaijan Republic). He is considered as one of the most heroic Persian freedom fighters in the Iranian history. He initiated the Khurramites movement against the Arab Caliph occupiers (Abbasid Dynasty at the time). At the time, Iranians resisted the brutal rulings of Abbasid Caliphs in different parts of Iran, similar to what is happening now under the ruling of Islamic republic. Many Iranians today compare the Islamic Republic with Omayyad and Abbasid rulers. The Khorramdin revolt expanded to every corner of Iran and lasted for twenty years before it was defeated. Babak was betrayed by Khaydar Afshin, a senior traitor general at the court of Abbasid Caliph. The Caliph ordered Babak's executions in public. Caliph's henchmen first cut off his legs and then his hands in order to see his paled face, but Babak heroically covered his face with the drained blood pouring out of his cuts. Babak's movement later on became known as "Babak Fortress," located in the Qarabaq Mountains. His heritage is celebrated by many Iranians, Azarbaijanis, and Tajiks.

the benefit of only a very small sect of the whole population. Some of the current leaders in Iran have become outrageously rich while the rest of the people have been suffering from the unhealthy economy for years. There is nothing benevolent about the Islamic Republic.

Benevolent dictatorships can be good and constructive but, in my humble opinion, in this era with modern communications technology increasing the awareness of the people, dictatorship in any shape or form is destructive and inefficient. I think Mohammad Reza Shah, as I mentioned before, was overall a good leader. I say this despite the hateful statements and loathsome feelings harbored many against him. However, his creation of SAVAK and firmly establishing its authority to suppress political freedom turned his regime into a malevolent dictatorship and cost him his throne.

Truly benevolent and strong political leaders never resort to violence against their people not even against their toughest opponents. Leaders and freedom fighters that have captured the hearts and souls of the people used their words and not their swords, to free their nations or to fight for a good cause. This is a fact in history.

Imagine being in prison for 27 years under the harshest conditions and after being released, shaking hands with the enemies and letting go of the past. That takes a lot of restraint, forgiveness, courage, and humanity. This person is none other than Nelson Mandela who outlawed the apartheid with self-sacrifice and his words, not with weapons. King Cyrus, the Great, Mahatma Gandhi, and Martin Luther King Junior are other good examples of such leaders.

At any rate, going back to my summer 1985 visit to Iran; After staying for about a week in Tehran, my mother, my brother Ahmad, and I decided to go up north to Shahsavar (Tonekabon) to visit my other sisters and relatives. We had a nice family reunion that was blessed with pleasant weather. I was overwhelmed and humbled by the warm reception, which included an assortment of the most delicious foods. We laughed, joked, and sang songs while the kids danced—though everyone was cautious about playing the music too loudly. They talked about the horrors of the war and the casualties inflicted upon the people of Iran. They all expressed how bad it had been when the two governments started the war of cities. Although their town was never hit, they were always anxious for their relatives in Tehran. Thankfully, the air attacks of the civilians had ceased—at least for a while.

After enjoying the company of my uncles, my cousins, and my sister Maasoomeh, we left for my sister Molook's house in Ghale Gardan, a town not too far from Shahsavar, to sleep. The weather was nice, so my brother Ahmad, my brother-in-law Jaafar, and I decided to spread out our futon mattresses on the balcony and sleep there. The rest of the family slept inside. We gazed at the beautiful stars and talked for a long while before dozing off. We had not been sleeping long before a tremendous sound shook my sister's house. My brother-in-law Jaafar moaned, "Here we go again! Damn it, Saddam!" We were all awake now. Jaafar, very calmly and gently, suggested that we go back to sleep. Again, there was a loud booming sound. I thought they were bombing Shahsavar. I was worried about my sister Maasoomeh. Jaafar said, "Don't be naïve; they are hitting Tehran, not Shahsavar." Jaafar was correct; the Iraqis were bombing Tehran, and we could hear it and feel it in my sister's house—almost 260 kilometers away from Tehran.

We started getting worried about my family back in Tehran. Unfortunately, my sister Molook did not have a phone at that time. I told my brother Ahmad that we needed to leave. We left right after breakfast. I told my mother to stay because it was safer there, but she insisted that she wanted to be with us. I was so worried that perhaps our house in Tehran or any of my close family's houses might have been hit. Ahmad was driving as fast as he could. Although the scenery was beautiful along the way but I was too worried to enjoy.

It was early afternoon when we got home. Luckily, no harm was done to anyone I knew, but my heart bled for those who lost their houses and their loved ones. I felt a deep sympathy for those people. The bombing of the city of Tehran by Iraqis via French-made Dassault Mirage F1, and attacks on other major cities in Iran, five or six times throughout the night, became a routine thereafter for the next three weeks that I stayed in Tehran. Words cannot describe the horror and terrifying experiences that I went through during those three weeks. It was horrifying and heartbreaking to watch TV or read stories about the victims of the bombings. The media in Iran would only depict parts of the facts about the casualties and the victims, not the whole picture. The people of Iran expressed their disenchantment and disdain for the war through sporadic demonstrations every time Tehran was hit, but the government would send their thugs to disperse and suppress the demonstrations from becoming widespread.

I remember one early morning one of my friends, who was a government employee, called, and asked me if I wanted to go to his workplace and keep him company at work. I accepted the offer. He said that he would come to pick me up in an hour or so. I got up and picked up my electric shaver, but my father cautioned me not to shave. "Why not?" I asked.

"You are going to a government building in which the employees don't shave," my father said.

I put my shaver back in the shaving bag. I took a quick shower, and put on my short-sleeved shirt. My father said, "Put on a long-sleeved shirt; they don't like it there, they are not going to let you in."

Then I jokingly picked up a tie and pretended that I was putting it on. "What are you doing?" My father asked. "Wearing a tie is not allowed in Government Buildings."

"What is so Islamic about an *aba* and a cloak and what is so un-Islamic about wearing a tie, or wearing a short-sleeved shirt, or shaving?" I asked. "The Prophet Muhammad was a well-dressed person and he always encouraged his people to dress properly. Didn't he?"

My father didn't have any answer to that. Anyhow, my friend showed up, and just before we left, my father cautioned me to be careful not to say certain words that might get me into trouble.

At work, my friend introduced me to all employees in his division. He was the supervisor of the division. Unlike the Shah's era, when normally all government employees were required to shave and to wear appropriate attire with a tie, these people were all unshaven, and they mostly looked much older than their age. In mid-morning, I noticed almost everyone was dozing off. I did not notice any female employees. Even the secretaries at that time were all men. I had taken a book with me and I was reading it, and I felt very tired myself. My friend who stepped out for a while came back and yelled at the employees to wake up. Poor guys were tired because of the lack of enough sleep due to all the nighttime bombings and the sirens that went off the night before. Just before lunch, we were all required to pray. After lunch, again, the employees were dozing off. They brought us tea, one after another. In the mid-afternoon, the main boss showed up, a tall, smiling mullah in his mid to late fifties. I was introduced to him as a doctoral student in the United States of America. "My son, what are you studying in the land of Satan?" he asked.

"I am studying mechanical engineering," I said.

He asked a few more questions and then shook my hand and said, "I hope you come back after you finish your doctoral degree."

"If you think that land is the land of Satan; I am going to be the product of that land, why do you want me to come back?" I asked. In an instant, his smiling face turned sour and left without saying a word. My friend and a couple of his deputies left with him. After he left the room, two of the employees came to me and started complaining about the situations in Iran.

One of them quietly said, "These bastards ruined our country and they think they own this land."

One of them said, "We are less fortunate than the people of South Africa! At least they are not being bombed every single night. In South Africa, there is apartheid of whites against blacks; here we have religious apartheid, the apartheid of mullahs against non-mullahs. If you don't think like they do, you are a non-Muslim; you are *a Kaafar*, an infidel."

"Why are you guys working for the government if you are not happy?" I asked.

"Who is going to feed our families? We are thankful that at least we have a job," they said. At this point, my friend and his other deputies came back, and those guys went back to their desks.

Another time, I asked the same friend to help me inquire about my job prospects in Iran after finishing my education in the United States. He made an appointment with an influential person in the office of the prime minister (Mr. Mousavi was the prime minister at that time) by the name of ST. Mr. ST was polite and very kind to me. He asked me a few questions about my background and my areas of expertise. He then made a few phone calls and then turned to me and said that he had an excellent idea. He could make me the director of the research center at the air force with excellent pay. Without any hesitation, I refused that offer. He mentioned about all kinds of benefits, including free housing, and again reiterated the excellent salary. Again, I said no. Mr. ST asked, "Could you tell me why you are so adamant about this job?"

"I will not work for the government," I said.

"May I ask why not?"

"I am going to keep my reasons to myself."

"Only those who don't approve of the government don't want to work for the government," he said.

Again, I said, "I will keep my reasons to myself."

"I respect that," he said. "What kinds of jobs do you like?"

"I would like to work for a university," I said.

"There are plenty of professorial jobs available. Go back to the United States, finish your education, come back, and see me again," he said.

My father was very curious about my meeting with Mr. ST and asked me to tell him all the details. I told him about my meetings and my remarks to my friend's boss about "the land of Satan." He did not like my remarks and became very upset with me, and we argued back and forth. My father and I got into arguments several times during my visits to Iran. He admired Khomeini and always thought of him as somewhat a divine person, as a person who defeated darkness and brought light and hope to life. He could never accept any criticism of Khomeini's regime and strongly believed in Khomeini's doctrine of *Velayat-e-Faghih* as the only way to fight against blasphemy and to defuse dictatorship and tyranny. He had the same sentiments and feelings about Khomeini's successor, Ali Khamenei.

I learned so much from my father and respected him as a genuinely patriotic, religious, and humanitarian person. He shed tears for young kids living in orphanages and for people living in poverty. He shared the sorrow of people who lost their loved ones in the war. He cared about humanity and people all over the world. He loved peace and hated war. He condemned terrorism and called it inhumane and un-Islamic. Yet he supported the Islamic Republic. During my visits to Iran and through my observations and talking to a wide cross-section of people, I was convinced of the undemocratic, corrupt, and brutal nature of the regime. I could not accept why anybody with a right mind would support such inhumane regime, let alone my own father! We argued occasionally and neither of us could convince the other. What I did not realize was the fact that about a decade before my father passed away; he was out of touch with the outside world and watched too much of the Islamic Republic's TV and believed their lies and propaganda machines. The rest of my family members, however, were too much involved with their daily grind of supporting their family, and they had no desire whatsoever to get involved with politics.

After staying in Iran for more than three weeks, observing the harsh circumstances, and experiencing the horror of nighttime bombings, I felt sad and helpless. It was time for me to go back. I figured the best thing for me to do was to go back to the United States, finish my education, and hope for a change of circumstances. My brother Ahmad took me to the international terminal, and I purchased my bus ticket back to Turkey for two days later. Those days coincided with the month of Ramadan. On the way back from the terminal, it was after lunchtime and we were both very hungry. All the restaurants and food centers were closed in commemoration of the month of Ramadan. He took me to a sandwich shop belonging to an Armenian. His shop windows were all covered with papers and mini blinds for the month of Ramadan. He knocked on the door; the shop owner would only open the door for those who he knew. We had to buy the sandwiches and leave immediately. According to the rules of the Islamic Republic, it was illegal to eat in public. Violators would be sentenced to jail or even more severe punishment. We had other things to do that day and had no choice but to eat the sandwiches in my brother's car. He drove to a quiet alley, parked the car, and we started eating the sandwiches inside the car. For every bite of the sandwich, we had to watch out for the police or the Revolutionary Guards. We finished our lunch cautiously and fearfully.

I felt so bad for my brother Ahmad; he was my youngest brother, he had finished his military service just before the Iran-Iraq war started, and he was working as an electrician. He was very talented and skillful in his profession. I thought he could do a lot better with his talent in the United States than wasting it under the harsh ruling of the Islamic Republic. My other brothers were married and had children. The laws in Iran were changing overnight. When Khomeini took over as the leader of the revolution, he reduced the military service from two years to one. After the war started, they changed the law again to what it used to be. Ahmad was among those who had served for only one year. In those days rumors spread that, those who served for only one year should go back to the military. Going back to the military meant being drafted to the war zone.

The war was not to defend the territory any longer. It turned to a war of Saddam and Khomeini. As mentioned before, Iranians very heroically defended their soil and recaptured all the occupied lands within the first couple of years of the war. Saddam and other Arab nations agreed to pay Iran for war reparation as mentioned before. Khomeini should have stopped the war then. He unjustifiably insisted that the war must continue.[138] Innocent people were being killed on both sides for no reason. I didn't want my brother to die for an unjust war. I became determined to get my youngest brother out of Iran before he was recalled for the military service and sent to the war zone.

The day of my departure to Turkey in early June 1985, I felt so depressed that I was leaving my family behind during the tense and stressful times. Saddam started hitting Tehran with ground-to-ground missiles in addition to his Mirage air attacks. My family members were fearful that the bus carrying me to Turkey might get hit, and I was worried that our house in Tehran might get hit. That day was probably the saddest day of my life. I cried hysterically and uncontrollably, not only for my family, but also for my people, and for my country. On the bus, I noticed mostly young Iranian boys (those who had finished their military duties) and some girls trying to get out of the country in the hopes of seeking a better future in Turkey or to seek political asylum in some European countries or in the United States. Most of them ended up living in Turkey in the harshest conditions.

After the June 12, 2009 presidential election in Iran, a huge number of young Iranian people left the country for Turkey. Among them were many young and honest journalists who spoke up and told the truth about the election fraud and

---

138 It wasn't until July of 1988 when the war came to a deadlock and Khomeini had no choice but accepting UN mediation for truce. He drank "the cup of poison" as he put it. The cost of the senseless war was approximately $300 billion (Encyclopedia of the Middle East/Ayatollah Ruhollah Khomeini).

many young freedom fighters who, participated in anti-government demonstrations. The government identified many of them and their pictures appeared in the government-controlled newspapers and on the Internet. Most of these refugees paid so much money to be smuggled to the city of Van in Turkey (the closest border city to Iran) to escape the death sentence and the brutality of the Islamic Republic. Yet they had to pay even more money to go to Istanbul in order to seek political asylum in other countries. These refugees in Turkey are not allowed to work, they are not allowed to participate in any political activities, and they have to pay temporary residency taxes. In addition, they have to pay at least $200 for rent in clay houses, plus utility bills, and from $200 to $300 per month for food.[139] Another tragedy is the mistreatment of the Greek government against Iranian political asylum seekers. There are 44 refugees in Athens consist of men, women, and children. These people have no shelters, cannot work, and cannot even open a bank account. Among the 44 refugees, several have sewn their mouths shut to further protest their unacceptable status in Athens as well as the regime in Tehran.[140]

Going back to my story, in the summer of 1985, after arriving in Istanbul, I went back to the American Consulate General the next day. I went to the guard again and asked him to find out whether they had received the Telex from their counterpart in Amsterdam. The guard came back shortly and said, "Yes, we have received the Telex, and you can come in." I was very happy that I did not have to stay in the big line. I sat in the waiting room until they called my name. My interviewer was a lady who loudly and impolitely said, "What makes you think, if they have accepted your visa applications in Amsterdam, we automatically grant you the visa? Go back and get the visa from them. Besides, you should have stayed in the line like everybody else anyway."

"Madam, why are you mad at me? Your guard told me that I could come in," I said. "Please give me my passport back and I will try to go back to Amsterdam."

I got my passport back and left. At the door, the guard asked me, "Did you get your visa?"

"No, she didn't give it to me," I said. "What is my chance of getting a visa to Amsterdam?"

"Very slim," he said. I had heard from other people that it was very difficult to get a visa to Holland.

---

139 www.iranhumanrights.org/.../asylum-in-turkey-futile-hopes-and-dreams.
140 www.freepressers.com/.../the-inhumanity-to-iranians-starts-in-iran-and-continues-for-refugees-to-greece-and-turkey

I was very disappointed with the way I was treated at the American Consulate. I started panicking and thinking, "My only chance of getting a visa back to the United States of America is through the American Consulate in Amsterdam. What if they don't give me a visa back to Holland?"

I immediately, went to the Dutch Consulate General in Istanbul. Luckily, I did not have to stay in a big line. It was still early morning. I went to the guard, explained my situation, and offered him some money if he could help me getting the visa to Amsterdam. I could tell that the Turkish guard was sympathetic; he gently and politely said, "Don't worry; I will get you a visa. I have a way of convincing the consular officers here. You don't have to give me money. Just pay for the processing fees and come back in the afternoon."

I went back in the afternoon and got my passport back, and I was so glad that my tourist visa back to Amsterdam was approved. I expressed my gratitude to the Turkish guard and insisted on giving him some money, but he refused. He only said, "I have high admiration for those who pursue higher education."

I went back to Amsterdam to the U.S. Consulate General there and got my visa back to the United States without any problem. I told the consular officer that I wanted to speak with the Consul General. He said, "You already got your visa, what do you need him for?"

"I just wanted to say a few words to him." I said. He showed up. I told him, "Sir, you have been so kind to Telex my applications to Istanbul, and I don't know how to express my appreciation to you. You are a man of your words."

"I wish you every success in the United States," he said.

I went back to Virginia. Because of my visa status, other circumstances, and the uncertainty of the situation in Iran, I delayed my graduation until the summer of 1987. I finished my PhD, thanks to my excellent professors Drs. Kandil, Ibrahim, Mei, and Thornton, who taught me well and guided me through my PhD dissertation. I am also thankful to Dr. Robert Ash, the department chair at the time, who was always so courteous and so helpful to all the students including me.

Just about a year before the completion of my degree, I went back to Fayetteville to visit my former professors and to explore the possibility of working at the University of Arkansas. Lisa, the strong-minded girl whom I mentioned earlier, picked me up from the Tulsa Airport, the closest airport to Fayetteville at that time. She took me to Fayetteville and was so kind as to let me stay at her place temporarily. At the time, she was separated from her husband, living with her two lovely kids; Julian and Joao, and in the process of getting divorced. After her divorce, we became romantically involved, got engaged, and married in August 1987. Unfortunately, the marriage did not last for more than seven years. But Lisa and I have remained as friends and have had joint legal custody of three children of our own, Saum, Sara, and Sina, whom we both love and adore.

The University of Arkansas did not have any openings, but I was lucky enough to have found employment at Embry Riddle Aeronautical University—one of the best and most student-oriented schools in the world. I have accomplished most of my personal dreams; I have the greatest and most rewarding job. I remarried to a beautiful and most caring wife. I have three greatest kids in the world. I live in a free country, in one of the most beautiful cities in the world—Daytona Beach, Florida. My last dream, however, has yet to come to fruition. I continue to yearn to see a free Iran—a democratic and peaceful Iran. The Persian people deserve a peaceful Persian government. I hope to see the hostile relationship between the two great nations of Iran and America to come to an end. I hope to see peace and prosperity in the two lands that I love and that I am proudly a citizen of—one being the land of my ancestors, and the other one the land of my descendents.

EPILOGUE

We all share the same planet and nations are becoming increasingly aware of their dependency on each other. The economy of the world is becoming global. Atmospheric changes are becoming a global concern. Energy shortage, poverty, and human rights are becoming important international issues. This is not a world controlled by capitalists or communists any longer. This world belongs to people of all races, religions, colors, languages, ethnicities, dialects, and cultures.

Today in the world of academics, the same concepts are used to educate people. In the world of technology, we share the same sources of energy. In the world of sports, different teams of different countries are now employing players and coaches of different origins. Yet, despite such commonality and interdependence, there still exists racism, discrimination, and religious bigotry. There are still rulers in the world who commit crimes against humanity.

In my humble opinion, the sacredness of humanity is above any law, any race, and any religion. Our prophets, our founding fathers, our philosophers, and our most revered religious leaders, all taught us to value, respect, and love one another. They all taught us the most fundamental principles of life, the value of humanity and human synergy. They have all taught us that we need to coexist in peace; that we need to feel each other's pain and suffering and help one another. The great Persian poet Saadi says:

The children of Adam are limbs to each other
Having been created of one essence.
If destiny brings pain to a limb,
Other limbs will not be at ease.

If you are not sorrowful from others' suffering,
You are not worthy of being called a human being.

When crimes against humanity occur in a part of the world, people of the whole world share the pain and suffering. The perpetrators of such crimes will eventually face the iron fist of their own people or that of the entire world. They will have the same fate as Adolf Hitler, Slobodan Milosevic, apartheid, Augusto Pinochet, Saddam Hussein, and other dictators.

The brutal crackdown on peaceful demonstration of the Iranian people against election fraud after the June 12, 2009 election was felt and condemned by peace-loving people and freedom seekers around the world. Some of the leaders of the Islamic Republic, for the past thirty-one years, have committed crimes against humanity. Occurrences of public hangings (including minors), the imprisonment of women for bad *hejabi*, the raping and then killing of female prisoners, mass executions, torturing and raping of political prisoners have increased in recent years, particularly after 2009 election. In addition, the persecution of minorities such as Jews and Baha'is, the labeling of people as spies and executing them, the imprisonment and execution of people who change their religion, and stoning people (mostly women) to death have increased in recent years.

Some of my family members and friends criticized me for speaking out and warned that I might get myself into trouble by voicing my opposition against the Islamic Republic. I have had the fortune of finishing my education to the highest degree in America. I have achieved most of my goals in this land of opportunity. I have had the freedom to express my feelings, wear any clothing I wanted, and even to criticize the U.S. government openly without the fear of being scrutinized. I have been admonished that I have lived a reasonably good life in America; therefore, I have no reason to be concerned about what goes on in Iran. My parents wanted me to be silent. My brothers and sisters wanted me to be silent. Some of my friends want me to be silent. Frankly, I think I have been silent for too long.

How can I be silent, while my compatriots in my motherland do not enjoy basic God-given freedom in life? As mentioned before, my compatriots do not have the freedom to talk about freedom, to read about freedom, to write about freedom, to struggle for freedom, and to blog about freedom. How can I be silent? I feel that it is a moral obligation and a social responsibility to express my outrage at the injustice, brutality, illegitimacy, totalitarianism, and murderous acts of the unlawful invaders who occupied my motherland for over three decades in the name of God and Islam. How can I be silent while my young brothers and sisters are being tortured and dying in prisons for my freedom and for the establishment of democracy in my motherland? How can I be silent when my people are being oppressed inside the country and unjustly labeled as terrorists outside? How can I be silent while the teenagers in my country are being arrested, raped, and murdered for doing nothing more than demanding justice and for participating in peaceful rallies? I cannot stay silent any longer. For goodness' sake, how can anybody be silent? Dr. Mossadeq once said, "If I sit silent, I have sinned." In a similar fashion, Dr. Martin Luther King, Jr., stated, "Our lives begin to end the day we become silent about things that matter."

The majority of the Iranian people appreciated President Obama's willingness to start a dialogue with Iranian authorities through diplomacy in order to resolve the nuclear standoffs with the regime of the Islamic Republic. The people of Iran have been the main victims of the hostilities and estrangements between the two countries. It is about time that both countries resolve their thirty-one-year-old differences through peaceful means, but not at the cost of betraying the people of Iran. I do appreciate diplomacy and peaceful negotiations over threatening propagandas to start a war or hostile invasion. However, it was proven to President Obama and to the world that the Islamic Republic is not a government for peace. A regime that represses its own people, a regime that has survived for thirty-one years by terrorizing its nation and by engaging in a long war—a regime whose rulers have ignored "sanctions" and "economic embargos" against their own people but made themselves multibillionaires, does not care about peace. This regime is not afraid of another war, and, in fact, it foresees its survival in creating another war so it can send more teenagers to the minefields and suppress all the opposition movements as it did in the eighties. The rulers of the Islamic Republic are not afraid of sanctions that did not work in the past. They are afraid of their own people, especially their young voices. They are afraid of freedom and democracy. They are afraid of the political and social awareness of the new generation in Iran. They are afraid of more uprising and more demonstrations. The sanctions in the past did not work; only the ordinary people suffered from such sanctions. I am not sure if the new sanctions would work, but I am certain that engaging in a war with Iran would only benefit the ruthless rulers of the Islamic Republic. A vast majority of Iranians believe that the invasion of Iranian territory might tear the country into pieces, and perhaps rally people behind the current government.

I believe, further political isolations of the regime, indictments of the rulers of the Islamic Republic for crimes against humanity, supporting the Iranian students inside the country opposing the Islamic Republic would work. I also believe that the moral support of the struggling people of Iran, demanding the release of all political prisoners, and solidarity with Iranian workers and their labor organizations opposing the Islamic Republic, would work. Furthermore, I believe dealing with the rulers of Islamic Republic the way the United States dealt with the government of South Africa during the apartheid era or the governments of Poland and East Germany during the Communist domination era or the way American government dealt with the Serbian government during the ruling of Slobodan Milosevic, minus the bombing, would work.

I trust that President Obama, and his administration will not ignore the will and determination of the struggling Iranian people for establishing a democratic government. I trust that they will put the Iranian people on top of their Iran foreign policy before coming to any compromise with the autocratic and illegitimate government of the Islamic Republic and its unelected ruler. I hope that the American government and the free world would give strong moral support to the Iranian people so that they can be in control of their own destiny this time. Given the moral backing and the promise of future self-determination and independence, the people of Iran will be quite capable of removing this repressive regime sooner rather than later. I only hope that the current agonizing struggle of Iranians for freedom would result in a bloodless transition of power from the dictatorship to a rather democratic government without the invasion by any foreign troops. This is the desire of all peace-loving Persian people as well.

Democracy cannot be dictated; it cannot be achieved by force, nor can it be achieved through invasion, and it cannot happen overnight. It can only be achieved through education, and education only. I believe that the Iranian people are ready to establish a democratic state on their own. They only need moral aid and they want their voice and their cry for freedom to be heard. They want the free world to cut ties with the criminal rulers in Iran. The whole world will benefit from the establishment of a democratic and peaceful government in Iran.